THE AMERICAN PURITANS

Their Prose and Poetry

THE
AMERICAN
PURITANS

THEIR
Prose and Poetry

Edited by Perry Miller

ANCHOR BOOKS
Doubleday & Company, Inc.
Garden City, New York

Cover and Typography by Edward Gorey

The Anchor Books edition is the first publication of
The American Puritans, edited by Perry Miller.

Anchor Books edition: 1956

Library of Congress Catalog Card Number 56–7536

CONTENTS

CHAPTER THREE

THIS WORLD AND THE NEXT

CHAPTER FOUR

PERSONAL NARRATIVE

CHAPTER FIVE

POETRY

CHAPTER SIX

LITERARY AND EDUCATIONAL IDEALS

Perry Miller was born in Chicago on February 25, 1905. He was educated at the University of Chicago where he received his Ph.D. degree in 1931. Since then Mr. Miller has been teaching at Harvard University and in 1946 became a Professor of American Literature there.

He is the author of *Orthodoxy in Massachusetts* (1933); *The New England Mind* (1939); *Jonathan Edwards* (1949); *Roger Williams* (1953); *The Raven and the Whale* (1956); and *Errand into the Wilderness* (1956).

Other volumes edited by Perry Miller available in Anchor Books editions are: *The American Transcendentalists* (A119), *The Legal Mind in America: From Independence to the Civil War* (A313), and *Margaret Fuller: American Romantic—A Selection From Her Writings and Correspondence* (A356).

FOREWORD

Puritanism may be described empirically as that point of view, that code of values, carried to New England by the first settlers. These were English Protestants, and in their fundamental convictions were at one with the Protestants, or at least with the Calvinistic Protestants, of all Europe. But the peculiar isolation of the New England colonies—the homogeneous people, the sparse soil, the climate, the economic struggle—quickly made these Protestants a peculiar people. Because their societies were tightly organized, and above all because they were a highly articulate people, the New Englanders established Puritanism —for better or worse—as one of the continuous factors in American life and thought. It has played so dominant a rôle because descendants of the Puritans have carried traits of the Puritan mind into a variety of pursuits and all the way across the continent. Many of these qualities have persisted even though the original creed is lost. Without some understanding of Puritanism, and that at its source, there is no understanding of America.

As a help toward such understanding I have brought together these selections from the writings of American Puritans, meaning by them the settlers of New England in roughly the first century of colonial life. After that, modifications imposed by history proceeded at such a pace we can hardly say the creed and mentality survived in the pristine form. Because space is limited, the pieces are carefully chosen, only essential portions reprinted, and the comment restricted. In general, I think, the extracts speak for themselves and need little exposition.

This book is based on a previous anthology that Thomas H. Johnson and I published in 1939, *The Puritans*, now out of print. A few items not in that volume are added, and I have tried to retain those that have proved of general interest. A few of these, because then for the first time made available to the modern reader, have in effect become standard passages in American literature. Of course many of the others had long ago found their places in the canon.

In one respect this anthology falls short, in that it omits one of the greatest and certainly the most engaging of the Puritans, Roger Williams. The primary consideration is lack of space, but also, while his is the essential Puritan conscience, he developed heretical ideas which make him a sport amid the "orthodox" mind on which I wish to concentrate. Furthermore, Williams cannot fairly be exhibited in only short extracts, and I am the less worried about doing him an injustice because in 1953, in the Makers of the American Tradition series (Bobbs-Merrill), I issued a full volume of his writings.

Following the lead of Samuel Eliot Morison in his edition of William Bradford, I assumed as regards Williams the privileges of an editor and prepared a modern—*not* a "modernized"—text. Here I have again exercised that prerogative. I have regularized the spelling and capitalization, omitted italics, broken up long paragraphs, and endeavored to refashion the punctuation so as at once to remain faithful to the spirit of the text and yet to assist the modern reader. Since writers and printers in the seventeenth century observed no consistent rules in these matters, the discretion permitted an editor is large. However, since they punctuated on a rhetorical rather than a logical system, to impose the strict laws of modern practice on their sentences would be folly. Still, just as few readers today would be comfortable in reading Shakespeare were he always presented in the exact style of the First Folio, so I have found that many are put off by the unfamiliarity of seventeenth-century typography.

In that sense, then, my text is modern, but I have otherwise reproduced exactly the words and phrases of my sources. In the hope that thus a larger audience than "specialists" in American history may find interest and even pleasure in these remarkable writings, I take particular delight in offering them through this convenient format.

NEW ENGLAND

——— Present-day State Boundaries

---------- Part of Long Island under
Connecticut Jurisdiction
until 1664

CONNECTICUT R.

Northfie.

Deerfield   Turners
Falls

Hatfield

Northampton   Hadley

MASSACHUSETTS

Brookfie

Westfield   Agawam
Springfield

HUDSON R.

Enfield

Kingston

Simsbury

Windsor

Newtown, Hartford   Pyquag,
Wethersfield

Farmington   Cante.

NEW YORK   Colchester

CONNECTICUT

Middletown   Norw

Wallingford   Haddam   Peq
Lon

Paugassett, Derby   E. Haven   Lyn
Killingworth

New Haven
Milford   Guilford   Saybro

Fairfield   Branford   Southold

Norwalk   Stratford

Merrinack   Stamford   LONG ISLAND SOUND   Sag Harbor

New Rochelle   Greenwich   Setauket
East Chester   Rye
Westchester

Huntington   LONG
New York   ISLAND   Southam

Flushing   Oyster Bay
Hempstead
Gravesend

STATEN I.   GREAT BAY

ATLANTIC

NEW JERSEY

MILES

0   5   10

HISTORY

1. WILLIAM BRADFORD, 1590–1657

[The Puritans acquired their name because they were
English Protestants who in the second half of the sixteenth
and the first half of the seventeenth centuries were resolved
to "purify" the Church of England. They determined to
continue the reformation begun under Henry VIII until
they duplicated in England the precise form of ecclesiastical polity they believed to be clearly set forth in the New
Testament. They would utterly extirpate everything in the
Church for which they could find no specific Biblical warrant, especially those features they considered the foul
heritage of medieval corruption. They would abolish the
episcopal hierarchy, the prayer book, all ritual, vestments,
and the celebration of Christmas.

However, by the "Elizabethan Settlement" of 1559 the
crown officially identified itself with that compromise between radical Protestantism and Roman Catholicism which
today constitutes the Church of England. Hence the Puritans were obliged to become opponents, even enemies, of
the state. The controversy became, decade after decade,
more bitter, until it flared into ferocious warfare in 1642.
By 1649 the Puritans had seized the power and had executed both the Archbishop of Canterbury and King
Charles I.

In the course of fighting this Civil War the Puritan forces
discovered to their dismay that they were divided into two
irreconcilable opinions about just what the Biblical pattern, supposedly so precise, really was. Furthermore, as this
division came into the open, they had to recognize that it

went back to the origins of the movement in the 1560's, that it had always been there, though it had been kept down by the long necessity of maintaining a united front against the prelates. But out of this hidden rift in the ranks, some two decades before the Puritans took up arms against King Charles, came the migration of certain adherents of the minority position to New England.

The majority of English Puritans believed that the pure church should be "national"—as was the Church of England —that it should include the entire population, and be made up of geographical parish units, with membership and attendance enforced by the state. But their national church was to be Presbyterian, on the model of Calvin's system in Geneva or the Church of Scotland. They would replace the hierarchy of archbishops, bishops, priests, with a hierarchy of governing bodies, from the national assembly down through the regional classis to the presbytery of the parish church, consisting of the minister and the elders.

The minority were what ultimately came to be called Congregationalists. They held that each church was "particular," being founded on a covenant formally entered into only by those who possessed the will power to confess their faith and to swear to the covenant. These they called the "visible saints." The churches were to be entirely self-governing; there would be no compelling agencies above them, neither bishop nor classis nor synod. The conception of a national church was to be rooted out as being the last stronghold of Antichrist. Each congregation was to choose its own pastor and officers, to administer the rites, accept or excommunicate members, while the masses—if unable to make a profession—would simply have to remain meekly outside. Uniformity of practice and doctrine would be guaranteed by the unanimity of the saints, while the civil authority would keep the unchurched in subjection and prevent the rise among them of any heresy or of any competing ecclesiastical proposals.

The sources of this Congregational philosophy are difficult to locate. The proponents thought it was sufficiently set forth in the New Testament, though Presbyterians could not find it there. We may now perceive, in the perspective of history, that many half-formed aspirations of the age and of the nation were obliquely or unwittingly embodied in the theory. Congregationalists vehemently denied Presbyterian charges that the plan was shockingly "democratical"; still, it did create within the confines of each particular church a democracy of the membership. But it aimed to achieve these islands of democratic Christians by deliberately excluding most of the populace, who had neither the wit nor the inclination to make a profession, as presumably unregenerate and therefore probably headed for damnation.

This conception of the covenanted church began its ferment among the Puritan ranks in the 1580's. As soon as a few zealots got the idea firmly in their heads, they faced a logical deduction that, if the true church is founded on the volition of the members and not on a geographical parish, they could no longer remain within a national church. They took the terrible step of "separating," an act equivalent in the legal system of the time to high treason. Several paid for this temerity with their lives, and one group was so harried that it fled to Holland and ultimately, as our first narrative tells, to New England, there to found the Plymouth colony and to become the "Pilgrims" of American legend.

The great body of Puritans, whether they were working for a Presbyterian or a Congregational purification of England, were horrified by the Separatists. These endangered the cause by seeming to prove to the government that Puritanism was really what the government said it was—subversive, anarchical, disloyal. The solid Puritans were not trying to achieve mere toleration as against an established church; they had no notion whatsoever that religious liberty was feasible or desirable within a society. They—whether of the Presbyterian or Congregational faction—were scheming and plotting for the day when *they* would oust the bishops and rule at Canterbury and York. Whichever of them won was predetermined to suppress the other, with methods as ruthless as those of Kings James and Charles, and also to deal even more severely with such dissidents as dared to attempt a separation.

So, the little band who eventually landed and suffered at Plymouth in 1620 are not quite representative. The large and well-organized body who settled Massachusetts Bay in 1630, though committed to the Congregational idea, stoutly maintained that they were not and never had been Separatists. This difference made for some distinctions between the characters of the two plantations, yet in another sense the Separatists, by the fact of their having withdrawn, were able to concentrate upon the essence of Puritanism. They may well be called the purest of the purifiers. The heart and soul of that disposition was its intense devotion to the Bible, to the letter and the spirit, to the Old Testament as well as the New, and an absolute dedication to performing in this life what seemed the will of God.

Fittingly and properly, therefore, our story begins with William Bradford's narrative of the Plymouth enterprise. Not only does this come first in any chronological account, but in Bradford himself, as man and writer, we find the innermost being of the Puritan—the mind, the prose style, the conception of providential history, the literalness, the pettiness, and also the strength, the indestructible nobility.

William Bradford, born in Austerfield, of Yorkshire yeoman stock, inherited a "comfortable" sum from his father, and might easily have grown into a substantial farmer had he not, at the age of twelve, become a serious reader of the Bible. Thus he found himself driven, against the wishes of his family, to join the group of Separatists who furtively met at the house of William Brewster in Scrooby. With John Robinson as their minister, this congregation fled to Amsterdam in 1609, and then to Leyden, where Bradford supported himself as a fustian weaver and say worker. He was a leader of the migration to New England in 1620, and was elected governor of the Plymouth Colony upon the death of John Carver, in April, 1621. He served in that office for thirty of his remaining thirty-six years, without salary until 1639, and thereafter for £20 a year. In his old age he undertook the study of Hebrew, in order to see "the ancient oracles of God in their native beauty." In the inventory of his estate there were a red waistcoat, a great silver "beer bowle," and a violet cloak. He commenced writing his history in 1630, probably finished it about 1650.

The text is reprinted from *Of Plymouth Plantation*, edited, with an Introduction and Notes, by Samuel Eliot Morison, by permission of Alfred A. Knopf, Inc. Copyright 1952 by Samuel Eliot Morison.]

OF PLYMOUTH PLANTATION

When as by the travail and diligence of some godly and zealous preachers, and God's blessing on their labors, as in other places of the land, so in the north parts, many became enlightened by the word of God and had their ignorance and sins discovered unto them, and began by His grace to reform their lives and make conscience of their ways; the work of God was no sooner manifest in them but presently they were both scoffed and scorned by the profane multitude; and the ministers urged with the yoke of subscription, or else must be silenced. And the poor people were so vexed with apparitors and pursuivants and the commissary courts, as truly their affliction was not small. Which, notwithstanding, they bore sundry years with much patience, till they were occasioned by the continuance and increase of these troubles, and other means which the Lord raised up in those days, to see further into things by the light of the word of God. How not only these base and beggarly ceremonies were unlawful, but also that the lordly and tyrannous power of the prelates ought not to be submitted unto; which thus, contrary to the freedom of the Gospel, would load and burden men's consciences and by their compulsive power make a profane mixture of persons and things in the worship of God. . . .

So many, therefore, of these professors as saw the evil of these things in these parts, and whose hearts the Lord had touched with heavenly zeal for His truth, they shook off this yoke of antichristian bondage, and as the Lord's free people joined themselves (by a covenant of the Lord) into a church estate, in the fellowship of the Gospel, to walk in all His ways made known, or to be made known unto them, according to their best endeavors, whatsoever it should cost them, the Lord assisting them. And that it cost them something, this ensuing history will declare. . . .

But after these things they could not long continue in any peaceable condition, but were hunted and persecuted on every side, so as their former afflictions were but as flea-bitings in comparison of these which now came upon them. For some were taken and clapped up in prison, others had their houses beset and watched night and day, and hardly escaped their hands; and the most were fain to flee and leave their houses and habitations, and the means of their livelihood.

Yet these, and many other sharper things which afterward befell them, were no other than they looked for, and therefore were the better prepared to bear them by the assistance of God's grace and spirit.

Yet seeing themselves thus molested, and that there was no hope of their continuance there, by a joint consent they resolved to go into the Low Countries, where they heard was freedom of religion for all men; as also how sundry from London and other parts of the land had been exiled and persecuted for the same cause, and were gone thither, and lived at Amsterdam and in other places of the land. So after they had continued together about a year, and kept their meetings every Sabbath in one place or other, exercising the worship of God amongst themselves, notwithstanding all the diligence and malice of their adversaries, they seeing they could no longer continue in that condition, they resolved to get over into Holland as they could. . . .

Being thus constrained to leave their native soil and country, their lands and livings, and all their friends and familiar acquaintance, it was much; and thought marvelous by many. But to go into a country they knew not but by hearsay, where they must learn a new language and get their livings they knew not how, it being a dear place and subject to the miseries of war, it was by many thought an adventure almost desperate; a case intolerable and a misery worse than death. Especially seeing they were not acquainted with trades nor traffic (by which that country doth subsist) but had only been used to a plain country life and the innocent trade of husbandry. But these things did not dismay them, though they did sometimes trouble them; for their desires were set on the ways of God and to enjoy His ordinances; but they rested on His providence, and knew whom they had believed. Yet this was not all, for though they could not stay, yet were they not suffered to go; but the ports and havens were shut against them, so as they were fain to seek secret means of conveyance, and to bribe and fee the mariners, and give extraordinary rates for their passages. And yet were they oftentimes betrayed, many of them; and both they and their goods intercepted and surprised, and thereby put to great trouble and charge, of which I will give an instance or two and omit the rest.

There was a large company of them purposed to get passage at Boston in Lincolnshire, and for that end had hired a ship wholly to themselves and made agreement with the master to be ready at a certain day, and take them and their goods in at a convenient place, where they accordingly would all attend in readiness. So after long waiting and large expenses, though he kept not day with them, yet he came at length and took them in, in the night. But when he had them and their goods aboard, he betrayed them, having beforehand complotted with the searchers and other officers so to do; who took them, and put them into open boats, and there rifled and ransacked them, searching to their shirts for money, yea even the women further than became modesty; and then carried them back into the town and made them a spectacle and wonder to the multitude which came flocking on all sides to behold them. Being thus first, by these catchpoll officers rifled and stripped of their money, books and much other goods, there were presented to the magistrates, and messengers sent to inform the Lords of the Council of them; and so they were committed to ward. Indeed the magistrates used them courteously and showed them what favor they could; but could not deliver them till order came from the Council table. But the issue was that after a month's imprisonment the greatest part were dismissed and sent to the places from whence they came; but seven of the principal were still kept in prison and bound over to the assizes.

The next spring after, there was another attempt made by some of these and others to get over at another place. And it so fell out that they light of a Dutchman at Hull, having a ship of his own belonging to Zeeland. They made agreement with him, and acquainted him with their condition, hoping to find more faithfulness in him than in the former of their own nation; he bade them not fear, for he would do well enough. He was by appointment to take them in between Grimsby and Hull, where was a large common a good way distant from any town. Now against the prefixed time, the women and children with the goods were sent to the place in a small bark which they had hired for that end; and the men were to meet them by land. But it so fell out that they were there a day before the ship came, and the sea being rough and the women very sick, prevailed with the seamen to put into a creek hard by where they lay on ground at low water. The next morning the ship came but they were fast and could not stir until about noon. In the meantime, the shipmaster, perceiving how the matter was, sent his boat to be getting the men aboard whom he saw ready, walking about the shore. But after the first boatful was got aboard and she was ready to go for more, the master espied a great company, both horse and foot, with bills and guns and other weapons, for the country was raised to take them. The Dutchman, seeing that, swore his country's oath *sacremente*, and having the wind fair, weighed his anchor, hoised sails, and away.

But the poor men which were got aboard were in great distress for their wives and children which they saw thus to be taken, and were left destitute of their helps; and themselves also, not having a cloth to shift them with, more than they had on their backs, and some scarce a penny about them, all they had being aboard the bark. It drew tears from their eyes, and anything they had they would have given to have been ashore again; but all in vain, there was no remedy, they must thus sadly part. . . .

The rest of the men that were in greatest danger made shift to escape away before the troop could surprise them, those only staying that best might be assistant unto the women. But pitiful it was to see the heavy case of these poor women in this distress; what weeping and crying on every side, some for their husbands that were carried away in the ship as is before related; others not knowing what should become of them and their little ones; others again melted in tears, seeing their poor little ones hanging about them, crying for fear and quaking with cold. Being thus apprehended, they were hurried from one place to another and from one justice to another, till in the end they knew not what to do with them; for to imprison so many women and innocent children for no other cause (many of them) but that they must go with their husbands, seemed to be unreasonable and all would cry out of them. And to send them home again was as difficult; for they alleged, as the truth was, they had no homes to go to, for they had either sold or otherwise disposed of their houses and livings. To be short, after they had been thus turmoiled a good while and conveyed from one constable to another, they were glad to be rid of them in the end upon any terms, for all were wearied and tired with them. Though in the meantime they (poor souls) endured misery enough; and thus in the end necessity forced a way for them. . . .

And in the end, notwithstanding all these storms of opposition, they all got over at length, some at one time and some at another, and some in one place and some in another, and met together again according to their desires, with no small rejoicing. . . .

Being now come into the Low Countries, they saw many goodly and fortified cities, strongly walled and guarded with troops of armed men. Also, they heard a strange and uncouth language, and beheld the different manners and customs of the people, with their strange fashions and attires; all so far differing from that of their plain country villages (wherein they were bred and had so long lived) as it seemed they were come into a new world. But these were not the things they much looked on, or long took up their thoughts, for they had other work in hand and another kind of war to wage and maintain. For although they saw fair and beautiful cities, flowing with abundance of all sorts of wealth and riches, yet it was not long before they saw the grim and grisly face of poverty coming upon them like an armed man, with whom they must buckle and encounter, and from whom they could not fly. But they were armed with faith and patience against him and all his encounters; and though they were sometimes foiled, yet by God's assistance, they prevailed and got the victory. . . .

After they had lived in this city about some eleven or twelve years (which is the more observable being the whole time of that famous truce between that state and the Spaniards) and sundry of them were taken away by death and many others began to be well stricken in years (the grave mistress of experience having taught them many things), those prudent governors with sundry of the sagest members began both deeply to apprehend their present dangers and wisely to foresee the future and think of timely remedy. In the agitation of their thoughts, and much discourse of things hereabout, at length they began to incline to this conclusion: of removal to some other place. Not out of any newfangledness or other such like giddy humor by which men are oftentimes transported to their great hurt and danger, but for sundry weighty and solid reasons, some of the chief of which I will here briefly touch.

And first, they saw and found by experience the hardness of the place and country to be such as few in comparison would come to them, and fewer that would bide it out and continue with them. For many that came to them, and many more that desired to be with them, could not endure that great labor and hard fare, with other inconveniences which they underwent and were contented with. But though they loved their persons, approved their cause and honored their sufferings, yet they left them as it were weeping, as Orpah did her mother-in-law Naomi, or as those Romans did Cato in Utica who desired to be excused and borne with, though they could not all be Catos. For many, though they desired to enjoy the ordinances of God in their purity and the liberty of the Gospel with them, yet (alas) they admitted of bondage with danger of conscience, rather than to endure these hardships. Yea, some preferred and chose the prisons in England rather than this liberty in Holland with these afflictions. But it was thought that if a better and easier place of living could be had, it would draw many and take away these discouragements. Yea, their pastor would often say that many of those who both wrote and preached now against them, if they were in a place where they might have liberty and live comfortably, they would then practice as they did.

Secondly. They say that though the people generally bore all these difficulties very cheerfully and with a resolute courage, being in the best and strength of their years, yet old age began to steal on many of them; and their great and continual labors, with other crosses and sorrows, hastened it before the time. So as it was not only probably thought, but apparently seen, that within a few years more they would be in danger to scatter, by necessities pressing them, or sink under their burdens, or both. And therefore according to the divine proverb, that a wise man seeth the plague when it cometh, and hideth himself (Prov. 22. 3), so they like skillful and beaten soldiers were fearful either to be entrapped or surrounded by their enemies so as they should neither be able to fight nor fly. And therefore thought it better to dislodge betimes to some place of better advantage and less danger if any such could be found.

Thirdly. As necessity was a taskmaster over them, so they were forced to be such, not only to their servants but in a sort to their dearest children, the which as it did not a little wound the tender hearts of many a loving father and mother, so it produced likewise sundry sad and sorrowful effects. For many of their children that were of best dispositions and gracious inclinations, having learned to bear the yoke in their youth and willing to bear part of their parents' burden, were oftentimes so oppressed with their heavy labors that though their minds were free and willing, yet their bodies bowed under the weight of the same, and became decrepit in their early youth, the vigor of nature being consumed in the very bud as it were. But that which was more lamentable, and of all sorrows most heavy to be borne, was that many of their children, by these occasions and the great licentiousness of youth in that country, and the manifold temptations of the place, were drawn away by evil examples into extravagant and dangerous courses, getting the reins off their necks and departing from their parents. Some became soldiers, others took upon them far voyages by sea, and others some worse courses tending to dissoluteness and the danger of their souls, to the great grief of their parents and dishonor of God. So that they saw their posterity would be in danger to degenerate and be corrupted.

Lastly (and which was not least), a great hope and inward zeal they had of laying some good foundation, or at least to make some way thereunto, for the propagating and advancing the Gospel of the kingdom of Christ in those remote parts of the world; yea, though they should be but even as stepping-stones unto others for the performing of so great a work.

These and some other like reasons moved them to undertake this resolution of their removal; the which they afterward prosecuted with so great difficulties, as by the sequel will appear.

The place they had thoughts on was some of those vast and unpeopled countries of America, which are fruitful and fit for habitation, being devoid of all civil inhabitants, where there are only savage and brutish men which range up and down, little otherwise than the wild beasts of the same. This proposition being made public and coming to the scanning of all, it raised many variable opinions amongst men and caused many fears and doubts amongst themselves. Some, from their reasons and hopes conceived, labored to stir up and encourage the rest to undertake and prosecute the same; others again, out of their fears, objected against it and sought to divert from it; alleging many things, and those neither unreasonable nor unprobable; as that it was a great design and subject to many unconceivable perils and dangers; as, besides the casualties of the sea (which none can be freed from), the length of the voyage was such as the weak bodies of women and other persons worn out with age and travail (as many of them were) could never be able to endure. And yet if they should, the miseries of the land which they should be exposed unto would be too hard to be borne and likely, some or all of them together, to consume and utterly to ruinate them. For there they should be liable to famine and nakedness and the want, in a manner, of all things. The change of air, diet and drinking of water would infect their bodies with sore sicknesses and grievous diseases. And also those which should escape or overcome these difficulties should yet be in continual danger of the savage people, who are cruel, barbarous and most treacherous, being most furious in their rage and merciless where they overcome; not being content only to kill and take away life, but delight to torment men in the most bloody manner that may be; flaying some alive with the shells of fishes, cutting off the members and joints of others by piecemeal and broiling on the coals, eat the collops of their flesh in their sight whilst they live, with other cruelties horrible to be related.

And surely it could not be thought but the very hearing of these things could not but move the very bowels of men to grate within them and make the weak to quake and tremble. It was further objected that it would require greater sums of money to furnish such a voyage and to fit them with necessaries, than their consumed estates would amount to; and yet they must as well look to be seconded with supplies as presently to be transported. Also many precedents of ill success and lamentable miseries befallen others in the like designs were easy to be found, and not forgotten to be alleged; besides their own experience, in their former troubles and hardships in their removal into Holland, and how hard a thing it was for them to live in that strange place, though it was a neighbor country and a civil and rich commonwealth.

It was answered, that all great and honorable actions are accompanied with great difficulties and must be both enterprised and overcome with answerable courages. It was granted the dangers were great, but not desperate. The difficulties were many, but not invincible. For though there were many of them likely, yet they were not certain. It might be sundry of the things feared might never befall; others by provident care and the use of good means might in a great measure be prevented; and all of them, through the help of God, by fortitude and patience, might either be borne or overcome. True it was that such attempts were not to be made and undertaken without good ground and reason, not rashly or lightly as many have done for curiosity or hope of gain, etc. But their condition was not ordinary, their ends were good and honorable, their calling lawful and urgent; and therefore they might expect the blessing of God in their proceeding. Yea, though they should lose their lives in this action, yet might they have comfort in the same and their endeavors would be honorable. . . .

These troubles being blown over, and now all being compact together in one ship, they put to sea again with a prosperous wind, which continued divers days together, which was some encouragement unto them; yet, according to the usual manner, many were afflicted with seasickness. And I may not omit here a special work of God's providence. There was a proud and very profane young man, one of the seamen, of a lusty, able body, which made him the more haughty; he would always be condemning the poor people in their sickness and cursing them daily with grievous execrations, and did not let to tell them that he hoped to help cast half of them overboard before they came to their journey's end, and to make merry with what they had; and if he were by any gently reproved, he would curse and swear most bitterly. But it pleased God before they came half seas over to smite this young man with a grievous disease, of which he died in a desperate manner, and so was himself the first that was thrown overboard. Thus his curses light on his own head, and it was an astonishment to all his fellows for they noted it to be the just hand of God upon him.

After they had enjoyed fair winds and weather for a season, they were encountered many times with cross winds and met with many fierce storms with which the ship was shrewdly shaken, and her upper works made very leaky; and one of the main beams in the midships was bowed and cracked, which put them in some fear that the ship could not be able to perform the voyage. So some of the chief of the company, perceiving the mariners to fear the sufficiency of the ship as appeared by their mutterings, they entered into serious consultation with the master and other officers of the ship, to consider in time of the danger, and rather to return than to cast themselves into a desperate and inevitable peril. And truly there was great distraction and difference of opinion amongst the mariners themselves; fain would they do what could be done for their wages' sake (being now near half the seas over) and on the other hand they were loath to hazard their lives too desperately. But in examining of all opinions, the master and others affirmed they knew the ship to be strong and firm under water; and for the buckling of the main beam, there was a great iron screw the passengers brought out of Holland which would raise the beam into his place; the which being done, the carpenter and master affirmed that with a post put under it, set firm in the lower deck and otherways bound, he would make it sufficient. And as for the decks and upper works, they would caulk them as well as they could, and though with the working of the ship they would not long keep staunch, yet there would otherwise be no great danger, if they did not overpress her with sails. So they committed themselves to the will of God and resolved to proceed.

In sundry of these storms the winds were so fierce and the seas so high, as they could not bear a knot of sail, but were forced to hull for divers days together. And in one of them, as they thus lay at hull in a mighty storm, a lusty young man called John Howland, coming upon some occasion above the gratings, was, with a roll of the ship, thrown into sea; but it pleased God that he caught hold of the topsail halyards which hung overboard and ran out at length. Yet he held his hold (though he was sundry fathoms under water) till he was hauled up by the same rope to the brim of the water, and then with a boat hook and other means got into the ship again and his life saved. And though he was something ill with it, yet he lived many years after and became a profitable member both in church and commonwealth. In all this voyage there died but one of the passengers, which was William Butten, a youth, servant to Samuel Fuller, when they drew near the coast.

But to omit other things (that I may be brief), after long beating at sea they fell with that land which is called Cape Cod; the which being made and certainly known to be it, they were not a little joyful. After some deliberation had amongst themselves and with the master of the ship, they tacked about and resolved to stand for the southward (the wind and weather being fair) to find some place about Hudson's River for their habitation. But after they had sailed that course about half the day, they fell amongst dangerous shoals and roaring breakers, and they were so far entangled therewith as they conceived themselves in great danger; and the wind shrinking upon them withal, they resolved to bear up again for the Cape and thought themselves happy to get out of those dangers before night overtook them, as by God's good providence they did. And the next day they got into the cape harbor where they rode in safety. . . .

Being thus arrived in a good harbor, and brought safe to land, they fell upon their knees and blessed the God of heaven who had brought them over the vast and furious ocean, and delivered them from all the perils and miseries thereof, again to set their feet on the firm and stable earth, their proper element. And no marvel if they were thus joyful, seeing wise Seneca was so affected with sailing a few miles on the coast of his own Italy, as he affirmed, that he had rather remain twenty years on his way by land than pass by sea to any place in a short time, so tedious and dreadful was the same unto him.

But here I cannot but stay and make a pause, and stand half amazed at this poor people's present condition; and so I think will the reader, too, when he well considers the same. Being thus passed the vast ocean, and a sea of troubles before in their preparation (as may be remembered by that which went before), they had now no friends to welcome them nor inns to entertain or refresh their weatherbeaten bodies; no houses or much less towns to repair to, to seek for succor. It is recorded in scripture, as a mercy to the apostle and his shipwrecked company, that

the barbarians showed them no small kindness in refreshing
them, but these savage barbarians, when they met with
them (as after will appear), were readier to fill their sides
full of arrows than otherwise. And for the season it was
winter, and they that know the winters of that country
know them to be sharp and violent, and subject to cruel
and fierce storms, dangerous to travel to known places,
much more to search an unknown coast. Besides, what
could they see but a hideous and desolate wilderness, full
of wild beasts and wild men—and what multitudes there
might be of them they knew not. Neither could they, as it
were, go up to the top of Pisgah to view from this wilderness a more goodly country to feed their hopes; for which
way soever they turned their eyes (save upward to the
heavens) they could have little solace or content in respect of any outward objects. For summer being done, all
things stand upon them with a weatherbeaten face, and
the whole country, full of woods and thickets, represented
a wild and savage hue. If they looked behind them, there
was the mighty ocean which they had passed and was
now as a main bar and gulf to separate them from all the
civil parts of the world. If it be said they had a ship to
succor them, it is true; but what heard they daily from the
master and company? But that with speed they should
look out a place (with their shallop) where they would be,
at some near distance; for the season was such as he would
not stir from thence till a safe harbor was discovered by
them, where they would be, and he might go without
danger; and that victuals consumed apace but he must and
would keep sufficient for themselves and their return. Yea,
it was muttered by some that if they got not a place in
time, they would turn them and their goods ashore and
leave them. Let it also be considered what weak hopes of
supply and succor they left behind them, that might bear
up their minds in this sad condition and trials they were
under; and they could not but be very small. It is true,
indeed, the affections and love of their brethren at Leyden
was cordial and entire towards them, but they had little
power to help them or themselves; and how the case stood

between them and the merchants at their coming away hath already been declared.

What could now sustain them but the spirit of God and His grace? May not and ought not the children of these fathers rightly say: "Our fathers were Englishmen which came over this great ocean, and were ready to perish in this wilderness; but they cried unto the Lord, and He heard their voice and looked on their adversity" (Deut. 26. 5, 7), "Let them therefore praise the Lord, because He is good: and His mercies endure forever." "Yea, let them which have been redeemed of the Lord, show how He hath delivered them from the hand of the oppressor. When they wandered in the desert wilderness out of the way, and found no city to dwell in, both hungry and thirsty, their soul was overwhelmed in them. Let them confess before the Lord His lovingkindness and His wonderful works before the sons of men" (Psal. 107. 1–5, 8). . . .

I shall a little return back, and begin with a combination made by them before they came ashore; being the first foundation of their government in this place. Occasioned partly by the discontented and mutinous speeches that some of the strangers amongst them had let fall from them in the ship: that when they came ashore they would use their own liberty, for none had power to command them, the patent they had being for Virginia and not for New England, which belonged to another government, with which the Virginia Company had nothing to do. And partly that such an act by them done, this their condition considered, might be as firm as any patent, and in some respects more sure.

The form was as followeth:

IN THE NAME OF GOD, AMEN.

We whose names are underwritten, the loyal subjects of our dread sovereign lord King James, by the grace of God of Great Britain, France, and Ireland, king, defender of the faith, etc.

Having undertaken, for the glory of God and advancement of the Christian faith and honor of our king and country, a voyage to plant the first colony in the northern

parts of Virginia, do by these presents solemnly and
mutually in the presence of God and one of another, covenant and combine ourselves together into a civil body
politic, for our better ordering and preservation and furtherance of the ends aforesaid; and by virtue hereof to
enact, constitute and frame such just and equal laws,
ordinances, acts, constitutions and offices, from time to time,
as shall be thought most meet and convenient for the general good of the colony, unto which we promise all due
submission and obedience. In witness whereof we have
hereunder subscribed our names at Cape Cod, the 11th of
November, in the year of the reign of our sovereign lord
King James, of England, France and Ireland the eighteenth, and of Scotland the fifty-fourth. *Anno Domini* 1620.

After this they chose, or rather confirmed, Mr. John
Carver (a man godly and well approved amongst them)
their governor for that year. And after they had provided
a place for their goods, or common store (which were long
in unloading for want of boats, foulness of the winter
weather and sickness of divers), and begun some small
cottages for their habitations; as time would admit, they
met and consulted of laws and orders, both for their civil
and military government as the necessity of their condition did require, still adding thereunto as urgent occasion
in several times, and as cases did require.

In these hard and difficult beginnings they found some
discontents and murmurings arise amongst some, and
mutinous speeches and carriages in others; but they were
soon quelled and overcome by the wisdom, patience, and
just equal carriage of things, by the governor and better
part, which clave faithfully together in the main.

But that which was most sad and lamentable was, that
in two or three months' time half of their company died,
especially in January and February, being the depth of
winter, and wanting houses and other comforts; being infected with the scurvy and other diseases which this long
voyage and their inaccommodate condition had brought
upon them. So as there died sometimes two or three of a

day in the foresaid time, that of one hundred and odd persons, scarce fifty remained. And of these, in the time of most distress, there was but six or seven sound persons who to their great commendations, be it spoken, spared no pains night nor day, but with abundance of toil and hazard of their own health, fetched them wood, made them fires, dressed them meat, made their beds, washed their loathsome clothes, clothed and unclothed them. In a word, did all the homely and necessary offices for them which dainty and queasy stomachs cannot endure to hear named; and all this willingly and cheerfully, without any grudging in the least, showing herein their true love unto their friends and brethren; a rare example and worthy to be remembered. Two of these seven were Mr. William Brewster, their reverend elder, and Myles Standish, their captain and military commander, unto whom myself and many others were much beholden in our low and sick condition. And yet the Lord so upheld these persons as in this general calamity they were not at all infected either with sickness or lameness. And what I have said of these I may say of many others who died in this general visitation, and others yet living; that whilst they had health, yea, or any strength continuing, they were not wanting to any that had need of them. And I doubt not but their recompense is with the Lord.

2. THOMAS SHEPARD, 1605–1649

[The tiny colony at Plymouth in 1620 was the work of a small band of battered wanderers who had no resources but their own dedication and industry. The Massachusetts Bay Company was the work of a determined group of powerful Puritans, financially well backed, equipped with a royal charter that gave them the right to exercise the prerogatives of the crown. The Company sent an advance guard to Salem in 1628; the fleet comprising the Great Migration arrived in 1630, immediately to organize the communities of Boston, Charlestown, Dorchester, Roxbury and Watertown, each around the precious center of a particular and covenanted church. John Winthrop was governor, the magistrates men of substance and accustomed to command, the clergy already famous as scholars and preachers. In the next ten years it is estimated that over 20,000 persons followed, bringing tools, cattle, clothes and pewter.

There is copious evidence that though the leaders were careful not to advertise the fact, they were fully committed to putting into practice, the moment they set foot on shore, the Congregational rather than the Presbyterian order. They skillfully concealed their intention in order not to alarm the English government, which would surely have prevented the move had it known. For decades Massachusetts and Connecticut solemnly contended that they had never, never separated from the Church of England, that they had only carried a piece of it to New England and there reformed it in the manner which sooner or later all England would follow. But furthermore, in 1630 they hid their purpose so as not to antagonize the multitude of their Puritan friends and supporters who assumed that of course the colonies would proceed to a Presbyterian reformation. Behind this façade of silence—of what later seemed downright duplicity—the leaders, both lay and clerical, had learned from a succession of English theologians (the greatest being William Ames) how to read the New Testament in a Congregational manner. The old myth to the contrary, they needed to learn nothing from Plymouth. "The New England Way," as it came to be called, was a fully developed blueprint in England which the Great Migration simply translated into actual churches.

Even before 1642, English Puritans became profoundly disturbed over rumors about the treasonable conduct of New England, and sent nervous questions asking if such horrid stories were true. To those of John Ball, the Rev. John Davenport returned in 1639 an *Answer* in the name of all the clergy; this convinced the Presbyterians that New England had betrayed the cause, and after it was published in 1643, Ball wrote an attack upon it.

By 1646, after the united Puritans had defeated the King, the conflict between the Presbyterian wing and the

Congregational—or, as they were known in England, the Independents—became virulent. Presbyterians took every occasion to heap abuse upon the New Englanders not only for having plotted in secret and so for having strengthened the Independents, but also for having cowardly deserted the field and so avoided doing their part in the holy war against the bishops. This was a serious charge: if that view were accepted by international Protestantism, the whole justification for the migration would be destroyed. It had proclaimed itself undertaken not for profit but for the mighty cause of the Reformation; if it was an escape from responsibility, then it was not part of the Reformation at all, and its peculiar experiment in church government was a ghastly mistake.

Thomas Shepard undertook to answer these Presbyterian accusations in *A Defence of the Answer made unto the Nine Questions or Positions sent from New-England against the reply thereto by Mr. John Ball,* the manuscript of which was sent to London and there printed in 1648. Shepard is one of the four or five greatest preachers in the first generation. Born in Towcester, the son of a grocer, he entered pensioner at Emmanuel College, Cambridge, receiving his M.A. in 1627. He was silenced by Bishop Laud, escaped to New England in 1635, and was chosen minister at Cambridge. He was particularly energetic in the suppression of the Antinomians; his works enjoyed great repute, one of them, *The Sincere Convert,* being continuously in print from 1641 to 1812.

Shepard defends the removal by recreating the desperate atmosphere of 1630, the year after King Charles had announced that Parliament would never meet again, when the cause of the Almighty Himself seemed lost in England. To Presbyterian ears Shepard's defense must have rung hollow because it is an indirect confession that the New Englanders had schemed from the beginning to execute their base design, but to us the preface is an invaluable summoning up, in the very swirl of the language, of the emotional and spiritual tensions out of which the design was born and energies were moblized to carry it out.]

A DEFENSE OF THE ANSWER

Let us entreat all the godly wise, to consider and look back upon the season of this great enterprise, undertaken by us, and the manner of our proceedings in it, with the admirable workings of God's providence first and last about it: and we think (though we were silent) they may easily satisfy themselves, whether this was of God or men: a sinful neglect of the cause of Christ or a manifest attestation to the truth, by open profession against corruptions of worship in use, and for the necessity of reformation of the church, and that confirmed by no small degree of sufferings for the same.

For was it not a time when human worship and inventions were grown to such an intolerable height that the consciences of God's saints and servants enlightened in the truth could no longer bear them? Was not the power of the tyrannical prelates so great that like a strong current carried all down stream before it, whatever was from the law or otherwise set in their way? Did not the hearts of men generally fail them? Where was the people to be found that would cleave to their godly ministers in their sufferings, but rather thought it their discretion to provide for their own quiet and safety? Yea, when some freely in zeal of the truth preached or professed against the corruptions of the times, did not some take offense at it, judge it rashness and to be against all rules of discretion, who since are ready to censure us for deserting the cause? Many then thought, it is an evil time, the prudent shall hold their peace, and might we not say, this is not our resting place? And what would men have us do in such a case? Must we study some distinctions to salve our consciences in complying with so manifold corruptions in God's worship? Or should we live without God's ordinances because we could not partake in the corrupt administration thereof? Or content ourselves to live without those ordinances of God's worship and communion of saints which He called us unto, and our souls breathed after?

Or should we forsake the public assemblies and join together in private separated churches? How unsufferable it would then have been, the great offense that now is taken at it is a full evidence. And if in cities or some such great towns, that might have been done, yet how was it possible for so many scattered Christians all over the country? It is true, we might have suffered; if we had sought it, we might easily have found the way to have filled the prisons, and some had their share therein.

But whether we were called thereunto when a wide door was set open of liberty otherwise, and our witness to the truth (through the malignant policy of those times) could not be open before the world, but rather smothered up in close prisons or some such ways, together with ourselves, we leave to be considered. We cannot see but the rule of Christ to his apostles and saints, and the practice of God's saints in all ages, may allow us this liberty as well as others: to fly into the wilderness from the face of the dragon. But if it had been so, that the godly ministers and Christians that fled to New England were the most timorous and faint-hearted of all their brethren that stayed behind, and that those sufferings were nothing in comparison of their brethrens' (for why should any boast of sufferings?), yet who doth not know that the spirit who gives various gifts, and all to profit withal, in such times doth single out every one to such work as He in wisdom intends to call them unto? And whom the Lord will honor by suffering for His cause, by imprisonment, etc., He gives them spirits suitable thereto; whom the Lord will reserve for other service or employ in other places, He inclines their hearts rather to fly, giving them an heart suitable to such a condition. It is a case of conscience frequently put and oft resolved by holy Bradford, Peter Martyr, Philpot, and others, in Queen Mary's bloody days, *viz.* whether it was lawful to flee out of the land: to which their answer was that if God gave a spirit of courage and willingness to glorify Him by sufferings, they should stay; but if they found not such a spirit they might lawfully fly: yea, they advised them thereunto. Those servants of Christ, though full of the spirit of glory and of Christ to outface the greatest persecutors in profession of the truth unto the death, yet did not complain of the cowardice of such as fled because they deserted them and the cause, but rather advised diverse so to do, and rejoiced when God gave liberty to their brethren to escape with their lives to the places of liberty, to serve the Lord according to His word. Neither were those faithful saints and servants of God useless and unprofitable in the church of God that fled from the bloody prelates.

The infinite and only wise God hath many works to do in the world, and He doth by His singular providence give gifts to His servants and disposeth them to His work as seemeth best to Himself. If the Lord will have some to bear witness by imprisonments, dismembering, etc., we honor them therein; if He will have others instrumental to promote reformation in England, we honor them and rejoice in their holy endeavors, praying for a blessing upon themselves and labors. And what if God will have His church and the kingdom of Christ go up also in these remote parts of the world, that His name may be known to the heathen, or whatsoever other end He hath, and to this end will send forth a company of weak-hearted Christians which dare not stay at home to suffer—why should we not let the Lord alone and rejoice that Christ is preached howsoever and wheresoever? And who can say that this work was not undertaken and carried on with sincere and right ends and in an holy serious manner, by the chief and the body of such as undertook the same?

The Lord knows whether the sincere desires of worshiping Himself according to His will, of promoting and propagating the Gospel, was not in the hearts of very many in this enterprise; and He that seeth in secret and rewardeth openly knows what prayers and tears have been poured out to God by many alone, and in days of fasting and prayer of God's servants together, for His counsel, direction, assistance, blessing in this work. How many longings and pantings of heart have been in many after the Lord Jesus, to see His goings in His sanctuary as the one thing their souls desired and requested of God, that they might dwell in His house forever; the fruit of which prayers and desires this liberty of New England hath been taken to be and thankfully received from God. Yea, how many serious consultations with one another, and with the faithful ministers and other eminent servants of Christ, have been taken about this work is not unknown to some; which clears us from any rash heady rushing into this place, out of discontent, as many are ready to conceive.

We will here say nothing of the persons whose hearts the Lord stirred up in this business: surely all were not rash, weak-spirited, inconsiderate of what they left behind, or of what it was to go into a wilderness. But if it were well known and considered, or if we were able to express and recount the singular workings of divine providence for the bringing on of this work to what it is come unto, it would stop the mouths of all that have not an heart to accuse and blaspheme the goodness of God in His glorious works: whatever many may say or think, we believe aftertimes will admire and adore the Lord herein, when all His holy ends and the ways He hath used to bring them about shall appear.

Look from one end of the heaven to another, whether the Lord hath assayed to do such a work as this in any nation, so to carry out a people of His own from so flourishing a state to a wilderness so far distant, for such ends and for such a work. Yea, and in a few years hath done for them, as He hath here done for His poor despised people. When we look back and consider what a strange poise of spirit the Lord hath laid upon many of our hearts, we cannot but wonder at ourselves, that so many, and some so weak and tender, with such cheerfulness and constant resolutions against so many persuasions of friends, discouragements from the ill report of this country, the straits, wants, and trials of God's people in it, yet should leave our accommodations and comforts, should forsake our dearest relations, parents, brethren, sisters, Christian friends and acquaintances, overlook all the dangers and difficulties of the vast seas, the thought whereof was a terror to many, and all this to go to a wilderness, where we could forecast nothing but care and temptations, only in hopes of enjoying Christ in his ordinances, in the fellowship of his people. Was this from a stupid senselessness or desperate carelessness what became of us or ours? Or want of natural affections to our dear country or nearest relations? No surely, with what bowels of compassion to our dear country, with what heart-breaking affections to our dear relations and Christian friends many of us at last came away, the Lord is witness.

What shall we say of the singular providence of God bringing so many shiploads of His people through so many dangers, as upon eagles' wings, with so much safety from year to year? The fatherly care of our God in feeding and clothing so many in a wilderness, giving such healthfulness and great increase of posterity? What shall we say of the work itself of the kingdom of Christ? And the form of a commonwealth erected in a wilderness, and in so few years brought to that state that scarce the like can be seen in any of our English colonies in the richest places of this America after many more years standing? That the Lord hath carried the spirits of so many of His people through all their toilsome labor, wants, difficulties, losses, etc., with such a measure of cheerfulness and contentation? But above all we must acknowledge the singular pity and mercies of our God that hath done all this and much more for a people so unworthy, so sinful, that by murmurings of many, unfaithfulness in promises, oppressions, and other evils which are found among us, have so dishonored His majesty, exposed His work here to much scandal and obloquy, for which we have cause forever to be ashamed that the Lord should yet own us and rather correct us in mercy than cast us off in displeasure and scatter us in this wilderness, which gives us cause with Micah 7.18 to say: "Who is a God like our God, that pardoneth iniquities, and passeth by the transgressions of the remnant of His heritage; even because He delighteth in mercy?"

Though we be a people of many weaknesses and wants, yet we acknowledge our God to have been to us a God of many mercies, in respect of that sweet peace which He hath taken away from so many nations, yet continuing the same to us; in respect also of that liberty we have in God's house, the blessed ministry of the word, the sweet unity and communion of God's churches and ministers, increase and multiplication of churches, Christian government in the commonwealth, and many other mercies we enjoy, but especially the gracious presence of Christ to many of our souls in all these.

But we will not insist much upon this subject, being persuaded it is in the consciences and hearts of many of our dear countrymen to think that we should be an object of love and tenderness to that state and people by whose laws and unkind usages we were driven out into a wilderness rather than to be judged as deserters of our brethren and the cause of Christ in hand: with whom (excuse us if we now speak plainly) it had been far more easy unto many of us to have suffered than to have adventured hither upon the wilderness sorrows we expected to have met withal: though we must confess the Lord hath sweetened it beyond our thoughts and utmost expectations of prudent men.

3. EDWARD JOHNSON, 1598–1672

[Edward Johnson was born in Canterbury, brought up to the trade of joiner, and went with the Great Migration to Boston. In 1640 he was a founder of Woburn, and served both town and colony in a variety of public offices. He began writing his history in 1650; it was published in London in 1654.

Though not of the humblest order, Johnson represents the rank and file of the enterprise. He had not, like the clergy, studied at the university and so had not acquired the learned "plain style" of the Puritan pulpit (cf. p. 165); he had read popular romances, and so uses a windy and ornate manner that is not characteristic of Puritan prose. Still, his *Wonder-Working Providence of Sions Saviour* tells the planting of New England as an episode in history in accordance with the Puritan conception of the universal narrative of mankind. This does not lack drama, intensity or anguish even though it be, from beginning to end, under the providential guidance of God. Johnson's re-enactment of the departure makes a striking complement to Shepard's passionate exposition of the reasons behind it.]

WONDER-WORKING PROVIDENCE
OF SION'S SAVIOR

CHAPTER I.

The Sad Condition of England,
When This People Removed.

When England began to decline in religion, like luke-warm Laodicea, and instead of purging out Popery, a far-ther compliance was sought, not only in vain idolatrous ceremonies but also in profaning the Sabbath and, by proc-lamation throughout their parish churches, exasperating lewd and profane persons to celebrate a Sabbath, like the heathen, to Venus, Bacchus and Ceres, insomuch that the multitude of irreligious lascivious and Popish affected per-sons spread the whole land like grasshoppers—in this very time, Christ, the glorious king of his churches, raises an army out of our English nation, for freeing his people from their long servitude under usurping prelacy. And because every corner of England was filled with the fury of malig-nant adversaries, Christ creates a new England to muster up the first of his forces in, whose low condition, little num-ber, and remoteness of place made these adversaries tri-umph, despising this day of small things. But in this height of their pride, the Lord Christ brought sudden and unex-pected destruction upon them. Thus have you a touch of the time when this work began.

Christ Jesus, intending to manifest his kingly office to-ward his churches more fully than ever yet the sons of men saw, even to the uniting of Jew and Gentile churches in one faith, begins with our English nation (whose former reformation being very imperfect), doth now resolve to cast down their false foundation of prelacy, even in the height of their domineering dignity. And therefore in the year 1628, he stirs up his servants as the heralds of a king to make this proclamation for volunteers, as followeth:

"Oh yes! oh yes! oh yes! All you, the people of Christ

that are here oppressed, imprisoned and scurrilously derided, gather yourselves together, your wives and little ones, and answer to your several names as you shall be shipped for his service, in the western world, and more especially for planting the united colonies of New England, where you are to attend the service of the king of kings, upon the divulging of this proclamation by his heralds at arms."

Many (although otherwise willing for this service) began to object as followeth:

"Can it possibly be the mind of Christ (who formerly enabled so many soldiers of his to keep their station unto the death here) that now so many brave soldiers, disciplined by Christ himself, the captain of our salvation, should turn their backs to the disheartening of their fellow soldiers and loss of further opportunity in gaining a great number of subjects to Christ's kingdom?"

Notwithstanding this objection, it was further proclaimed as followeth: "What creature wilt not know that Christ thy king crusheth with a rod of iron the pomp and pride of man; and must he, like man, cast and contrive to take his enemies at advantage? No, of purpose he causeth such instruments to retreat as he hath made strong for himself, that so, his adversaries glorying in the pride of their power, insulting over the little remnant remaining, Christ causeth them to be cast down suddenly forever. And we find in stories reported, earth's princes have passed their armies at need over seas and deep torrents. Could Caesar so suddenly fetch over fresh forces from Europe to Asia, Pompey to foil? How much more shall Christ, who createth all power, call over this nine hundred league ocean at his pleasure such instruments as he thinks meet to make use of in this place, from whence you are now to depart? But further, that you may not delay the voyage intended, for your full satisfaction know this is the place where the Lord will create a new heaven and a new earth in, new churches and a new commonwealth together."

CHAPTER II.

*The Commission of the People of Christ Shipped for
New England, and First of Their Gathering
into Churches.*

"Wherefore, attend to your commission, all you that are
or shall hereafter be shipped for this service. Ye are with
all possible speed to embark yourselves; and as for all such
worthies who are hunted after as David was by Saul and
his courtiers, you may change your habit and ship you with
what secrecy you can, carrying all things most needful for
the voyage and service you are to be employed in after
your landing. But as soon as you shall be exposed to danger of tempestuous seas, you shall forthwith show whose
servants you are by calling on the name of your God, sometimes by extraordinary seeking His pleasing face in times
of deep distress, and publishing your Master's will and
pleasure to all that voyage with you, and that [it] is His
mind to have purity in religion preferred above all dignity
in the world. Your Christ hath commanded the seas they
shall not swallow you, nor pirates imprison your persons or
possess your goods. At your landing, see you observe the
rule of His word, for neither larger nor stricter commission
can He give by any; and therefore at first filling the land
whither you are sent, with diligence search out the mind
of God both in planting and continuing church and civil
government. But be sure they be distinct, yet agreeing and
helping the one to the other. Let the matter and form of
your churches be such as were in the primitive times (before Antichrist's kingdom prevailed), plainly pointed out
by Christ and his apostles in most of their epistles to be
neither national nor provincial, but gathered together in
covenant of such a number as might ordinarily meet together in one place, and built of such living stones as outwardly appear saints by calling. You are also to ordain
elders in every church: make you use of such as Christ
hath endowed with the best gifts for that end; their call
to office small be mediate from you, but their authority and

commission shall be immediate from Christ revealed in his word—which, if you shall slight, despise or condemn, he will soon frustrate your call by taking the most able among you to honor with an everlasting crown, whom you neglected to honor on earth double as their due, or he will carry them remote from you to more infant churches. You are not to put them upon anxious cares for their daily bread, for assuredly (although it may now seem strange) you shall be fed in this wilderness whither you are to go with the flower of wheat, and wine shall be plentiful among you (but be sure you abuse it not). These doctrines, delivered from the word of God, embrace. And let not Satan delude you by persuading their learned skill is unnecessary: soon then will the word of God be slighted as translated by such, and you shall be left bewildered with strange revelations of every fantastic brain."

CHAPTER III.

Of the Voluntary Banishment, Chosen by This People of Christ, and Their Last Farewell Taken of Their Country and Friends.

And now behold, the several regiments of these soldiers of Christ, as they are shipped for his service in the western world, part thereof being come to the town and port of Southampton in England, where they were to be shipped that they might prosecute this design to the full, one ship, called the *Eagle*, they wholly purchase, and many more they hire, filling them with the seed of man and beast to sow this yet untilled wilderness withal, making sale of such land as they possess, to the great admiration of their friends and acquaintance, who thus expostulate with them: "What, will not the large income of your yearly revenue content you, which in all reason cannot choose but be more advantageous both to you and yours, than all that rocky wilderness, whither you are going, to run the hazard of your life? Have you not here your tables filled with great variety of food, your coffers filled with coin, your houses beautifully built and filled with all rich furniture?" Or otherwise: "Have you not such a gainful trade as none the like in the town where you live? Are you not enriched daily? Are not your children very well provided for as they come to years? Nay, may you not here as pithily practice the two chief duties of a Christian (if Christ give strength), namely mortification and sanctification, as in any place of the world? What helps can you have there that you must not carry from hence?"

With bold resolvedness, these stout soldiers of Christ reply: "As death, the king of terror with all his dreadful attendance, inhumane and barbarous tortures doubled and trebled by all the infernal furies, have appeared but light and momentary to the soldiers of Christ Jesus, so also the pleasure, profits and honors of this world set forth in their most glorious splendor and magnitude by the alluring lady of delight, proffering pleasant embraces, cannot entice with her siren songs such soldiers of Christ, whose aims are elevated by him many millions above that brave warrier Ulysses."

Now, seeing all can be said will but barely set forth the immovable resolutions that Christ continued in these men, pass on and attend with tears, if thou hast any, the following discourse, while these men, women and children are taking their last farewell of their native country, kindred, friends and acquaintance, while the ships attend them. Many make choice of some solitary place to echo out their bowel-breaking affections in bidding their friends farewell. "Dear friends," says one, "as near as my own soul doth thy love lodge in my breast, with thought of the heart-burning ravishments that thy heavenly speeches have wrought. My melting soul is poured out at present with these words."

Both of them had their farther speech strangled from the depth of their inward dolor, with breast-breaking sobs, till leaning their heads each on others' shoulders, they let fall the salt-dropping dews of vehement affection, striving to exceed one another, much like the departure of David and Jonathan. Having a little eased their hearts with the still streams of tears, they recovered speech again. "Ah! my much honored friend, hath Christ given thee so great a charge as to be leader of his people into that far remote and vast wilderness? Ay, oh, and alas! thou must die there and never shall I see thy face in the flesh again! Wert thou called to so great a task as to pass the precious ocean and hazard thy person in battle against thousands of malignant enemies there? There were hopes of thy return with triumph. But now after two, three, or four months spent with daily expectation of swallowing waves and cruel pirates, you are to be landed among barbarous Indians, famous for nothing but cruelty, where you are like to spend your days in a famishing condition for a long space!"

Scarce had he uttered this, but presently he locks his friend fast in his arms; holding each other thus for some space of time, they weep again. But, as Paul to his beloved flock, the other replies: "What do you weeping and breaking my heart? I am now pressed for the service of our Lord Christ, to rebuild the most glorious edifice of Mount Sion in a wilderness; and as John Baptist, I must cry, 'Prepare ye the way of the Lord, make His paths straight, for behold, He is coming again!' He is coming to destroy Antichrist and give the whore double to drink the very dregs of His wrath! Then, my dear friend, unfold thy hands, for thou and I have much work to do, I and all Christian soldiers of the world throughout."

Then hand in hand they lead each other to the sandy banks of the brinish ocean, when clenching their hands fast, they unloose not till enforced to wipe their watery eyes, whose constant streams forced a watery path upon their cheeks, which to hide from the eyes of others they shun society for a time. But being called by occasion, whose bald back-part none can lay hold on, they thrust in among the throng now ready to take ship, where they beheld the like affections with their own among diverse relations. Husbands and wives, with mutual consent, are now purposed to part for a time nine hundred leagues asunder; since some providence at present will not suffer them to go together, they resolve their tender affections shall not hinder this work of Christ. The new married and betrothed man, exempt by the law of God from war, now will not claim their privilege, but being constrained by the love of Christ, lock up their natural affections for a time, till the Lord shall be pleased to give them a meeting in this western world, sweetly mixing it with spiritual love. In the meantime, many fathers now take their young Samuels and give them to this service of Christ all their lives. Brethren, sisters, uncles, nephews, nieces, together with all kindred of blood that binds the bowels of affection in a true lovers knot, can now take their last farewell, each of other, although natural affection will still claim her right, and manifest herself to be in the body by looking out at the windows in a mournful manner.

Among this company, thus disposed, doth many reverend and godly pastors of Christ present themselves, some in a seaman's habit. And their scattered sheep, coming as a poor convoy, loftily take their leave of them as followeth: "What doleful days are these, when the best choice our orthodox ministers can make is to take up a perpetual banishment from their native soil, together with their wives and children? We their poor sheep they may not feed but by stole-dread, should they abide here. Lord Christ, here they are at thy command: they go, this is the door thou hast opened upon our earnest request, and we hope it shall never be shut. For England's sake they are going from England, to pray without ceasing for England. O England! thou shalt find New England prayers prevailing with their God for thee; but now, woe alas! what great hardship must these our endeared pastors endure for a long season!"

With these words they lifted up their voices and wept, adding many drops of salt liquor to the ebbing ocean. Then shaking hands they bid adieu with much cordial affection to all their brethren and sisters in Christ. Yet now the scorn and derision of those times, and for this their great enterprise counted as so many cracked brains: but Christ will make all the earth know the wisdom he hath endued them with shall overtop all the human policy in the world, as the sequel we hope will show.

4. JOHN WINTHROP, 1588–1649

[The grandfather of John Winthrop was a wealthy clothier who, in the dissolution of the monasteries, acquired in 1544 the manor of Groton in Norfolk. The family perfectly exemplify those middle-class Englishmen who thus profited financially by Henry VIII's "reformation" of the Church of England. The father was a successful lawyer, and John Winthrop was sent to Trinity College, Cambridge, which he left in his second year in order to be married. He was justice of the peace, and was admitted in 1628 to the Inner Temple. Had he remained in England, this squire of Groton Manor would have become a power in the Long Parliament.

However, upon King Charles' abrogation of Parliament in 1629 he was deprived of his attorneyship. Already a convert to the Congregational ideal of reformation, Winthrop signed the agreement at Cambridge, on August 26, 1629, promising to migrate to New England on condition that the royal charter could be transferred thither. Chosen governor in October, he superintended the tumultuous work of the departure, which we have heard Edward Johnson metaphorically describe. He sailed in March, 1630, as commander-in-chief, aboard the flagship of the Great Migration, the *Arbella*.

As the fleet assembled in Southampton Water, off the Isle of Wight, Governor Winthrop, conscious that he was the chosen Moses of a new and even mightier Exodus, commenced a *Journal*. He may have hoped someday to rework it into a formal history, which then would have been Massachusetts' counterpart to Bradford's *Of Plymouth Plantation,* but the myriad pressures of his offices kept Winthrop from doing more than occasional jottings. Yet for that very reason the collection has an immediacy which an organized treatment would lack; it shows how to the Puritan mind great events and trivial ones were of like importance as significations of God's dealings with mankind.

Sailing from England in March, the fleet reached Salem (called by the Indians Nahumkeck) in June, to be welcomed by John Endecott and the Rev. Samuel Skelton, leaders of the advance guard sent out in 1628. Winthrop went with the main body of the migration to Charlestown, moved across the Charles to Boston in 1631.

With characteristic objectivity, Winthrop speaks of himself in the third person, so that he is "the governor" or "the deputy," depending on his office. In 1636 he was demoted to deputy-governor as the electorate hoped to curry favor with the home government by electing Sir Henry Vane, son of a Privy Councillor. Winthrop dispassionately tells how factions thereupon arose out of a supposed (and probably a real) tension between himself and his nearest rival, Thomas Dudley (father of Anne Bradstreet), who displaced him as governor in 1634, 1640, and 1645. The reply of the servant quoted on April 13, 1645, is the nearest approach to humor in the *Journal,* but in the margin of his record Winthrop wrote "insolent." The synod of 1648, in the last quotation, framed the codification of New England's peculiar church polity, entitled *The Cambridge Platform.*]

JOURNAL

[June 12, 1630.] About four in the morning we were near our port. We shot off two pieces of ordnance, and sent our skiff to Mr. Peirce his ship (which lay in the harbor, and had been there [*blank*] days before). About an hour after, Mr. Allerton came aboard us in a shallop as he was sailing to Pemaquid. As we stood towards the harbor, we saw another shallop coming to us; so we stood in to meet her, and passed through the narrow strait between Baker's Isle and Little Isle, and came to an anchor a little within the islands.

After Mr. Peirce came aboard us, and returned to fetch Mr. Endecott, who came to us about two of the clock, and with him Mr. Skelton and Capt. Levett. We that were of the assistants, and some other gentlemen, and some of the women, and our captain, returned with them to Nahumkeck, where we supped with a good venison pasty and good beer, and at night we returned to our ship, but some of the women stayed behind.

In the meantime most of our people went on shore upon the land of Cape Ann, which lay very near us, and gathered store of fine strawberries.

An Indian came aboard us and lay there all night. . . .

[February 10, 1631.] The frost brake up; and after that, though we had many snows and sharp frost, yet they continued not, neither were the waters frozen up as before. It hath been observed, ever since this bay was planted by Englishmen, *viz.* seven years, that at this day the frost hath broken up every year.

The poorer sort of people (who lay long in tents, etc.) were much afflicted with the scurvy, and many died, especially at Boston and Charlestown; but when this ship came and brought store of juice of lemons, many recovered speedily. It hath been always observed here, that such as fell into discontent, and lingered after their former conditions in England, fell into the scurvy and died. . . .

[October 11, 1631.] The governor, being at his farmhouse at Mystic, walked out after supper, and took a piece in his hand supposing he might see a wolf (for they came daily about the house, and killed swine and calves, etc.;) and, being about half a mile off, it grew suddenly dark, so as, in coming home, he mistook his path, and went till he came to a little house of Sagamore John, which stood empty. There he stayed, and having a piece of match in his pocket (for he always carried about him match and a compass, and in summertime snake-weed,) he made a good fire near the house, and lay down upon some old mats, which he found there, and so spent the night, sometimes walking by the fire, sometimes singing psalms, and sometimes getting wood, but could not sleep. It was (through God's mercy) a warm night; but a little before day it began to rain, and, having no cloak, he made shift by a long pole to climb up into the house. In the morning, there came thither an Indian squaw, but perceiving her before she had opened the door, he barred her out; yet she stayed there a great while essaying to get in, and at last she went away, and he returned safe home, his servants having been much perplexed for him, and having walked about, and shot off pieces, and hallooed in the night, but he heard them not. . . .

[January 18, 1636.] Mr. Vane and Mr. Peter, finding some distraction in the commonwealth, arising from some difference in judgment, and withal some alienation of affection among the magistrates and some other persons of quality, and that hereby factions began to grow among the people, some adhering more to the old governor, Mr. Winthrop, and others to the late governor, Mr. Dudley—the former carrying matters with more lenity, and the latter with more severity—they procured a meeting, at Boston, of the governor, deputy, Mr. Cotton, Mr. Hooker, Mr. Wilson, and there was present Mr. Winthrop, Mr. Dudley, and themselves; where, after the Lord had been sought, Mr. Vane declared the occasion of this meeting (as is before noted), and the fruit aimed at, *viz.* a more firm and friendly uniting of minds, etc., especially of the said Mr. Dudley and Mr. Winthrop, as those upon whom the weight of the affairs did lie, etc., and therefore desired all present to take up a resolution to deal freely and openly with the parties, and they each with other, that nothing might be left in their breasts, which might break out to any jar or difference hereafter (which they promised to do). Then Mr. Winthrop spake to this effect: that when it pleased Mr. Vane to acquaint him with what he had observed, of the dispositions of men's minds inclining to the said faction, etc., it was very strange to him, professing solemnly that he knew not of any breach between his brother Dudley and himself, since they were reconciled long since, neither did he suspect any alienation of affection in him or others from himself, save that, of late, he had observed, that some newcomers had estranged themselves from him, since they went to dwell at Newtown; and so desired all the company, that, if they had seen anything amiss in his government or otherwise, they would deal freely and faithfully with him, and for his part he promised to take it in good part, and would endeavor, by God's grace, to amend it. Then Mr. Dudley spake to this effect: that for his part he came thither a mere patient, not with any intent to charge his brother Winthrop with anything; for though there had been formerly some differences and breaches between them, yet they had been healed, and, for his part, he was not willing to renew them again; and so left it to others to utter their own complaints. Whereupon the governor, Mr. Haynes, spake to this effect: that Mr. Winthrop and himself had been always in good terms, etc.; therefore he was loath to give any offense to him, and he hoped that, considering what the end of this meeting was, he would take it in good part, if he did deal openly and freely, as his manner ever was. Then he spake of one or two passages, wherein he conceived that [he] dealt too remissly in point of justice; to which Mr. Winthrop answered, that his speeches and carriage had been in part mistaken; but withal professed, that it was his judgment, that in the infancy of plantation, justice should be administered with more lenity than in a settled state, because people were then more apt to transgress, partly of ignorance of new laws and orders, partly through oppression of business and other straits; but, if it might be made clear to him, that it was an error, he would be ready to take up a stricter course. Then the ministers were desired to consider of the question by the next morning, and to set down a rule in the case. The next morning, they delivered their several reasons, which all sorted to this conclusion, that strict discipline, both in criminal offenses and in martial affairs, was more needful in plantations than in a settled state, as tending to the honor and safety of the Gospel. Whereupon Mr. Winthrop acknowledged that he was convinced, that he had failed in over much lenity and remissness, and would endeavor (by God's assistance) to take a more strict course hereafter. . . .

[September 25, 1638.] The Court, taking into consideration the great disorder general through the country in costliness of apparel, and following new fashions, sent for the elders of the churches, and conferred with them about it, and laid it upon them, as belonging to them, to redress it, by urging it upon the consciences of their people, which they promised to do. But little was done about it; for divers of the elders' wives, etc., were in some measure partners in this general disorder. . . .

[May 26, 1639.] Mr. Hooker being to preach at Cambridge, the governor and many others went to hear him (though the governor did very seldom go from his own congregation upon the Lord's day). He preached in the afternoon, and having gone on, with much strength of voice and intention of spirit, about a quarter of an hour, he was at a stand, and told the people that God had deprived him both of his strength and matter, etc., and so went forth, and about half an hour after returned again, and went on to very good purpose about two hours. . . .

[December 15, 1640.] About this time there fell out a thing worthy of observation. Mr. Winthrop the younger, one of the magistrates, having many books in a chamber where there was corn of divers sorts, had among them one wherein the Greek testament, the psalms and the common prayer were bound together. He found the common prayer eaten with mice, every leaf of it, and not any of the two other touched, nor any other of his books, though there were above a thousand.

[April 13, 1641.] A godly woman of the church of Boston, dwelling sometimes in London, brought with her a parcel of very fine linen of great value, which she set her heart too much upon, and had been at charge to have it all newly washed, and curiously folded and pressed, and so left it in press in her parlor overnight. She had a Negro maid went into the room very late, and let fall some snuff of the candle upon the linen, so as by the morning all the linen was burned to tinder, and the boards underneath, and some stools and a part of the wainscot burned, and never perceived by any in the house, though some lodged in the chamber overhead, and no ceiling between. But it pleased God that the loss of this linen did her much good, both in taking off her heart from worldly comforts, and in preparing her for a far greater affliction by the untimely death of her husband, who was slain not long after at Isle of Providence.

[September 15, 1641.] A great training at Boston two days. About 1200 men were exercised in most sorts of land service; yet it was observed that there was no man drunk, though there was plenty of wine and strong beer in the town, not an oath sworn, no quarrel, nor any hurt done.

[September 22, 1642.] The sudden fall of land and cattle, and the scarcity of foreign commodities, and money, etc., with the thin access of people from England, put many into an unsettled frame of spirit, so as they concluded there would be no subsisting here, and accordingly they began to hasten away, some to the West Indies, others to the Dutch, at Long Island, etc. (for the governor there invited them by fair offers), and others back for England. . . .

. . . They fled for fear of want, and many of them fell into it, even to extremity, as if they had hastened into the misery which they feared and fled from, besides the depriving themselves of the ordinances and church fellowship, and those civil liberties which they enjoyed here; whereas, such as stayed in their places, kept their peace and ease, and enjoyed still the blessing of the ordinances, and never tasted of those troubles and miseries, which they heard to have befallen those who departed. Much disputation there was about liberty of removing for outward advantages, and all ways were sought for an open door to get out at; but it is to be feared many crept out at a broken wall. For such as come together into a wilderness, where are nothing but wild beasts and beastlike men, and there confederate together in civil and church estate, whereby they do, implicitly at least, bind themselves to support each other, and all of them that society, whether civil or sacred, whereof they are members, how they can break from this without free consent, is hard to find, so as may satisfy a tender or good conscience in time of trial. Ask thy conscience, if thou wouldst have plucked up thy stakes, and brought thy family 3000 miles, if thou hadst expected that all, or most, would have forsaken thee there? Ask again, what liberty thou hast towards others, which thou likest not to allow others towards thyself? For if one may go, another may, and so the greater part, and so church and commonwealth may be left destitute in a wilderness, exposed to misery and reproach, and all for thy ease and pleasure; whereas these all, being now thy brethren, as

near to thee as the Israelites were to Moses, it were much
safer for thee, after his example, to choose rather to suffer
affliction with thy brethren, than to enlarge thy ease and
pleasure by furthering the occasion of their ruin.

[July 5, 1643.] There arose a sudden gust at N.W. so
violent for half an hour, as it blew down multitudes of trees.
It lifted up their meeting house at Newbury, the people
being in it. It darkened the air with dust, yet through God's
great mercy it did no hurt, but only killed one Indian with
the fall of a tree.

[January 18, 1644.] The 18th of this month two lights
were seen near Boston (as is before mentioned), and a
week after the like was seen again. A light like the moon
arose about the N.E. point in Boston, and met the former
at Nottles Island, and there they closed in one, and then
parted, and closed and parted divers times, and so went
over the hill in the island and vanished. Sometimes they
shot out flames and sometimes sparkles. This was about
eight of the clock in the evening, and was seen by many.
About the same time a voice was heard upon the water
between Boston and Dorchester, calling out in a most
dreadful manner, "Boy, boy, come away, come away," and
it suddenly shifted from one place to another a great distance, about twenty times. It was heard by divers godly
persons. About 14 days after, the same voice in the same
dreadful manner was heard by others on the other side of
the town towards Nottles Island.

These prodigies having some reference to the place
where Captain Chaddock's pinnace was blown up a little
before, gave occasion of speech of that man who was the
cause of it, who professed himself to have skill in necro-
mancy, and to have done some strange things in his way
from Virginia hither, and was suspected to have murdered
his master there; but the magistrates here had not notice
of him till after he was blown up. This is to be observed
that his fellows were all found, and others who were blown
up in the former ship were also found, and others also who
have miscarried by drowning, etc., have usually been
found, but this man was never found. . . .

[March 21, 1644.] One Dalkin and his wife dwelling near

Medford coming from Cambridge, where they had spent their Sabbath, and being to pass over the river at a ford, the tide not being fallen enough, the husband adventured over, and finding it too deep, persuaded his wife to stay awhile, but it raining very sore, she would needs adventure over, and was carried away with the stream past her depth. Her husband, not daring to go help her, cried out, and thereupon his dog, being at his house near by, came forth, and seeing something in the water, swam to her, and she caught hold on the dog's tail, so he drew her to the shore and saved her life.

[July 15, 1644.] A poor man of Hingham, one Painter, who had lived at New Haven and at Rowley and Charlestown, and been scandalous and burdensome by his idle and troublesome behavior to them all, was now on the sudden turned Anabaptist, and having a child born, he would not suffer his wife to bring it to the ordinance of baptism, for she was a member of the church, though himself were not. Being presented for this, and enjoined to suffer the child to be baptized, he still refusing, and disturbing the church, he was again brought to the Court not only for his former contempt, but also for saying that our baptism was antichristian; and in the open Court he affirmed the same. Whereupon after much patience and clear conviction of his error, etc., because he was very poor, so as no other but corporal punishment could be fastened upon him, he was ordered to be whipped, not for his opinion, but for reproaching the Lord's ordinance, and for his bold and evil behavior both at home and in the Court. He endured his punishment with much obstinacy, and when he was loosed, he said boastingly, that God had marvelously assisted him. Whereupon two or three honest men, his neighbors, affirmed before all the company, that he was of very loose behavior at home, and given much to lying and idleness, etc. Nor had he any great occasion to gather God's assistance from his stillness under the punishment, which was but moderate, for divers notorious malefactors had showed the like, and one the same Court.

[April 13, 1645.] Mr. Hopkins, the governor of Hartford upon Connecticut, came to Boston, and brought his wife with him (a godly young woman, and of special parts), who was fallen into a sad infirmity, the loss of her understanding and reason, which had been growing upon her divers years, by occasion of her giving herself wholly to reading and writing, and had written many books. Her husband, being very loving and tender of her, was loath to grieve her; but he saw his error, when it was too late. For if she had attended her household affairs, and such things as belong to women, and not gone out of her way and calling to meddle in such things as are proper for men, whose minds are stronger, etc., she had kept her wits, and might have improved them usefully and honorably in the place God had set her. He brought her to Boston, and left her with her brother, one Mr. Yale, a merchant, to try what means might be had here for her. But no help could be had.

[April 13, 1645.] The wars in England kept servants from coming to us, so as those we had could not be hired, when their times were out, but upon unreasonable terms, and we found it very difficult to pay their wages to their content (for money was very scarce). I may upon this occasion report a passage between one of Rowley and his servant. The master, being forced to sell a pair of his oxen to pay his servant his wages, told his servant he could keep him no longer, not knowing how to pay him the next year. The servant answered, he would serve him for more of his cattle. "But how shall I do," saith the master, "when all my cattle are gone?" The servant replied, "You shall then serve me, and so you may have your cattle again."

[July 3, 1645.] Divers free schools were erected, as at Roxbury (for maintenance whereof every inhabitant bound some house or land for a yearly allowance forever) and at Boston (where they made an order to allow forever 50 pounds to the master and an house and 30 pounds to an usher, who should also teach to read and write and cipher, and Indians' children were to be taught freely, and the charge to be by yearly contribution, either by voluntary allowance, or by rate of such as refused, etc., and this order was confirmed by the General Court) . . . Other towns did the like, providing maintenance by several means.

[July, 1646.] Great harm was done in corn (especially wheat and barley) in this month by a caterpillar, like a black worm about an inch and a half long. They ate up first the blades of the stalk, then they ate up the tassels, whereupon the ear withered. It was believed by divers good observers, that they fell in a great thunder shower, for divers yards and other bare places, where not one of them was to be seen an hour before, were presently after the shower almost covered with them, besides grass places where they were not so easily discerned. They did the most harm in the southern parts, as Rhode Island, etc., and in the eastern parts in their Indian corn. In divers places the churches kept a day of humiliation, and presently after the caterpillars vanished away.

[September 20, 1646.] There fell a sad affliction upon the country this year, though it more particularly concerned New Haven and those parts. A small ship of about 100 tons set out from New Haven in the middle of the eleventh month last (the harbor there being so frozen, as they were forced to hew her through the ice near three miles). She was laden with pease and some wheat, all in bulk, with about 200 West India hides, and store of beaver, and plate, so as it was estimated in all at 5000 pounds. There were in her about seventy persons, whereof divers were of very precious account, as Mr. Grigson, one of their magistrates, the wife of Mr. Goodyear, another of their magistrates (a right godly woman), Captain Turner, Mr. Lamberton, master of the ship, and some seven or eight others, members of the church there. The ship never went voyage before, and was very crank-sided, so as it was conceived, she was overset in a great tempest, which happened soon after she put to sea, for she was never heard of after. . . .

[June 28, 1648.] There appeared over the harbor at New Haven, in the evening, the form of the keel of a ship with three masts, to which were suddenly added all the tackling and sails, and presently after, upon the top of the poop, a man standing with one hand akimbo under his left side, and in his right hand a sword stretched out toward the sea. Then from the side of the ship which was from the town arose a great smoke, which covered all the ship, and in that smoke she vanished away; but some saw her keel sink into the water. This was seen by many, men and women, and it continued about a quarter of an hour. . . .

[June 4, 1647.] An epidemical sickness was through the country among Indians and English, French and Dutch. It took them like a cold, and a light fever with it. Such as bled or used cooling drinks died; those who took comfortable things, for most part recovered, and that in few days. Wherein a special providence of God appeared, for not a family, nor but few persons escaping it, had it brought all so weak as it did some, and continued so long, our hay and corn had been lost for want of help; but such was the mercy of God to his people, as few died, not above forty or fifty in the Massachusetts, and near as many at Connecticut. But that which made the stroke more sensible and grievous, both to them and to all the country, was the death of that faithful servant of the Lord, Mr. Thomas Hooker, pastor of the church in Hartford, who, for piety, prudence, wisdom, zeal, learning, and what else might make him serviceable in the place and time he lived in, might be compared with men of greatest note; and he shall need no other praise: the fruits of his labors in both Englands shall preserve an honorable and happy remembrance of him forever.

[June 14.] In this sickness the governor's wife, daughter of Sir John Tindal, Knight, left this world for a better, being about fifty-six years of age: a woman of singular virtue, prudence, modesty, and piety, and specially beloved and honored of all the country.

[August 15, 1648.] The synod met at Cambridge by adjournment from the 4 [June] last. Mr. Allen of Dedham preached out of Acts 15, a very godly, learned, and particular handling of near all the doctrines and applications concerning that subject with a clear discovery and refutation of such errors, objections, and scruples as had been raised about it by some young heads in the country.

It fell out, about the midst of his sermon, there came a snake into the seat, where many of the elders sat behind the preacher. It came in at the door where people stood thick upon the stairs. Divers of the elders shifted from it, but Mr. Thomson, one of the elders of Braintree (a man of much faith), trode upon the head of it, and so held it with his foot and staff with a small pair of grains, until it was killed. This being so remarkable, and nothing falling out but by divine providence, it is out of doubt, the Lord discovered somewhat of His mind in it. The serpent is the devil; the synod, the representative of the churches of Christ in New England. The devil had formerly and lately attempted their disturbance and dissolution; but their faith in the seed of the woman overcame him and crushed his head.

5. JOHN WINTHROP, 1588–1649

[Mistress Anne Hutchinson, wife of William and mother of many children, hung with rapture upon the preaching of John Cotton at Boston in Lincolnshire, and so followed him, with her family, to the Boston of Massachusetts in 1634. Winthrop tells, as an integral part of the *Journal,* the tragic consequences of her passionate devotion to Cotton, which in 1636, when the incompetent Vane was governor, almost wrecked the colony. There are other records of the crisis (see Charles Francis Adams, *Antinomianism in the Colony of Massachusetts Bay,* 1894), but Winthrop's is the most dramatic because it was he who fought with cold ferocity the heresy propounded by Mistress Anne and her brother-in-law, John Wheelwright. Winthrop ousted Vane from the governorship in May, 1637, and then relentlessly forced through the ecclesiastical excommunication (ironically pronounced by John Cotton himself) and the civil banishment in March, 1638.

Though disguised to modern ears by the technical language of theology, the purport of the Antinomian heresy is clear. Protestant orthodoxy held that men are saved by their faith in Christ, not their good works, that Christ has fulfilled the law, satisfied the vengeance of God, so that his righteousness is "imputed" to the saints for their salvation. This legal ascribing of Christ's virtue to an individual's account is his "justification." A justified person would thereafter strive to achieve a perfect Christian life, which would be his "sanctification," though in this existence it is bound to be, at best, imperfect. However, the creation of any degree of ability so to strive is, according to the orthodox view, a work of the Holy Ghost; yet at the same time, the individuality of the saint is respected and his efforts toward sanctification must emanate from his own genuine exertions.

The version of this doctrine worked out by Mrs. Hutchinson and her adherents is a vitalistic, mystical restatement. By maintaining that "the Holy Ghost dwells in a justified person" she concluded that the saint in the moment of justification receives an influx of energy which overwhelms and obliterates his individuality, carrying him on a wave of ecstasy. Consequently she argued that it makes no difference whether he achieves any sanctification whatsoever, that his good or bad conduct is irrelevant. The saint is to surrender his will to the promptings and propulsions from within. To Winthrop this doctrine led to an abandonment of all individual moral responsibility, to an ethical anarchy which would have the most dangerous of social consequences.

From the orthodox point of view, Mrs. Hutchinson's admission before the General Court that she received special revelations direct from God was proof positive that she had been seduced by Satan. Direct revelation had come to an end with the completion of the Bible, and though God continues to indicate His wishes through the providential management of the world, no mortal can pretend that he or she receives commands in so many words. Conversion gives the saint an ability to comprehend and believe the truths of the Bible, but it imparts no content of truth. If Mrs. Hutchinson had been allowed to "vent" her revelations, the fabric of the Puritan state would have been torn to shreds.

Banished to Rhode Island, Mrs. Hutchinson moved in 1642 (after the death of her husband) to what is now New Rochelle, New York, and there in August of 1643 was butchered by the Indians, the news of her death being

greeted in Massachusetts Bay as a divine confirmation of
the community's sentence upon her.]

THE ANTINOMIAN CRISIS

[October 21, 1636.] One Mrs. Hutchinson, a member of
the church of Boston, a woman of a ready wit and bold
spirit, brought over with her two dangerous errors: 1. That
the person of the Holy Ghost dwells in a justified person.
2. That no sanctification can help to evidence to us our
justification. From these two grew many branches; as: our
union with the Holy Ghost, so as a Christian remains dead
to every spiritual action, and hath no gifts nor graces, other
than such as are in hypocrites, nor any other sanctification
but the Holy Ghost himself.

There joined with her in these opinions a brother of hers,
one Mr. Wheelwright, a silenced minister sometimes in
England.

[October 25.] The other ministers in the Bay, hearing of
these things, came to Boston at the time of a General Court,
and entered conference in private with them, to the end
they might know the certainty of these things; that if need
were, they might write to the church of Boston about them,
to prevent (if it were possible) the dangers, which seemed
hereby to hang over that and the rest of the churches. At
this conference, Mr. Cotton was present, and gave satisfaction to them, so as he agreed with them all in the point
of sanctification, and so did Mr. Wheelwright; so as they
all did hold, that sanctification did help to evidence justification. The same he had delivered plainly in public,
divers times; but, for the indwelling of the person of the
Holy Ghost, he held that still, as some others of the ministers did, but not union with the person of the Holy Ghost
(as Mrs. Hutchinson and others did), so as to amount to a
personal union. . . .

[November 17.] The governor, Mr. Vane, a wise and
godly gentleman, held, with Mr. Cotton and many others,
the indwelling of the person of the Holy Ghost in a believer,
and went so far beyond the rest, as to maintain a personal

union with the Holy Ghost; but the deputy [Winthrop], with the pastor [Wilson] and divers others, denied both; and the question proceeded so far by disputation (in writing, for the peace sake of the church, which all were tender of), as at length they could not find the person of the Holy Ghost in scripture, nor in the primitive churches three hundred years after Christ. So that, all agreeing in the chief matter of substance, *viz.* that the Holy Ghost is God, and that he doth dwell in the believers (as the Father and Son both are said also to do), but whether by His gifts and power only, or by any other manner of presence, seeing the scripture doth not declare it, it was earnestly desired, that the word person might be forborn, being a term of human invention, and tending to doubtful disputation in this case. . . .

[December 10.] At this Court the elders of the churches were called, to advise with them about discovering and pacifying the differences among the churches in point of opinion. The governor having declared the occasion to them, Mr. Dudley desired that men would be free and open, etc. Another of the magistrates spake, that it would much further the end they came for, if men would freely declare what they held different from others, as himself would freely do, in what point soever he should be opposed. The governor said that he would be content to do the like, but that he understood the ministers were about it in a church way, etc., which he spake upon this occasion: the ministers had met, a little before, and had drawn into heads all the points, wherein they suspected Mr. Cotton did differ from them, and had propounded them to him, and pressed him to a direct answer, affirmative or negative, to every one; which he had promised, and taken time for. This meeting being spoke of in the Court the day before, the governor took great offense at it, as being without his privity, etc., which this day Mr. Peter told him as plainly of (with all due reverence), and how it had sadded the ministers' spirits, that he should be jealous of their meetings, or seem to restrain their liberty, etc. The governor excused his speech, as sudden and upon a mistake. Mr. Peter told him also that before he came, within less than two years since, the churches were in peace, etc. The governor answered that the light of the Gospel brings a sword, and the children of the bondwoman would persecute those of the freewoman. Mr. Peter also besought him humbly to consider his youth and short experience in the things of God, and to beware of peremptory conclusions, which he perceived him to be very apt unto. . . .

Mr. Wilson made a very sad speech of the condition of our churches and the inevitable danger of separation, if these differences and alienations among brethren were not speedily remedied; and laid the blame upon these new opinions risen up amongst us, which all the magistrates, except the governor and two others, did confirm, and all the ministers but two. . . .

The speech of Mr. Wilson was taken very ill by Mr. Cotton and others of the same church, so as he and divers of them went to admonish him. But Mr. Wilson and some others could see no breach of rule, seeing he was called by the Court about the same matter with the rest of the elders, and exhorted to deliver their minds freely and faithfully, both for discovering the danger, and the means to help; and the things he spake of were only in general, and such as were under a common fame. And being questioned about his intent, he professed he did not mean Boston church, nor the members thereof, more than others. But this would not satisfy, but they called him to answer publicly, [December] 31; and there the governor pressed it violently against him, and all the congregation, except the deputy and one or two more, and many of them with much bitterness and reproaches; but he answered them all with words of truth and soberness, and with marvelous wisdom. It was strange to see how the common people were led, by example, to condemn him in that, which (it was very probable) divers of them did not understand, nor the rule which he was supposed to have broken; and that such as had known him so long, and what good he had done for that church, should fall upon him with such bitterness for justifying himself in a good cause; for he was a very holy, upright man, and for faith and love inferior to none in the country, and most dear to all men. The teacher joined with the church in their judgment of him (not without some appearance of prejudice), yet with much wisdom and moderation. They were eager to proceed to present censure, but the teacher stayed them from that, telling them he might not do it, because some opposed it, but gave him a grave exhortation. The next day Mr. Wilson preached, notwithstanding, and the Lord so assisted him, as gave great satisfaction, and the governor himself gave public witness to him. . . .

[January 20, 1637.] The differences in the said points of religion increased more and more, and the ministers of both sides (there being only Mr. Cotton of one party) did publicly declare their judgments in some of them, so as all men's mouths were full of them. And there being, [February] 3, a ship ready to go for England, and many passengers in it, Mr. Cotton took occasion to speak to them about the differences, etc., and willed them to tell our countrymen that all the strife amongst us was about magnifying the grace of God; one party seeking to advance the grace of God within us, and the other to advance the grace of God towards us (meaning by the one justification, and by the other sanctification); and so bade them tell them that, if there were any among them that would strive for grace, they should come hither; and so declared some particulars. Mr. Wilson spake after him, and declared that he knew none of the elders or brethren of the churches, but did labor to advance the free grace of God in justification, so far as the word of God required; and spake also about the doctrine of sanctification, and the use and necessity, etc., of it; by occasion whereof no man could tell (except some few, who knew the bottom of the matter) where any difference was: which speech, though it offended those of Mr. Cotton's party, yet it was very seasonable to clear the rest, who otherwise should have been reputed to have opposed free grace. Thus every occasion increased the contention, and caused great alienation of minds; and the members of Boston (frequenting the lectures of other ministers) did make much disturbance by public questions, and objections to their doctrines, which did any way disagree from their opinions; and it began to be as common here to distinguish between men, by being under a covenant of grace or a covenant of works, as in other countries between Protestants and Papists. . . .

[March 9.] Mr. Wheelwright, one of the members of Boston, preaching at the last fast, inveighed against all that walked in a covenant of works, as he described it to be, *viz.* such as maintain sanctification as an evidence of justification, etc., and called them Antichrists, and stirred up the people against them with much bitterness and vehemency. For this he was called into the Court, and his sermon being produced, he justified it, and confessed he did mean all that walk in such a way. Whereupon the elders of the rest of the churches were called, and asked whether they, in their ministry, did walk in such a way. They all acknowledged they did. So, after much debate, the Court adjudged him guilty of sedition, and also of contempt, for that the Court had appointed the fast as a means of reconciliation of the differences, etc., and he purposely set himself to kindle and increase them. The governor and some few more (who dissented) tendered a protestation, which, because it wholly justified Mr. Wheelwright and condemned the proceedings of the Court, was rejected. The church of Boston also tendered a petition in his behalf, justifying Mr. Wheelwright's sermon. The Court deferred sentence till the next Court, and advised with the ministers, etc., whether they might enjoin his silence, etc. They answered that they were not clear in that point, but desired rather that he might be commended to the church of Boston to take care of him, etc., which accordingly was done, and he enjoined to appear at the next Court. Much heat of contention was this Court between the opposite parties; so as it was moved, that the next Court might be kept at Newtown. . . .

[May 17.] Our Court of elections was at Newtown. So soon as the Court was set, being about one of the clock, a petition was preferred by those of Boston. The governor would have read it, but the deputy said it was out of order; it was a Court for elections, and those must first be dispatched, and then their petitions should be heard. Divers others also opposed that course, as an ill precedent, etc.;

and the petition, being about pretense of liberty, etc.
(though intended chiefly for revoking the sentence given
against Mr. Wheelwright), would have spent all the day in
debate, etc.; but yet the governor and those of that party
would not proceed to election, except the petition was
read. Much time was already spent about this debate, and
the people crying out for election, it was moved by the
deputy that the people should divide themselves, and the
greater number must carry it. And so it was done, and
the greater number by many were for election. But the
governor and that side kept their place still, and would
not proceed. Whereupon the deputy told him that, if he
would not go to election, he and the rest of that side would
proceed. Upon that, he came from his company, and they
went to election; and Mr. Winthrop was chosen governor,
Mr. Dudley deputy and Mr. Endecott of the standing
council; and Mr. Israel Stoughton and Mr. Richard Sal-
tonstall were called in to be assistants; and Mr. Vane, Mr.
Coddington, and Mr. Dummer (being all of that faction)
were left quite out.

There was great danger of a tumult that day; for those
of that side grew into fierce speeches, and some laid hands
on others; but seeing themselves too weak, they grew quiet.
They expected a great advantage that day, because the
remote towns were allowed to come in by proxy; but it
fell out, that there were enough beside. . . .

[August 30.] The synod, called the assembly, began at
Newtown. There were all the teaching elders through the
country, and some new come out of England, not yet called
to any place here, as Mr. Davenport, etc.

The assembly began with prayer, made by Mr. Shepard,
the pastor of Newtown. Then the erroneous opinions, which
were spread in the country, were read (being eighty in
all); next the unwholesome expressions; then the scriptures
abused. Then they chose two moderators for the next day,
viz. Mr. Bulkeley and Mr. Hooker, and these were continued in that place all the time of the assembly. There
were about eighty opinions, some blasphemous, others erroneous, and all unsafe, condemned by the whole assembly;
whereto near all the elders, and others sent by the

churches, subscribed their names; but some few liked not subscription, though they consented to the condemning of them. . . .

[November 1.] There was great hope that the late general assembly would have had some good effect in pacifying the troubles and dissensions about matters of religion; but it fell out otherwise. For though Mr. Wheelwright and those of his party had been clearly confuted and confounded in the assembly, yet they persisted in their opinions, and were as busy in nourishing contentions (the principal of them) as before. Whereupon the General Court, being assembled in the 2 of [November], and finding, upon consultation, that two so opposite parties could not contain in the same body, without apparent hazard of ruin to the whole, agreed to send away some of the principal. . . . Then the Court sent for Mr. Wheelwright, and, he persisting to justify his sermon, and his whole practice and opinions, and refusing to leave either the place or his public exercisings, he was disfranchised and banished. Upon which he appealed to the king, but neither called witnesses, nor desired any act to be made of it. The Court told him that an appeal did not lie; for by the king's grant we had power to hear and determine without any reservation, etc. So he relinquished his appeal, and the Court gave him leave to go to his house, upon his promise that, if he were not gone out of our jurisdiction within fourteen days, he would render himself to one of the magistrates.

The Court also sent for Mrs. Hutchinson, and charged her with divers matters, as her keeping two public lectures every week in her house, whereto sixty or eighty persons did usually resort, and for reproaching most of the ministers (viz. all except Mr. Cotton) for not preaching a covenant of free grace, and that they had not the seal of the spirit, nor were able ministers of the New Testament; which were clearly proved against her, though she sought to shift it off. And, after many speeches to and fro, at last she was so full as she could not contain, but vented her revelations; amongst which this was one, that she had it revealed to her, that she should come into New England, and should here be persecuted, and that God would ruin us and our posterity, and the whole state, for the same. So the Court proceeded and banished her; but, because it was winter, they committed her to a private house, where she was well provided, and her own friends and the elders permitted to go to her, but none else. . . .

After this, many of the church of Boston, being highly offended with the governor for this proceeding, were earnest with the elders to have him called to account for it; but they were not forward in it, and himself, understanding their intent, thought fit to prevent such a public disorder, and so took occasion to speak to the congregation to this effect:

. . . He did nothing in the cases of the brethren, but by the advice and direction of our teacher and other of the elders. For in the oath, which was administered to him and the rest, etc., there was inserted: "In all causes wherein you are to give your vote, etc., you are to give your vote as in your judgment and conscience you shall see to be most for the public good, etc." And so for his part he was persuaded that it would be most for the glory of God, and the public good, to pass sentence as they did.

He would give them one reason, which was a ground for his judgment, and that was, for that he saw that those brethren, etc., were so divided from the rest of the country in their judgment and practice, as it could not stand with the public peace, that they should continue amongst us. So, by the example of Lot in Abraham's family, and after Hagar and Ishmael, he saw they must be sent away. . . .

[March 1, 1638.] While Mrs. Hutchinson continued at Roxbury, divers of the elders and others resorted to her, and finding her to persist in maintaining those gross errors beforementioned, and many others, to the number of thirty or thereabout, some of them wrote to the church at Boston, offering to make proof of the same before the church, etc., [March] 15; whereupon she was called (the magistrates being desired to give her license to come), and the lecture was appointed to begin at ten. . . . When she appeared, the errors were read to her. . . . These were also clearly confuted, but yet she held her own; so as the church (all but two of her sons) agreed she should be admonished, and because her sons would not agree to it, they were admonished also.

Mr. Cotton pronounced the sentence of admonition with great solemnity, and with much zeal and detestation of her errors and pride of spirit. The assembly continued till eight at night, and all did acknowledge the special presence of God's spirit therein; and she was appointed to appear again the next lecture day. . . .

[March 22.] Mrs. Hutchinson appeared again (she had been licensed by the Court, in regard she had given hope of her repentance, to be at Mr. Cotton's house, that both he and Mr. Davenport might have the more opportunity to deal with her); and the articles being again read to her, and her answer required, she delivered it in writing, wherein she made a retraction of near all, but with such explanations and circumstances as gave no satisfaction to the church; so as she was required to speak further to them. Then she declared that it was just with God to leave her to herself, as He had done, for her slighting His ordinances, both magistracy and ministry; and confessed that what she had spoken against the magistrates at the Court (by way of revelation) was rash and ungrounded; and desired the church to pray for her. This gave the church good hope of her repentance; but when she was examined about some particulars, as that she had denied inherent righteousness, etc., she affirmed that it was never her judgment; and though it was proved by many testimonies, that she had been of that judgment, and so had persisted, and maintained it by argument against divers, yet she impudently persisted in her affirmation, to the astonishment of all the assembly. So that, after much time and many arguments had been spent to bring her to see her sin, but all in vain, the church, with one consent, cast her out. Some moved to have her admonished once more; but, it being for manifest evil in matter of conversation, it was agreed otherwise; and for that reason also the sentence was denounced by the pastor, matter of manners belonging properly to his place.

After she was excommunicated, her spirits, which seemed before to be somewhat dejected, revived again, and she gloried in her sufferings, saying that it was the greatest happiness, next to Christ, that ever befell her. Indeed, it was a happy day to the churches of Christ here, and to many poor souls who had been seduced by her, who, by what they heard and saw that day, were (through the grace of God) brought off quite from her errors, and settled again in the truth. . . .

After two or three days, the governor sent a warrant to Mrs. Hutchinson to depart this jurisdiction before the last of this month, according to the order of Court, and for that end set her at liberty from her former constraint, so as she was not to go forth of her own house till her departure; and upon the 28th she went by water to her farm at the Mount, where she was to take water, with Mr. Wheelwright's wife and family, to go to Pascataquack; but she changed her mind, and went by land to Providence, and so to the island in the Naragansett Bay, which her husband and the rest of that sect had purchased of the Indians, and prepared with all speed to remove unto. For the Court had ordered that, except they were gone with their families by such a time, they should be summoned to the General Court.

6. COTTON MATHER, 1663–1728

[Cotton Mather, son of Increase and grandson of both Richard Mather and John Cotton, was born to the heritage of clerical leadership and extensive erudition. He fought hard against changing times to maintain the first, and in the second achieved a staggering success. Posterity remembers him as the persecutor of witches, though all he had to do with the miserable proceedings at Salem in 1692 was —and this is reprehensible enough—urge the Court on and then write a defense of its actions after everybody, including Cotton Mather, realized that it had been caught in a panic and had proceeded on fallacious legal principles.

In historical fact, his book defending the procedure, *The Wonders of the Invisible World*, was only a minor episode in Mather's long career (1684–1728) as minister of the Second Church in Boston (until 1723 as colleague with his father), and as author of over five hundred printed titles. The most massive of these is *Magnalia Christi Americana* ("The Great Achievements of Christ in America"), a folio published in London in 1702. It is a prodigious gathering from survivors or from the papers of the founders of everything that happened in New England since the settlement of Plymouth and Boston.

For our purposes, it is important as exemplifying (although in a style more recondite, not to say more tormented, than the normal ideal of the "plain") the Puritan conception of history, the theory of which is set forth in "A General Introduction." Because the Puritan writer held that everything that has happened has been under divine control, then every event, the minutest as well as the greatest, has a significance. The historian was duty-bound to record everything, even if he could not make it intelligible. But on the other hand, God regulates the universe for conscious purposes, and so the function of the historian was not only to relate facts but to interpret them. Thus Puritan history was peculiarly obliged to be concrete and at the same time to strain after design. While it must be heavily (sometimes tediously) specific, it must also be didactic. (In recent times, Henry Adams inherited the mantle of Cotton Mather.) A history of New England would need to be also a sermon to New Englanders. The historian would be what Urian Oakes in 1673 called "a Lord's remembrancer or recorder," though he had to be that while maintaining a conscientious respect for accuracy. This difficult task, in its entirety, Cotton Mather took upon himself in the *Magnalia*, and in his introduction set forth his and the people's philosophy.]

A GENERAL INTRODUCTION

1. I write the wonders of the Christian religion, flying from the depravations of Europe to the American strand; and, assisted by the holy author of that religion, I do, with all conscience of truth, required therein by Him who is the

truth itself, report the wonderful displays of His infinite power, wisdom, goodness, and faithfulness, wherewith His divine providence hath irradiated an Indian wilderness.

I relate the considerable matters that produced and attended the first settlement of colonies which have been renowned for the degree of reformation professed and attained by evangelical churches, erected in those ends of the earth; and a field being thus prepared, I proceed unto a relation of the considerable matters which have been acted thereupon.

I first introduce the actors that have in a more exemplary manner served those colonies, and give remarkable occurrences in the exemplary lives of many magistrates, and of more ministers, who so lived as to leave unto posterity examples worthy of everlasting remembrance.

I add hereunto the notables of the only Protestant university that ever shone in that hemisphere of the New World, with particular instances of Criolians in our biography provoking the whole world with virtuous objects of emulation.

I introduce then the actions of a more eminent importance that have signalized those colonies, whether the establishments, directed by their synods, with a rich variety of synodical and ecclesiastical determinations, or the disturbances with which they have been from all sorts of temptations and enemies tempestuated, and the methods by which they have still weathered out each horrible tempest.

And into the midst of these actions, I interpose an entire book wherein there is, with all possible veracity, a collection made of memorable occurrences and amazing judgments and mercies befalling many particular persons among the people of New England.

Let my readers expect all that I have promised them in this bill of fare; and it may be they will find themselves entertained with yet many other passages, above and beyond their expectation, deserving likewise a room in history; in all which there will be nothing but the author's too mean way of preparing so great entertainments to reproach the invitation.

2. The reader will doubtless desire to know what it was that

> . . . *tot volvere casus*
> *Insignes pietate viros, tot adire labores,*
> *Impulerit.*

[". . . drove men eminent in piety to endure so many calamities and to undertake so many hardships" (*Aeneid,* I, 9–11).] And our history shall, on many fit occasions which will be therein offered, endeavor with all historical fidelity and simplicity, and with as little offense as may be, to satisfy him. The sum of the matter is that from the beginning of the Reformation in the English nation there hath always been a generation of godly men, desirous to pursue the reformation of religion, according to the word of God and the example of the best reformed churches, and answering the character of good men given by Josephus in his paraphrase on the words of Samuel to Saul, μηδὲν ἄλλο πραχθήσεσθαι καλῶς ὑφ᾽ ἑαυτῶν νομίζοντες ἤ ὅτι ἄν ποιήσωσι τοῦ Θεοῦ κεκελευκότος ["They think they do nothing right in the service of God but what they do according to the command of God"]. And there hath been another generation of men, who have still employed the power which they have generally still had in their hands, not only to stop the progress of the desired reformation but also, with innumerable vexations, to persecute those that most heartily wish well unto it. There were many of the reformers who joined with the Rev. John Fox in the complaints, which he then entered in his *Martyrology,* about the baits of Popery yet left in the church, and in his wishes: God take them away or ease us from them, for God knows they be the cause of much blindness and strife amongst men! They zealously decried the policy of complying always with the ignorance and vanity of the people, and cried out earnestly for purer administrations in the House of God, and more conformity to the law of Christ and primitive Christianity, while others would not hear of going any further than the first essay of reformation. 'Tis very certain that the first reformers never intended that what they did should be the absolute boundary of reformation, so that it should be a sin to proceed any further; as, by their own going beyond Wiclif, and changing and growing in their own models also, and the confessions of Cranmer, with the *Scripta Anglicana* of Bucer, and a thousand other things was abundantly demonstrated. But after a fruitless expectation, wherein the truest friends of the Reformation long waited, for to have that which Heylin himself owns to have been the design of the first reformers, followed as it should have been, a party very unjustly arrogated to themselves the venerable name of "The Church of England," by numberless oppressions grievously smote those their fellow servants. Then 'twas that, as our great Owen hath expressed it: "Multitudes of pious, peaceable Protestants were driven, by their severities, to leave their native country, and seek a refuge for their lives and liberties, with freedom for the worship of God, in the wilderness in the ends of the earth."

3. It is the history of these Protestants that is here attempted—Protestants that highly honored and affected the Church of England, and humbly petition to be a part of it; but by the mistake of a few powerful brethren driven to seek a place for the exercise of the Protestant religion, according to the light of their consciences, in the deserts of America. And in this attempt I have proposed not only to preserve and secure the interest of religion in the churches of that little country, New England, so far as the Lord Jesus Christ may please to bless it for that end, but also to offer unto the churches of the Reformation, abroad in the world, some small memorials that may be serviceable unto the designs of reformation, whereto, I believe, they are quickly to be awakened. I am far from any such boast concerning these churches, that they have need of nothing; I wish their works were more perfect before God. Indeed, that which Austin called "the perfection of Christians" is like to be, until the term for the Antichristian apostasy be expired, "the perfection of churches" too. *Ut agnoscant se nunquam esse perfectas* ["That they acknowledge themselves never to be perfect"]. Nevertheless, I persuade myself that, so far as they have attained, they have given great examples of the methods and measures wherein an

evangelical reformation is to be prosecuted, and of the qualifications requisite in the instruments that are to prosecute it, and of the difficulties which may be most likely to obstruct it, and the most likely directions and remedies for those obstructions.

It may be 'tis not possible for me to do a greater service unto the churches on the best island of the universe than to give a distinct relation of those great examples which have been occurring among churches of exiles, that were driven out of that island into an horrible wilderness, merely for their being well-willers unto the Reformation. When that blessed martyr, Constantine, was carried, with other martyrs, in a dungcart, unto the place of execution, he pleasantly said, "Well, yet we are a precious odor to God in Christ." Though the reformed churches in the American regions have, by very injurious representations of their brethren (all which they desire to forget and forgive!), been many times thrown into a dungcart, yet as they have been a precious odor to God in Christ, so, I hope, they will be a precious odor unto His people—and not only precious, but useful also, when the history of them shall come to be considered. A reformation of the church is coming on, and I cannot but thereupon say, with the dying Cyrus to his children in Xenophon, Ἐκ τῶν προγεγεννημένων μανθάνετε, αὐτὴ γὰρ ἀρίστη διδασκαλία ["Learn from the things that have been done already, for this is the best way of learning"].

The reader hath here an account of the things that have been done already. Bernard upon that clause in the Canticles—"O thou fairest among women"—has this ingenious gloss: Pulchram, non omnimode quidem, sed pulchram inter mulieres eam docet, videlicet cum distinctione, quatenus ex hoc amplius reprimatur, et sciat quid desit sibi ["He calls her fair, not absolutely, but fair among women, that is to say with a distinction, so that she may thereby be more restrained, and may know her deficiencies"]. Thus I do not say that the churches of New England are the most regular that can be, yet I do say, and am sure, that they are very like unto those that were in the first ages of Christianity. And if I assert that in the reformation of the church, the state of it in those ages is not a little to be considered, the great Peter Ramus, among others, has emboldened me. For when the Cardinal of Lorrain, the Maecenas of that great man, was offended at him for turning Protestant, he replied, *Inter opes illas, quibus me ditasti, has etiam in aeternam recordabor, quod beneficio, Poessiacae responsionis tuae didici, de quindecim a Christo saeculis, primum vere esse aureum reliqua, quo longius abscederent esse nequiora, atque deteriora: Tum igitur cum fieret optio, aurem saeculum delegi* ["Among those riches with which you enriched me, this I was mindful of always, which I learned from your reply at Poissy—that of the fifteen centuries since Christ, the first is truly golden. The rest, the farther they are removed from the first, are the more worthless and degenerate. Therefore when choice was to be made, I chose the golden age"]. In short, the first age was the golden one; to return unto that will make a man a Protestant, and I may add, a Puritan. 'Tis possible that our Lord Jesus Christ carried some thousands of reformers into the retirements of an American desert on purpose that, with an opportunity granted unto many of his faithful servants, to enjoy the precious liberty of their ministry, tho' in the midst of many temptations all their days, he might there, to them first, and then by them, give a specimen of many good things which he would have his churches elsewhere aspire and arise unto. And this being done, he knows whether there be not all done that New England was planted for, and whether the plantation may not, soon after this, come to nothing. Upon that expression in the sacred scriptures, "Cast the unprofitable Servant into Outer Darkness," it hath been imagined by some that the *Regiones Exterae* of America are the *Tenebrae Exteriores* which the unprofitable are condemned unto. No doubt the authors of those ecclesiastical impositions and severities which drove the English Christians into the dark regions of America esteemed those Christians to be a very unprofitable sort of creatures. But behold, ye European churches, there are golden candlesticks (more than twice seven times seven!) in the midst of this outer darkness; unto the upright children of Abraham, here hath arisen light in dark-

ness. And let us humbly speak it, it shall be profitable for
you to consider the light, which from the midst of this
outer darkness is now to be darted over unto the other
side of the Atlantic ocean. But we must therewithal ask
your prayers that these golden candlesticks may not
quickly be removed out of their place!

4. But whether New England may live anywhere else
or no, it must live in our history!

History, in general, hath had so many and mighty commendations from the pens of those numberless authors who,
from Herodotus to Howel, have been the professed writers
of it, that a tenth part of them transcribed would be a furniture for a *polyanthea* in folio. We, that have neither liberty
nor occasion to quote those commendations of history, will
content ourselves with the opinion of one who was not
much of a profess'd historian, expressed in that passage
whereto all mankind subscribe: *Historia est testis tem-
porum, nuntia vetustatis, lux veritatis, vita memoriae, ma-
gistra vitae* ["History is the witness of periods of time, the
messenger of antiquity, the light of truth, the life of memory, the instructress of life" (Cicero, *De Oratore,* II, 9)].
But of all history it must be confessed that the palm is to
be given unto church history, wherein the dignity, the
suavity, and the utility of the subject is transcendent. I
observe that for the description of the whole world in the
Book of Genesis, that first-born of all historians, the great
Moses, employs but one or two chapters, whereas he implies it may be seven times as many chapters in describing
that one little pavilion, the tabernacle. And when I am
thinking what may be the reason of this difference, methinks it intimates unto us that the church, wherein the
service of God is performed, is much more precious than
the world, which was indeed created for the sake and use
of the church. 'Tis very certain that the greatest entertainments must needs occur in the history of the people whom
the Son of God hath redeemed and purified unto himself
as a peculiar people, and whom the spirit of God, by super-
natural operations upon their minds, does cause to live like
strangers in this world, conforming themselves unto the
truths and rules of his holy word, in expectation of a king-

dom whereto they shall be in another and a better world advanced. Such a people our Lord Jesus Christ hath procured and preserved in all ages visible, and the dispensations of his wondrous providence towards this people (for, O Lord, thou do'st lift them up, and cast them down!), their calamities, their deliverances, the dispositions which they have still discovered, and the considerable persons and actions found among them, cannot but afford matters of admiration and admonition, above what any other story can pretend unto; 'tis nothing but atheism in the hearts of men that can persuade them otherwise.

Let any person of good sense peruse the *History* of Herodotus, which, like a river taking rise where the sacred records of the Old Testament leave off, runs along smoothly and sweetly, with relations that sometimes want an apology, down until the Grecians drive the Persians before them. Let him then peruse Thucydides, who from acting betook himself to writing, and carries the ancient state of the Grecians down to the twenty-first year of the Peloponnesian Wars in a manner which Casaubon judges to be *mirandum potius quam imitandum* ["rather to be admired than imitated"]. Let him next revolve Xenophon, that "Bee of Athens," who continues a narrative of the Greek affairs from the Peloponnesian Wars to the battle of Mantinea, and gives us a Cyrus into the bargain, at such a rate that Lipsius reckons the character of a *suavi, fidus et circumspectus scriptor* ["pleasant, faithful and accurate writer"] to belong unto him. Let him from hence proceed unto Diodorus Siculus, who, besides a rich treasure of Egyptian, Assyrian, Lybian and Grecian and other antiquities, in a phrase which according to Photius's judgment is ἱστορίᾳ μάλιστὰ, πρεπούσῃ ["of all most becoming an historian"], carries on the thread begun by his predecessors until the end of the hundred and nineteenth Olympiad; and where he is defective, let it be supplied from Arianus, from Justin, and from Curtius, who in the relish of Colerus is *quovis melle dulcior* ["sweeter than honey"]. Let him hereupon consult Polybius, and acquaint himself with the birth and growth of the Roman Empire, as far as 'tis described, in the five and forty books composed by an author who, with a learned professor of history, is *prudens scriptor, si quis alius* ["a prudent writer, if ever there was one"]. Let him now run over the table of the Roman affairs compendiously given by Lucius Florus, and then let him consider the transactions of above three hundred years reported by Dionysius Halicarnassaeus who, if the censure of Bodin may be taken, *Graecos omnes et Latinos superasse videatur* ["seems to have surpassed all Greek and Latin authors"]. Let him from hence pass to Livy, of whom the famous critic says, *Hoc solum ingenium (de historicis loquor) populus Romanus par imperio suo habuit* ["In him alone (to speak of historians) the Roman people had a genius worthy of their empire"], and supply those of his *Decads* that are lost, from the best fragments of antiquity, in others (and especially Dion and Sallust) that lead us on still further in our way. Let him then proceed unto the writers of the Caesarean times, and first revolve Suetonius, then Tacitus, then Herodian, then a whole army more of historians, which now crowd into our library; and unto all the rest, let him not fail of adding the incomparable Plutarch, whose books, they say, Theodore Gaza preferred above any in the world, next to the inspired oracles of the Bible. But if the number be still too little to satisfy an historical appetite, let him add Polyhistor unto the number, and all the chronicles of the following ages. After all, he must sensibly acknowledge that the two short books of ecclesiastical history written by the Evangelist Luke hath given us more glorious entertainments than all these voluminous historians, if they were put all together. The achievements of one Paul, particularly, which that Evangelist hath emblazoned, have more true glory in them than all the acts of those execrable plunderers and murderers, and irresistible banditti of the world, which have been dignified with the name of conquerors. Tacitus counted *ingentia bella, expugnationes urbium, fusos captosque reges* ["great wars, the storming of cities, kings put to flight and captured"] —the ravages of war and the glorious violences whereof great warriors make a wretched ostentation—to be the noblest matter for an historian. But there is a nobler, I humbly conceive, in the planting and forming of evangelical churches, and the temptations, the corruptions, the afflictions, which assault them, and their salvations from those assaults, and the exemplary lives of those that heaven employs to be patterns of holiness and usefulness upon earth.

And unto such it is that I now invite my readers: things in comparison whereof the subjects of many other histories are of as little weight as the questions about Z, the last letter of our alphabet, and whether H is to be pronounced with an aspiration, whereabout whole volumes have been written, and of no more account than the composure of Didymus.

But for the manner of my treating this matter, I must now give some account unto him.

5. Reader! I have done the part of an impartial historian, albeit not without all occasion perhaps for the rule which a worthy writer in his *Historica* gives to every reader: *Historici legantur cum moderatione et venia et cogitetur fieri non posse ut in omnibus circumstantiis Lyncei sint* ["Historians are to read with moderation and kindness, and it is to be remembered that they can not be in all circumstances like Lynceus"]. Polybius complains of those historians who always made either the Carthaginians brave and the Romans base, or *è contra*, in all their actions, as their affection for their own party led them. I have endeavored with all good conscience to decline this writing merely for a party, or doing like the dealer in history whom Lucian derides for always calling the captain of his own party an Achilles, but of the adverse party a Thersites; nor have I added unto the just provocations for the complaint made by the Baron Maurier, that the greatest part of histories are but so many panegyrics composed by interested hands, which elevate iniquity to the heavens, like Paterculus and like Machiavel, who propose Tiberius Caesar and Caesar Borgia as examples fit for imitation, whereas true history would have exhibited them as horrid monsters—as very devils. 'Tis true, I am not of the opinion that one cannot merit the name of an impartial historian except he write bare matters of fact, without all reflection; for I can tell where to find this given as the definition of

history, *Historia est rerum gestarum, cum laude aut vituperatione, narratio* ["History is the narrative of great actions with praise or blame"]; and if I am not altogether a Tacitus, when virtues or vices occur to be matters of reflection as well as of relation, I will, for my vindication, appeal to Tacitus himself, whom Lipsius calls one of the prudentest (though Tertullian, long before, counts him the lyingest) of them who have enriched the world with history; he says, *Præcipuum munus annalium reor ne virtutes sileantur utque pravis dictis factisque ex posteritate et infamia metus sit* ["I believe it is the principal function of history not to be silent respecting virtues, and to hold up before depravity, both in word and deed, the dread of infamy with posterity"].

I have not commended any person but when I have really judged, not only that he deserved it, but also that it would be a benefit unto posterity to know wherein he deserved it; and my judgment of desert hath not been biased by persons' being of my own particular judgment in matters of disputation among the churches of God. I have been as willing to wear the name of Simplicius Verinus throughout my whole undertaking as he that, before me, hath assumed it; nor am I like Pope Zachary, impatient so much as to hear of any Antipodes. The spirit of a Schlusselbergius, who falls foul with fury and reproach on all who differ from him; the spirit of an Heylin, who seems to count no obloquy too hard for a reformer; and the spirit of those (folio-writers there are, some of them, in the English nation!) whom a noble historian stigmatizes as "those hotheaded, passionate bigots, from whom 'tis enough if you be of a religion contrary unto theirs to be defamed, condemned, and pursued with a thousand calumnies"—I thank Heaven I hate it with all my heart. But how can the lives of the commendable be written without commending them? Or is that law of history, given in one of the eminentest pieces of antiquity we now have in our hands, wholly antiquated: *Maxime proprium est historiæ laudem rerum egregie gestarum persequi* ["It is most proper to history to praise eminent deeds"]? Nor have I, on the other side, forborne to mention many censurable things, even in the

best of my friends, when the things in my opinion were
not good; or so bore away for Placentia, in the course of
our story as to pass by Verona; but been mindful of the
direction which Polybius gives to the historian: "It becomes
him that writes an history, sometimes to extol enemies in
his praises, when their praiseworthy actions bespeak it,
and at the same time to reprove the best friends, when
their deeds appear worthy of a reproof; inasmuch as history is good for nothing, if truth (which is the very eye of
the animal) be not in it."

Indeed I have thought it my duty upon all accounts
(and if it have proceeded unto the degree of a fault, there
is, it may be, something in my temper and nature that has
betrayed me therein) to be more sparing and easy in thus
mentioning of censurable things than in my other liberty;
a writer of church history should, I know, be like the
builder of the temple, one of the tribe of Naphthali; and
for this I will also plead my Polybius in my excuse: "It is
not the work of an historian to commemorate the vices and
villainies of men so much as their just, their fair, their honest actions; and the readers of history get more good by
the objects of their emulation than of their indignation."
Nor do I deny that, though I cannot approve the conduct
of Josephus (whom Jerome not unjustly nor ineptly calls
"The Greek Livy") when he left out of his *Antiquities* the
story of the golden calf, and I don't wonder to find
Chamier, and Rivet, and others taxing him for his partiality
towards his countrymen; yet I have left unmentioned some
censurable occurrences in the story of our colonies, as
things no less unuseful than improper to be raised out of
the grave, wherein oblivion hath now buried them: lest I
should have incurred the pasquil bestowed upon Pope
Urban, who employing a committee to rip up the old errors
of his predecessors, one clapped a pair of spurs upon the
heels of the statue of St. Peter; and a label from the statue
of St. Paul opposite thereunto, upon the bridge, asked him,
"Whither he was bound?" St. Peter answered, "I apprehend some danger in staying here; I fear they'll call me in
question for denying my master." And St. Paul replied,
"Nay, then I had best be gone too, for they'll question me

also, for persecuting the Christians before my conversion."

Briefly, my pen shall reproach none that can give a good word unto any good man that is not of their own faction, and shall fall out with none but those that can agree with nobody else except those of their own schism. If I draw any sort of men with charcoal, it shall be because I remember a notable passage of the best queen that ever was in the world, our late Queen Mary. Monsieur Jurieu, that he might justify the Reformation in Scotland, made a very black representation of their old Queen Mary; for which a certain sycophant would have incensed our Queen Mary against that reverend person, saying, "Is it not a shame that this man, without any consideration for your royal person, should dare to throw such infamous calumnies upon a queen from whom your royal highness is descended?" But that excellent princess replied, "No, not at all; is it not enough that by fulsome praises great persons be lulled asleep all their lives, but must flattery accompany them to their very graves? How should they fear the judgment of posterity, if historians be not allowed to speak the truth after their death?" But whether I do myself commend, or whether I give my reader an opportunity to censure, I am careful above all things to do it with truth; and as I have considered the words of Plato: *Deum indigne et graviter ferre cum quis ei similem, id est virtute præstantem, vituperet aut laudet contrarium* ["It is offensive to God when anyone who is like Him, excelling in virtue, is dishonored, or praise given to the contrary"], so I have had the ninth Commandment of a greater lawgiver than Plato to preserve my care of truth from first to last. If any mistake have been anywhere committed, it will be found merely circumstantial, and wholly involuntary; and let it be remembered that, though no historian ever merited better than the incomparable Thuanus, yet learned men have said of his work what they never shall truly say of ours, that it contains *multa falsissima et indigna* ["much that is most false and unworthy"].

I find Erasmus himself mistaking one man for two when writing of the ancients. And even our own English writers too are often mistaken, and in matters of a very late importance, as Baker and Heylin and Fuller (professed historians) tell us that Richard Sutton, a single man, founded the Charterhouse; whereas his name was Thomas, and he was a married man. I think I can recite such mistakes, it may be *sans* number, occurring in the most credible writers; yet I hope I shall commit none such. But although I thus challenge, as my due, the character of an impartial, I doubt I may not challenge that of an elegant historian. I cannot say whether the style wherein this church history is written will please the modern critics; but if I seem to have used ἁπλουστάτῃ συντάξει γραφῆς, a simple, submiss, humble style, 'tis the same that Eusebius affirms to have been used by Hegesippus, who, as far as we understand, was the first author (after Luke) that ever composed an entire body of ecclesiastical history, which he divided into five books, and entitled ὑπομνήματα τῶν ἐκκλησιαστικῶν πραξέων ["memoirs of ecclesiastical transactions"]. Whereas others, it may be, will reckon the style embellished with too much of ornament by the multiplied references to other and former concerns, closely couched, for the observation of the attentive, in almost every paragraph; but I must confess that I am of his mind who said, *Sicuti sal modice cibis aspersus condit et gratiam saporis addit, ita, si paulum antiquitatis admiscueris, oratio fit venustior* ["Just as salt discreetly sprinkled on food flavors it, and adds to the pleasure of the relish, so if you mingle a little of antiquity, the oration is made more lovely"]. And I have seldom seen that way of writing faulted but by those who, for a certain odd reason, sometimes find fault that the grapes are not ripe. These embellishments (of which yet I only *veniam pro laude peto* ["beg pardon for this self-praise"]) are not the puerile spoils of Polyanthea's; but I should have asserted them to be as choice flowers as most that occur in ancient or modern writings, almost unavoidably putting themselves into the author's hand while about his work, if those words of Ambrose had not a little frightened me, as well as they did Baronius: *Unumquemque fallunt sua scripta* ["Every writer is in error about his own writings"].

I observe that learned men have been so terrified by the

reproaches of pedantry, which little smatterers at reading
and learning have by their quoting humors brought upon
themselves, that, for to avoid all approaches towards that
which those feeble creatures have gone to imitate, the best
way of writing has been most injuriously deserted. But
what shall we say? The best way of writing under heaven
shall be the worst, when Erasmus his monosyllable tyrant
will have it so! And if I should have resigned myself wholly
to the judgment of others what way of writing to have
taken, the story of the two statues made by Polyclitus tells
me what may have been the issue: he contrived one of
them according to the rules that best pleased himself, and
the other according to the fancy of every one that looked
upon his work; the former was afterwards applauded by
all, and the latter derided by those very persons who had
given their directions for it. . . .

6. I hope 'tis a right work that I have done. But we have
not yet arrived unto the day wherein God will bring every
work in judgment (the day of the kingdom that was promised unto David); and a son of David hath as truly as
wisely told us that until the arrival of that happy day, this
is one of the vanities attending human affairs: "For a right
work, a man shall be envied of his neighbor." It will not be
so much a surprise unto me if I should live to see our
church history vexed with "anie-mad-versions" of calum-
nious writers as it would have been unto Virgil to read his
Bucolics reproached by the anti-bucolica of a nameless
scribbler, and his *Aeneids* travestied by the *Aeneidomastix*
of Carbilius, or Herennius taking pains to make a collection
of the faults, and Faustinus of the thefts, in his incomparable composures. Yea, Pliny and Seneca, and our Jerome,
reproaching him as a man of no judgment, nor skill, in
sciences, while Paedianus affirms of him that he was himself, *Usque adeo invidiae expers, ut si quid erudite dictum
inspiceret alterius, non minus gauderet ac si suum esset*
["He was so incapable of envy that if he came upon any
elegant expression of another's, it pleased him not less than
if it had been his own"].

How should a book, no better labored than this of ours,
escape Zoilean outrages, when in all ages the most exquisite

works have been as much vilified as Plato's by Scaliger and
Aristotle's by Lactantius? In the time of our King Edward
VI there was an order to bring in all the teeth of St.
Apollonia, which the people of his one kingdom carried
about them for the cure of the toothache: and they were
so many that they almost filled a tun. Truly, envy hath as
many teeth as Madame Apollonia would have had, if all
those pretended reliques had been really hers. And must
all these teeth be fastened on thee, O my book? It may
be so! And yet the book, when ground between these
teeth, will prove like Ignatius in the teeth of the furious
tigers: "The whiter manchet for the churches of God."

The greatest and fiercest rage of envy is that which I
expect from those Idumaeans whose religion is all ceremony, and whose charity is more for them who deny the
most essential things in the Articles and Homilies of the
Church of England than for the most conscientious men in
the world who manifest their being so by their dissent in
some little ceremony. Or those persons whose hearts are
notably expressed in those words used by one of them
('tis Howell in his *Familiar Letters* . . .): "I rather pity
than hate Turk or infidel, for they are of the same metal
and bear the same stamp as I do, though the inscriptions
differ; if I hate any, 'tis those schismatics that puzzle the
sweet peace of our Church; so that I could be content to
see an Anabaptist go to hell on a Brownist's back." The
writer whom I last quoted hath given us a story of a young
man in High Holborn who, being after his death dissected,
there was a serpent with divers tails found in the left
ventricle of his heart. I make no question that our church
history will find some reader disposed like that writer, with
an heart as full of serpent and venom as ever it can hold.
Nor indeed will they be able to hold, but the tongues and
pens of those angry folks will scourge me as with scorpions
and cause me to feel (if I will feel) as many lashes as
Cornelius Agrippa expected from their brethren, for the
book in which he exposed their vanities. . . .

However, all these things, and an hundred more such
things which I think of, are very small discouragements for
such a service as I have here endeavored. I foresee a rec-

ompense which will abundantly swallow up all discouragements! It may be Strato the philosopher counted himself well recompensed for his labors, when Ptolemy bestowed fourscore talents on him. It may be Archimelus the poet counted himself well recompensed when Hiero sent him a thousand bushels of wheat for one little epigram; and Saleius the poet might count himself well recompensed when Vespasian sent him twelve thousand and five hundred philippics, and Oppian the poet might count himself well recompensed when Caracalla sent him a piece of gold for every line that he had inscribed unto him. As I live in a country where such recompenses never were in fashion, it hath no preferments for me; and I shall count that I am well rewarded in it if I can escape without being heavily reproached, censured and condemned for what I have done.

So I thank the Lord, I should exceedingly scorn all such mean considerations. I seek no out for benefactors to whom these labors may be dedicated. There is ONE to whom all is due! From Him I shall have a recompense. And what recompense? The recompense whereof I do, with inexpressible joy, assure myself is this: that these my poor labors will certainly serve the churches and interests of the Lord Jesus Christ. And I think I may say that I ask to live no longer than I count a service unto the Lord Jesus Christ and his churches to be itself a glorious recompense for the doing of it. When David was contriving to build the house of God, there was that order given from heaven concerning him: "Go tell David, my servant." The adding of that more than royal title unto the name of David was a sufficient recompense for all his contrivance about the house of God. In our whole church history, we have been at work for the house of the Lord Jesus Christ (even that Man who is the Lord God, and whose form seems on that occasion represented unto his David). And herein 'tis recompense enough that I have been a servant unto that heavenly Lord. The greatest honor, and the sweetest pleasure out of heaven is to serve our illustrious Lord Jesus Christ, who hath loved us and given himself for us, and unto whom it is infinitely reasonable that we should give ourselves and all that have and are. And it may be the angels in heaven, too, aspire not after an higher felicity.

Unto thee, therefore, O thou Son of God and King of heaven, and Lord of all things, whom all the glorious angels of light unspeakably love to glorify, I humbly offer up a poor history of churches which own thee alone for their head and prince and lawgiver: churches which thou hast purchased with thy own blood, and with wonderful dispensations of thy providence hitherto protected and preserved; and of a people which thou didst form for thyself, to show forth thy praises. I bless thy great name, for thy inclining of me to, and carrying of me through, the work of this history. I pray thee to sprinkle the book of this history with thy blood, and make it acceptable and profitable unto thy churches, and serve thy truths and ways among thy people, by that which thou hast here prepared: for 'tis thou that has prepared it for them. Amen.

Quid sum? Nil. Quis sum? Nullus. Sed gratia Christi,
Quod sum, quod vivo, quodque laboro, facit.

["But what am I? Nothing. Who am I? No one. But the grace of Christ makes what I am, what I live, what I do."]

CHAPTER TWO

STATE AND SOCIETY

1. JOHN WINTHROP, 1588–1649

[On the deck of the flagship *Arbella*, in the middle of the Atlantic, during, as the manuscript describes it, "his passage (with the great company of religious people, of which Christian tribes he was the brave leader and famous governor) from the island of Great Britain to New England in the North America," Governor Winthrop delivered this lay sermon. While for the heart of Puritan piety we must go to Bradford's *Of Plymouth Plantation*, we find the essence of the Puritan social ideal in Winthrop's exposition. Along with Bradford's narrative, it is the fundamental document for comprehending the Puritan mind.

To the Congregational segment of the Puritan party, the basic idea was the covenant. This was primarily a grandiose theological conception (see pp. 143–44), but as a consequence of the Puritan alliance with Parliament against King James and King Charles, it became also a theory of society. In the Puritan formulation, it held that a body politic could be constituted only out of the consent of the governed, yet also out of an agreement not to terms of the people's own divising but only to the pre-stated terms of God's eternal law of justice and subordination. In order to expound to the immigrants (some of whom may already have begun to dream dreams of economic prosperity and social advancement in the New World) just how they had committed themselves—out of their free and sanctified will —to the rule of social righteousness, Winthrop framed this masterful discourse.

Though he was not a cleric, Winthrop could thus speak in the conventional form of a Puritan sermon because, according to Congregational doctrine, nobody was a clergyman until ordained by a settled congregation. In the broad Atlantic, halfway between the Old World and the New, nothing was settled; for the moment there were no churches and no ministers, so that Governor Winthrop spoke in the character—which for nineteen years he was to maintain—of the leader who united both the secular and spiritual aspirations of the plantation.]

A MODEL OF CHRISTIAN CHARITY

God Almighty in His most holy and wise providence hath so disposed of the condition of mankind as in all times some must be rich, some poor; some high and eminent in power and dignity, others mean and in subjection.

The reason hereof:

First, to hold conformity with the rest of His works, being delighted to show forth the glory of His wisdom in the variety and difference of the creatures and the glory of His power, in ordering all these differences for the preservation and good of the whole, and the glory of His greatness: that as it is the glory of princes to have many officers, so this great King will have many stewards, counting Himself more honored in dispensing His gifts to man by man than if He did it by His own immediate hand.

Secondly, that He might have the more occasion to manifest the work of His Spirit: first, upon the wicked in moderating and restraining them, so that the rich and mighty should not eat up the poor, nor the poor and despised rise up against their superiors and shake off their yoke; secondly, in the regenerate, in exercising His graces in them—as in the great ones, their love, mercy, gentleness, temperance, etc., in the poor and inferior sort, their faith, patience, obedience, etc.

Thirdly, that every man might have need of other, and from hence they might be all knit more nearly together in the bond of brotherly affection. From hence it appears plainly that no man is made more honorable than another or more wealthy, etc., out of any particular and singular respect to himself, but for the glory of his creator and the common good of the creature, man. Therefore God still reserves the property of these gifts to Himself (Ezek. 16. 17). He there calls wealth His gold and His silver, etc. (Prov. 3. 9). He claims their service as His due: "Honor the Lord with thy riches." All men being thus (by divine providence) ranked into two sorts, rich and poor, under the first are comprehended all such as are able to live comfortably by their own means duly improved, and all others are poor, according to the former distribution.

There are two rules whereby we are to walk, one towards another: justice and mercy. These are always distinguished in their act and in their object, yet may they both concur in the same subject in each respect: as sometimes there may be an occasion of showing mercy to a rich man in some sudden danger of distress, and also doing of mere justice to a poor man in regard of some particular contract.

There is likewise a double law by which we are regulated in our conversation, one towards another: in both the former respects, the law of nature and the law of grace, or the moral law or the law of the Gospel—to omit the rule of justice as not properly belonging to this purpose, otherwise than it may fall into consideration in some particular cases. By the first of these laws, man, as he was enabled so, withal [is] commanded to love his neighbor as himself; upon this ground stand all the precepts of the moral law, which concerns our dealings with men. To apply this to the works of mercy, this law requires two things: first, that every man afford his help to another in every want or distress; secondly, that he perform this out of the same affection which makes him careful of his own good according to that of our savior (Matt. 7. 12): "Whatsoever ye would that men should do to you." This was practiced by Abraham and Lot in entertaining the angels and the old man of Gibea.

The law of grace or the Gospel hath some difference

from the former, as in these respects: first, the law of nature was given to man in the estate of innocency, this of the Gospel in the estate of regeneracy. Secondly, the former propounds one man to another as the same flesh and image of God, this as a brother in Christ also, and in the communion of the same spirit, and so teacheth us to put a difference between Christians and others. "Do good to all, especially to the household of faith." Upon this ground the Israelites were to put a difference between the brethren of such as were strangers though not of the Canaanites. Thirdly, the law of nature could give no rules for dealing with enemies, for all are to be considered as friends in the estate of innocency; but the Gospel commands love to an enemy. Proof: "If thine enemy hunger, feed him; love your enemies, do good to them that hate you" (Matt. 5. 44).

This law of the Gospel propounds likewise a difference of seasons and occasions. There is a time when a Christian must sell all and give to the poor as they did in the apostles' times; there is a time also when a Christian, though they give not all yet, must give beyond their ability, as they of Macedonia (II Cor. 8). Likewise, community of perils calls for extraordinary liberality, and so doth community in some special service for the church. Lastly, when there is no other means whereby our Christian brother may be relieved in this distress, we must help him beyond our ability, rather than tempt God in putting him upon help by miraculous or extraordinary means. . . .

1. For the persons, we are a company professing ourselves fellow members of Christ, in which respect only, though we were absent from each other many miles, and had our employments as far distant, yet we ought to account ourselves knit together by this bond of love, and live in the exercise of it, if we would have comfort of our being in Christ. This was notorious in the practice of the Christians in former times, as is testified of the Waldenses from the mouth of one of the adversaries, Aeneas Sylvius: *Mutuo solent amare penè antequam norint*—they used to love any of their own religion even before they were acquainted with them.

2. For the work we have in hand, it is by mutual consent, through a special overruling providence and a more than an ordinary approbation of the churches of Christ, to seek out a place of cohabitation and consortship, under a due form of government both civil and ecclesiastical. In such cases as this, the care of the public must oversway all private respects by which not only conscience but mere civil policy doth bind us; for it is a true rule that particular estates cannot subsist in the ruin of the public.

3. The end is to improve our lives to do more service to the Lord, the comfort and increase of the body of Christ whereof we are members, that ourselves and posterity may be the better preserved from the common corruptions of this evil world, to serve the Lord and work out our salvation under the power and purity of His holy ordinances.

4. For the means whereby this must be effected, they are twofold: a conformity with the work and the end we aim at; these we see are extraordinary, therefore we must not content ourselves with usual ordinary means. Whatsoever we did or ought to have done when we lived in England, the same must we do, and more also where we go. That which the most in their churches maintain as a truth in profession only, we must bring into familiar and constant practice: as in this duty of love we must love brotherly without dissumulation, we must love one another with a pure heart fervently, we must bear one another's burdens, we must not look only on our own things but also on the things of our brethren. Neither must we think that the Lord will bear with such failings at our hands as He doth from those among whom we have lived. . . .

Thus stands the cause between God and us: we are entered into covenant with Him for this work; we have taken out a commission, the Lord hath given us leave to draw our own articles. We have professed to enterprise these actions upon these and these ends; we have hereupon besought Him of favor and blessing. Now if the Lord shall please to hear us and bring us in peace to the place we desire, then hath He ratified this covenant and sealed our Commission, [and] will expect a strict performance of the articles contained in it. But if we shall neglect the observation of these articles which are the ends we have propounded, and dissembling with our God, shall fall to embrace this present world and prosecute our carnal intentions, seeking great things for ourselves and our posterity, the Lord will surely break out in wrath against us, be revenged of such a perjured people, and make us know the price of the breach of such a covenant.

Now the only way to avoid this shipwreck and to provide for our posterity is to follow the counsel of Micah: to do justly, to love mercy, to walk humbly with our God. For this end, we must be knit together in this work as one man. We must entertain each other in brotherly affection; we must be willing to abridge ourselves of our superfluities, for the supply of others' necessities; we must uphold a familiar commerce together in all meekness, gentleness, patience and liberality. We must delight in each other, make others' conditions our own, rejoice together, mourn together, labor and suffer together: always having before our eyes our commission and community in the work, our community as members of the same body. So shall we keep the unity of the spirit in the bond of peace, the Lord will be our God and delight to dwell among us, as His own people, and will command a blessing upon us in all our ways, so that we shall see much more of His wisdom, power, goodness, and truth than formerly we have been acquainted with. We shall find that the God of Israel is among us, when ten of us shall be able to resist a thousand of our enemies, when He shall make us a praise and glory, that men shall say of succeeding plantations: "The Lord make it like that of New England." For we must consider that we shall be as a city upon a hill, the eyes of all people are upon us. So that if we shall deal falsely with our God in this work we have undertaken, and so cause Him to withdraw His present help from us, we shall be made a story and a by-word through the world: we shall open the mouths of enemies to speak evil of the ways of God and all professors for God's sake; we shall shame the faces of many of God's worthy servants, and cause their prayers to be turned into curses upon us, till we be consumed out of the good land whither we are going.

And to shut up this discourse with that exhortation of Moses, that faithful servant of the Lord, in his last farewell to Israel (Deut. 30): Beloved, there is now set before us life and good, death and evil, in that we are commanded this day to love the Lord our God, and to love one another, to walk in His ways and to keep His commandments and His ordinance and His laws and the articles of our covenant with Him, that we may live and be multiplied, and that the Lord our God may bless us in the land whither we go to possess it: but if our hearts shall turn away so that we will not obey, but shall be seduced and worship . . . other gods, our pleasures and profits, and serve them, it is propounded unto us this day, we shall surely perish out of the good land whither we pass over this vast sea to possess it.

Therefore, let us choose life,
that we, and our seed,
may live; by obeying His
voice and cleaving to Him,
for He is our life and
our prosperity.

2. JOHN COTTON, 1584-1652

[The social compact, as the Congregational Puritans conceived it, was not so much the creation of a society by mutual agreement among men as it was a covenant, an agreement to particular terms, between rulers and people. Government in some form or other was imposed upon man after the Fall of Adam by divine decree in order to restrain what otherwise would be the anarchic ravages of depravity; hence there was a necessity for the compact which, though men entered it voluntarily, could not be escaped. To this extent, society was founded on "nature." But the specific terms of each compact—the peculiar laws by which the community is to be governed—are determined arbitrarily and so are "positive" rather than natural.

The best exposition in the New England literature of this doctrine is by John Cotton. In the American legend he is supposed to be chief of the "theocracy" and is presented as a reactionary in contrast to the "liberal" Thomas Hooker. Actually, there is no difference whatsoever between them in the realm of political theory; all orthodox leaders in both Massachusetts and Connecticut would as a matter of course subscribe to what Cotton here says.

John Cotton took his M.A. at Emmanuel College, Cambridge, in 1606. As vicar of St. Botolph's in Boston, Lincolnshire, he was for twenty years a Puritan leader, renowned both as theologian and preacher. He fled to New England in 1633 and was immediately chosen teacher of the Boston church, so that he was in the central position to advise and to speak for the civil government.]

LIMITATION OF GOVERNMENT

This may serve to teach us the danger of allowing to any mortal man an inordinate measure of power to speak great things: to allow to any man uncontrollableness of speech; you see the desperate danger of it.

Let all the world learn to give mortal men no greater power than they are content they shall use—for use it they will. And unless they be better taught of God, they will use it ever and anon: it may be, make it the passage of their proceeding to speak what they will. And they that have liberty to speak great things, you will find it to be true, they will speak great blasphemies. No man would think what desperate deceit and wickedness there is in the hearts of men. And that was the reason why the beast did speak such great things; he might speak and nobody might control him: "What," saith the Lord (in Jer. 3. 5), "thou hast spoken and done evil things as thou couldst." If a church or head of a church could have done worse, he would have done it. This is one of the strains of nature: it affects boundless liberty, and to run to the utmost extent. Whatever power he hath received, he hath a corrupt nature that will improve it in one thing or other; if he have liberty, he will think why may he not use it?

Set up the Pope as Lord Paramount over kings and

princes, and they shall know that he hath power over them; he will take liberty to depose one and set up another. Give him power to make laws, and he will approve and disapprove as he list: what he approves is canonical, what he disapproves is rejected. Give him that power, and he will so order it at length, he will make such a state of religion, that he that so lives and dies shall never be saved; and all this springs from the vast power that is given to him and from the deep depravation of nature. He will open his mouth: "His tongue is his own, who is Lord over him" (Psal. 12. 3, 4).

It is therefore most wholesome for magistrates and officers in church and commonwealth never to affect more liberty and authority than will do them good, and the people good: for whatever transcendent power is given will certainly overrun those that give it and those that receive it. There is a strain in a man's heart that will sometime or other run out to excess, unless the Lord restrain it; but it is not good to venture it.

It is necessary, therefore, that all power that is on earth be limited, church-power or other. If there be power given to speak great things, then look for great blasphemies, look for a licentious abuse of it. It is counted a matter of danger to the state to limit prerogatives; but it is a further danger not to have them limited: they will be like a tempest if they be not limited. A prince himself cannot tell where he will confine himself, nor can the people tell; but if he have liberty to speak great things, then he will make and unmake, say and unsay, and undertake such things as are neither for his own honor nor for the safety of the state.

It is therefore fit for every man to be studious of the bounds which the Lord hath set: and for the people, in whom fundamentally all power lies, to give as much power as God in His word gives to men. And it is meet that magistrates in the commonwealth, and so officers in churches, should desire to know the utmost bounds of their own power, and it is safe for both. All intrenchment upon the bounds which God hath not given, they are not enlargements, but burdens and snares; they will certainly lead the spirit of a man out of his way, sooner or later.

It is wholesome and safe to be dealt withal as God deals with the vast sea: "Hitherto shalt thou come, but there shalt thou stay thy proud waves." And therefore if they be but banks of simple sand, they will be good enough to check the vast, roaring sea. And so for imperial monarchies: it is safe to know how far their power extends; and then if it be but banks of sand, which is most slippery, it will serve as well as any brazen wall. If you pinch the sea of its liberty, though it be walls of stone or brass, it will beat them down. So it is with magistrates: stint them where God hath not stinted them, and if they were walls of brass, they would beat them down, and it is meet they should; but give them the liberty God allows, and if it be but a wall of sand it will keep them.

As this liquid air in which we breathe, God hath set it for the waters of the clouds to the earth; it is a firmament, it is the clouds, yet it stands firm enough; because it keeps the climate where they are, it shall stand like walls of brass. So let there be due bounds set—and I may apply it to families: it is good for the wife to acknowledge all power and authority to the husband, and for the husband to acknowledge honor to the wife; but still give them that which God hath given them, and no more nor less. Give them the full latitude that God hath given, else you will find you dig pits, and lay snares, and cumber their spirits, if you give them less; there is never peace where full liberty is not given, nor never stable peace where more than full liberty is granted. Let them be duly observed, and give men no more liberty than God doth, nor women, for they will abuse it. The devil will draw them, and God's providence lead them thereunto; therefore give them no more than God gives.

And so for children and servants, or any others you are to deal with: give them the liberty and authority you would have them use, and beyond that stretch not the tether; it will not tend to their good nor yours. And also, from hence gather and go home with this meditation: that certainly here is this distemper in our natures, that we cannot tell how to use liberty, but we shall very readily corrupt ourselves. Oh, the bottomless depth of sandy earth!

of a corrupt spirit, that breaks over all bounds, and loves inordinate vastness! That is it we ought to be careful of.

3. THOMAS HOOKER, 1586–1647

[Thomas Hooker was the rival of John Cotton as theologian and surpassed him in moving pulpit eloquence. Taking his M.A. at Emmanuel College in 1611, he held various charges in the county of Essex and became so prominent a Puritan that in 1630 he was obliged to flee to Holland. He came to New England in 1633 in the same ship with Cotton and was ordained pastor at Newtown (later Cambridge). In 1636 he led his people out of Massachusetts and into the Connecticut Valley, there to found Hartford. The reasons for this removal are obscure: the people were land hungry, and probably the small colony was not yet large enough to contain two such giants as Cotton and Hooker.

Finding themselves outside the Massachusetts patent and having no charter, the Connecticut settlers put the Puritan machinery into action, created a government by social compact, and drew up a set of positive laws, the *Fundamental Orders*. At the first election, in 1638, Hooker preached a sermon, only the notes of which survive. They are enough to fill out the orthodox doctrine of the ideal Christian society. Nineteenth-century readers, unfamiliar with the general theory, thought this sermon a "liberal" assertion against the autocratic regime of John Winthrop; in fact, it is a summary of what all Puritans maintained against the Stuart regime in England.]

HARTFORD ELECTION SERMON

Text (Deut. 1. 13): "Take you wise men, and understanding, and known among your tribes, and I will make them rulers over you." Captains over thousands, and captains over hundreds—over fifties, over tens, etc.

Doctrine. I. That the choice of public magistrates belongs unto the people by God's own allowance.

II. The privilege of election, which belongs to the people, therefore must not be exercised according to their humors, but according to the blessed will and law of God.

III. They who have the power to appoint officers and magistrates, it is in their power also to set the bounds and limitations of power and place unto which they call them.

Reasons. 1. Because the foundation of authority is laid, firstly, in the free consent of the people.

2. Because by a free choice the hearts of the people will be more inclined to the love of the persons [chosen] and more ready to yield [obedience].

3. Because of that duty and engagement of the people.

Uses. The lesson taught is threefold:

First. There is matter of thankful acknowledgment in the [appreciation] of God's faithfulness towards us, and the permission of these measures that God doth command and vouchsafe.

Secondly. Of reproof: to dash the conceits of all those that shall oppose it.

Thirdly. Of exhortation: to persuade us, as God hath given us liberty, to take it.

And lastly: as God hath spared our lives and given them in liberty, so to seek the guidance of God, and to choose in God and for God.

4. JOHN WINTHROP, 1588–1649

[Just how far the Puritan adoption of the political tenet of fundamental law enshrined in a compact was from meaning democracy or equalitarian individualism, Winthrop explained in a classic speech of 1645. In that year a squabble broke out in Hingham; Winthrop, then lieutenant governor and so a magistrate, intervened and committed one faction for contempt. The lower house of the General Court impeached him for having exceeded his commission and for having violated fundamental law. He was acquitted on July 3, and then, in order to drive home the moral of his victory, he made the citizens sit there and listen to him.

As these Puritans saw it, a man who receives the grace of God employs his liberty to enter a compact with the Deity, promising to abide by God's laws. He does not formulate his own terms, he accepts those given. By analogy, Winthrop argues that individuals in a natural state are at absolute liberty to do anything they can; obviously natural men, being what they are, will lie, steal, murder, rape. The civil state is, so to speak, a state of social regeneration, where all men (whether or not individually saved) are at liberty to do only what God commands. The government is brought into being by the act of the people, but the institution itself is from God. The governors are elected by the people, but elected into an office that has its warrant from heaven. As one of the ministers, John Davenport, the clerical leader of the New Haven settlement, put it: "In regular actings of the creature, God is the first Agent: there are not two several and distinct actings, one of God, another of the people: but in one and the same action, God, by the people's suffrages, makes such an one governor, or magistrate, and not another." So the liberty which Puritan citizens exercised by bringing into being the organized societies of New England they could further exercise only in doing, not their own wills, but that which is inherently good, just and honest—which is to say, those things that qualified magistrates like Winthrop and learned clergymen like Cotton and Hooker defined as the good, just and honest.]

SPEECH TO THE GENERAL COURT

I suppose something may be expected from me, upon this charge that is befallen me, which moves me to speak now to you. Yet I intend not to intermeddle in the proceedings of the Court, or with any of the persons concerned therein. Only I bless God that I see an issue of this troublesome business. I also acknowledge the justice of the Court, and, for mine own part, I am well satisfied, I was publicly charged, and I am publicly and legally acquitted, which is all I did expect or desire.

And though this be sufficient for my justification before men, yet not so before God, who hath seen so much amiss in my dispensations (and even in this affair) as calls me to be humble. For to be publicly and criminally charged in this Court is matter of humiliation (and I desire to make a right use of it), notwithstanding I be thus acquitted. If her father had spit in her face (saith the Lord concerning Miriam), should she not have been ashamed seven days? Shame had lien upon her, whatever the occasion had been. I am unwilling to stay you from your urgent affairs; yet give me leave (upon this special occasion) to speak a little more to this assembly. It may be of some good use, to inform and rectify the judgments of some of the people, and may prevent such distempers as have arisen amongst us.

The great questions that have troubled the country are about the authority of the magistrates and the liberty of the people. It is yourselves who have called us to this office; and being called by you, we have our authority from God, in way of an ordinance, such as hath the image of God eminently stamped upon it, the contempt and violation whereof hath been vindicated with examples of divine vengeance. I entreat you to consider that when you choose magistrates, you take them from among yourselves, men subject to like passions as you are. Therefore, when you see infirmities in us, you should reflect upon your own; and that would make you bear the more with us, and not be severe censurers of the failings of your magistrates, when you have continual experience of the like infirmities in yourselves and others. We account him a good servant who breaks not his covenant. The covenant between you and us is the oath you have taken of us, which is to this purpose, that we shall govern you and judge your causes by the rules of God's law and our own, according to our best skill. When you agree with a workman to build you a ship or house, etc., he undertakes as well for his skill as for his faithfulness, for it is his profession, and you pay him for both. But when you call one to be a magistrate, he doth not profess nor undertake to have sufficient skill for that office, nor can you furnish him with gifts, etc.; therefore you must run the hazard of his skill and ability. But if he fail in faithfulness, which by his oath he is bound unto, that he must answer for. If it fall out that the case be clear to common apprehension and the rule clear also, if he transgress here, the error is not in the skill but in the evil of the will: it must be required of him. But if the case be doubtful or the rule doubtful to men of such understanding and parts as your magistrates are, if your magistrates should err here, yourselves must bear it.

For the other point concerning liberty, I observe a great mistake in the country about that. There is a twofold liberty—natural (I mean as our nature is now corrupt), and civil or federal. The first is common to man, with beasts and other creatures. By this, man, as he stands in relation to man simply, hath liberty to do what he lists; it is a liberty to evil as well as to good. This liberty is incompatible and inconsistent with authority, and cannot endure the least restraint of the most just authority. The exercise and maintaining of this liberty makes men grow more evil and in time to be worse than brute beasts: *omnes sumus licentia deteriores* ["We are all worse for liberty"]. This is that great enemy of truth and peace, that wild beast, which all the ordinances of God are bent against to restrain and subdue it.

The other kind of liberty I call civil or federal; it may also be termed moral, in reference to the covenant between God and man in the moral law, and the politic covenants and constitutions amongst men themselves. This liberty is the proper end and object of authority and cannot subsist without it; and it is a liberty to that only which is good, just, and honest. This liberty you are to stand for, with the hazard not only of your goods, but of your lives, if need be. Whatsoever crosseth this is not authority, but a distemper thereof. This liberty is maintained and exercised in a way of subjection to authority; it is of the same kind of liberty wherewith Christ hath made us free. The woman's own choice makes such a man her husband; yet being so chosen, he is her lord, and she is to be subject to him, yet in a way of liberty, not of bondage; and a true wife accounts her subjection her honor and freedom, and would not think her condition safe and free but in her subjection to her husband's authority. Such is the liberty of the church under the authority of Christ, her king and husband; his yoke is so easy and sweet to her as a bride's ornaments; and if through frowardness or wantonness, etc., she shake it off at any time, she is at no rest in her spirit until she take it up again; and whether her lord smiles upon her and embraceth her in his arms, or whether he frowns or rebukes, or smites her, she apprehends the sweetness of his love in all, and is refreshed, supported, and instructed by every such dispensation of his authority over her. On the other side, ye know who they are that complain of this yoke and say, let us break their bands, etc., we will not have this man to rule over us.

Even so, brethren, it will be between you and your magistrates. If you stand for your natural, corrupt liberties and will do what is good in your own eyes, you will not endure the least weight of authority, but will murmur, and oppose, and be always striving to shake off that yoke. But if you will be satisfied to enjoy such civil and lawful liberties, such as Christ allows you, then will you quietly and cheerfully submit unto that authority which is set over you, in all the administrations of it, for your good. Wherein, if we fail at any time, we hope we shall be willing, by God's assistance, to hearken to good advice from any of you or in any other way of God. So shall your liberties be preserved, in upholding the honor and power of authority amongst you.

5. NATHANIEL WARD, 1578–1652

[Within a year or two after the outbreak of the war prevented either king or Parliament from maintaining a firm control over England, sect after sect emerged, until by 1645 the religious situation, from the old point of view, was entirely out of hand. The Independents, faced with extermination by the Presbyterians, formed an alliance with these sectaries by converting themselves to the idea of toleration. Oliver Cromwell became the Independents' leader and dictator of the nation in order to enforce religious liberty with the sword.

This transformation of the English brethren utterly astounded New England Congregationalists. They had come to the wilderness assuming, as the wisdom of several centuries had assumed, that the notion of a state's permitting different religions or polities to exist side by side was unthinkable. In 1635 Massachusetts exiled Roger Williams for propounding this dangerous absurdity, and remained convinced that the unruly groups he tried to organize into the plantation of Rhode Island would end in savage anarchy. Now in the 1640's they beheld their own group in England following Williams's lead and treating him as a great man.

The New Englanders had not been fighting at home for any milk-and-water toleration. They were assured that they knew the exact truth, just as it is in the Bible; when they could not impose this truth on England, they came to America where they could establish their own society and within it make God's Word prevail forever. They were in no sense pioneers of religious liberty, and when their English counterparts went whoring after this strange perversion of political orthodoxy, they resolved to stand all the more resolutely in New England for an absolute uniformity, for a rigorous suppression of all dissent, by capital punishment if necessary.

Nathaniel Ward took his M.A. at Emmanuel College in 1603, but studied law and traveled on the Continent before becoming a minister in 1618. He came to New England in 1634 and served as minister in Ipswich (of which the Indian name was Aggawam). In 1641 he drew up the first codification of Massachusetts statutes, *The Body of Liberties*. He returned to England in 1648 and ended his days as a minister in Essex. He wrote his book in 1645; it was published in London in 1647 with a lengthy and spirited title:

The Simple Cobler of Aggawam in America. Willing to help 'mind his Native Country, lamentably tattered, both

*in the upper-Leather and sole, with all the honest stiches
he can take.*

*And as willing never to bee paid for his work, by Old
English wonted pay.*

It is his Trade to patch all the year long, gratis

Therefore I pray Gentlemen keep your purses.

It was announced as by "Theodore de la Guard."

Because Ward had a larger secular experience than most
of the clergy, he could write in a more worldly vein, and
his digression on women's fashion, as well as his whole
tenor, show that Puritans possessed their full share of that
vitality and exuberance to which we apply the adjective
"Elizabethan."]

THE SIMPLE COBLER OF AGGAWAM

Either I am in an apoplexy, or that man is in a lethargy
who does not now sensibly feel God shaking the heavens
over his head and the earth underneath his feet—the
heavens so as the sun begins to turn into darkness, the
moon into blood, the stars to fall down to the ground so
that little light of comfort or counsel is left to the sons of
men; the earth so as the foundations are failing, the righteous scarce know where to find rest, the inhabitants stagger
like drunken men; it is in a manner dissolved both in religions and relations, and no marvel, for they have defiled
it by transgressing the laws, changing the ordinances, and
breaking the everlasting covenant. The truths of God are
the pillars of the world whereon states and churches may
stand quiet if they will; if they will not, He can easily
shake them off into delusions and distractions enough.

Satan is now in his passions, he feels his passions approaching, he loves to fish in roiled waters. Though that
dragon cannot sting the vitals of the elect mortally, yet
that Beelzebub can fly-blow their intellectuals miserably.
The finer religion grows, the finer he spins his cobwebs;
he will hold pace with Christ so long as his wits will serve
him. He sees himself beaten out of gross idolatries, heresies, ceremonies, where the light breaks forth with power.

He will, therefore, bestir him to prevaricate evangelical truths and ordinances, that if they will needs be walking yet they shall *laborare varicibus* ["work with straddlings"] and not keep their path, he will put them out of time and place, assassinating for his engineers, men of Paracelsian parts, well complexioned for honesty; for such are fittest to mountebank his chemistry into sick churches and weak judgments.

Nor shall he need to stretch his strength overmuch in this work. Too many men, having not laid their foundations sure nor ballasted their spirits deep with humility and fear, are pressed enough of themselves to evaporate their own apprehensions. Those that are acquainted with history know it has ever been so in new editions of churches: such as are least able are most busy to pudder in the rubbish and to raise dust in the eyes of more steady repairers. Civil commotions make room for uncivil practices; religious mutations, for irreligious opinions; change of air discovers corrupt bodies; reformation of religion, unsound minds. He that has any well-faced fancy in his crown and does not vent it now, fears the pride of his own heart will dub him dunce forever. Such a one will trouble the whole Israel of God with his most untimely births, though he makes the bones of his vanity stick up, to the view and grief of all that are godly wise. The devil desires no better sport than to see light heads handle their heels and fetch their careers in a time when the roof of liberty stands open.

The next perplexed question with pious and ponderous men will be: What should be done for the healing of these comfortless exulcerations? I am the unablest adviser of a thousand, the unworthiest of ten thousand; yet I hope I may presume to assert what follows without just offense.

First, such as have given or taken any unfriendly reports of us New English should do well to recollect themselves. We have been reputed a colluvies of wild opinionists, swarmed into a remote wilderness to find elbow room for our fanatic doctrines and practices. I trust our diligence past and constant sedulity against such persons and courses will plead better things for us. I dare take upon me to be the herald of New England so far as to proclaim to the world, in the name of our colony, that all Familists, Antinomians, Anabaptists, and other enthusiasts shall have free liberty to keep away from us; and such as will come to be gone as fast as they can, the sooner the better.

Secondly, I dare aver that God does nowhere in His word tolerate Christian states to give toleration to such adversaries of His truth, if they have power in their hands to suppress them.

Here is lately brought us an extract of a Magna Carta, so called, compiled between the sub-planters of a West Indian island, whereof the first article of constipulation firmly provides free stableroom and litter for all kind of consciences, be they never so dirty or jadish, making it actionable—yea, treasonable—to disturb any man in his religion or to discommend it, whatever it be. We are very sorry to see such professed profaneness in English professors, as industriously to lay their religious foundations on the ruin of true religion, which strictly binds every conscience to contend earnestly for the truth; to preserve unity of spirit, faith, and ordinances; to be all like minded, of one accord, every man to take his brother into his Christian care, to stand fast with one spirit, with one mind, striving together for the faith of the Gospel; and by no means to permit heresies or erroneous opinions. But God, abhorring such loathsome beverages, has in His righteous judgment blasted that enterprise, which might otherwise have prospered well, for aught I know; I presume their case is generally known ere this.

If the devil might have his free option, I believe he would ask nothing else but liberty to enfranchise all false religions and to embondage the truth; nor should he need. It is much to be feared that lax tolerations upon state pretenses and planting necessities will be the next subtle stratagem he will spread to dista[s]te the truth of God and supplant the peace of the churches. Tolerations in things tolerable, exquisitely drawn out by the lines of the scripture and pencil of the spirit, are the sacred favors of truth, the due latitudes of love, the fair compartments of Christian fraternity; but irregular dispensations, dealt forth by the facilities of men, are the frontiers of error, the redoubts of schism, the perilous irritaments of carnal and spiritual enmity.

My heart has naturally detested four things: the standing of the Apocrypha in the Bible; foreigners dwelling in my country to crowd out native subjects into the corners of the earth; alchemized coins; tolerations of divers religions, or of one religion in segregant shapes. He that willingly assents to the last, if he examines his heart by daylight, his conscience will tell him he is either an atheist or a heretic or a hypocrite, or at best a captive to some lust. Poly-piety is the greatest impiety in the world. True religion is *ignis probationis* ["fire of proof"], which doth *congregare homogenea & segregare heterogenea* ["unite the homogeneous and separate the heterogeneous"].

Not to tolerate things merely indifferent to weak consciences argues a conscience too strong; pressed uniformity in these causes much disunity. To tolerate more than indifferents is not to deal indifferently with God; he that does it takes His scepter out of His hand and bids Him stand by. Who hath to do to institute religion but God? The power of all religion and ordinances lies in their purity, their purity in their simplicity; then are mixtures pernicious. I lived in a city where a Papist preached in one church, a Lutheran in another, a Calvinist in a third; a Lutheran one part of the day, a Calvinist the other, in the same pulpit. The religion of that place was but motley and meager, their affections leopard-like.

If the whole creature should conspire to do the Creator a mischief or offer Him an insolency, it would be in nothing more than in erecting untruths against His truth, or by sophisticating His truths with human medleys. The removing of some one iota in scripture may draw out all the life and traverse all the truth of the whole Bible; but to authorize an untruth by a toleration of state is to build a sconce against the walls of heaven, to batter God out of His chair. To tell a practical lie is a great sin, but yet transient; but to set up a theoretical untruth is to warrant every lie that lies from its root to the top of every branch it hath, which are not a few.

I would willingly hope that no member of the Parliament

has skillfully ingratiated himself into the hearts of the House that he might watch a time to midwife out some ungracious toleration for his own turn; and for the sake of that, some other, I would also hope that a word of general caution should not be particularly misapplied. I am the freer to suggest it because I know not one man of that mind. My aim is general, and I desire may be so accepted. Yet, good gentlemen, look well about you and remember how Tiberius played the fox with the senate of Rome and how Fabius Maximus cropped his ears for his cunning.

That state is wise that will improve all pains and patience rather to compose than tolerate differences in religion. There is no divine truth but hath much celestial fire in it from the spirit of truth, nor no irreligious untruth without its proportion of antifire from the spirit of error to contradict it: the zeal of the one, the virulency of the other, must necessarily kindle combustions. Fiery diseases seated in the spirit embroil the whole frame of the body; others more external and cool are less dangerous. They which divide in religion, divide in God; they who divide in Him, divide beyond *genus generalissimum* ["the most general genus"], where there is no reconciliation without atonement: that is, without uniting in Him who is one, and in His truth which is also one.

Wise are those men who will be persuaded rather to live within the pale of truth where they may be quiet than in the purlieus where they are sure to be hunted ever and anon, do authority what it can. Every singular opinion hath a singular opinion of itself, and he that holds it a singular opinion of himself, and a simple opinion of all contrasentients. He that confutes them must confute all three at once, or else he does nothing—which will not be done without more stir than the peace of the state or church can endure.

And prudent are those Christians that will rather give what may be given than hazard all by yielding nothing. To sell all peace of country to buy some peace of conscience unseasonably is more avarice than thrift, imprudence than patience: they deal not equally that set any truth of God at such a rate; but they deal wisely that will stay till the market is fallen.

My prognostics deceive me not a little if, once within three seven years, peace prove not such a pennyworth at most marts in Christendom that he that would not lay down his money, his lust, his opinion, his will—I had almost said the best flower of his crown—for it while he might have had it will tell his own heart he played the very ill husband.

Concerning tolerations I may further assert:

That persecution of true religion and toleration of false are the *Jannes* and *Jambres* to the kingdom of Christ, whereof the last is far the worst. Augustine's tongue had not owed his mouth one pennyrent though it had never spake word more in it but this; *Nullum malum pejus libertate errandi* ["No evil is worse than liberty for the erring"].

He that is willing to tolerate any religion or discrepant way of religion besides his own, unless it be in matters merely indifferent, either doubts of his own or is not sincere in it.

He that is willing to tolerate any unsound opinion, that his own may also be tolerated, though never so sound, will for a need hang God's Bible at the devil's girdle.

Every toleration of false religions or opinions hath as many errors and sins in it as all the false religions and opinions it tolerates; and one sound, one more.

That state that will give liberty of conscience in matters of religion must give liberty of conscience and conversation in their moral laws, or else the fiddle will be out of tune and some of the strings crack.

He that will rather make an irreligious quarrel with other religions than try the truth of his own valuable arguments and peaceable sufferings, either his religion or himself is irreligious.

Experience will teach churches and Christians that it is far better to live in a state united, though somewhat corrupt, than in a state whereof some part is incorrupt and all the rest divided.

I am not altogether ignorant of the eight rules given by

orthodox divines about giving tolerations, yet with their favor I dare affirm:

That there is no rule given by God for any state to give an affirmative toleration to any false religion or opinion whatsoever; they must connive in some cases, but may not concede in any.

That the state of England (so far as my intelligence serves) might in time have prevented with ease, and may yet without any great difficulty deny both toleration, and connivances *salva Republica* ["without violation of the state"].

That if the state of England shall either willingly tolerate or weakly connive at such courses, the church of that kingdom will sooner become the devil's dancing-school than God's temple, the civil state a bear-garden than an exchange, the whole realm a *pays bas* than an England. And what pity it is that the country which hath been the staple of truth to all Christendom should now become the aviary of errors to the whole world, let every fearing heart judge. . . .

Concerning novelties of opinions, I shall express my thoughts in these brief passages: First, that truth is the best boon God ever gave the world; there is nothing in the world any further than truth makes it so; it is better than any created *Ens* or *Bonum*, which are but truth's twins. Secondly, the least truth of God's kingdom doth in its place uphold the whole kingdom of His Truths; take away the least *vericulum* ["javelin"] out of the world, and it unworlds all potentially, and may unravel the whole texture actually, if it be not conserved by an arm of extraordinary power. Thirdly, the least evangelical truth is more worth than all the civil truths in the world, that are merely so. Fourthly, that truth is the parent of all liberty, whether political or personal: so much untruth, so much thralldom (John 8. 32).

Hence it is that God is so jealous of His truths, that He hath taken order in His due justice: First, that no practical sin is so sinful as some error in judgment; no men so accursed with indelible infamy and dedolent impenitency as authors of heresy. Secondly, that the least error, if grown sturdy and pressed, shall set open the spittle-door of all the squint-eyed, wry-necked, and brazen-faced errors that are or ever were of that litter; if they be not enough to serve its turn, it will beget more, though it hath not one crust of reason to maintain them. Thirdly, that that state which will permit errors in religion shall admit errors in policy unavoidably. Fourthly, that that policy which will suffer irreligious errors shall suffer the loss of so much liberty in one kind or other: I will not exempt Venice, Rhaguse, the Netherlands, or any.

An easy head may soon demonstrate that the prementioned planters by tolerating all religions had immazed themselves in the most intolerable confusions and inextricable thralldoms the world ever heard of. I am persuaded the devil himself was never willing with their proceedings, for fear it would break his wind and wits to attend such a province. I speak it seriously according to my meaning. How all religions should enjoy their liberty, justice its due regularity, civil cohabitation, moral honesty, in one and the same jurisdiction, is beyond the artique of my comprehension. If the whole conclave of hell can so compromise exadverse and diametrial contradictions as to compolitize such a multimonstrous maufrey of heteroclytes and quicquidlibets quietly, I trust I may say with all humble reverence, they can do more than the senate of heaven. My *modus loquendi* ["mode of speaking"] pardoned, I entirely wish much welfare and more wisdom to that plantation. . . .

[*On Women's Fashions*]

Should I not keep promise in speaking a little to women's fashions, they would take it unkindly. I was loath to pester better matter with such stuff; I rather thought it meet to let them stand by themselves, like the *Quae Genus* in the grammar, being deficients, or redundants, not to be brought under any rule. I shall therefore make bold for this once to borrow a little of their loose-tongued liberty, and misspend a word or two upon their long-waisted but short-skirted patience. A little use of my stirrup will do no harm.

Ridentem dicere verum, quid prohibet? ["What prohibits speaking truth with a smile?"]

> Gray gravity itself can well beteam
> That language be adapted to the theme.
> He that to parrots speaks, must parrotize;
> He that instructs a fool, may act th' unwise.

It is known more than enough that I am neither niggard nor cynic to the due bravery of the true gentry; if any man mislikes a bullimong drassock more than I, let him take her for his labor; I honor the woman that can honor herself with her attire; a good text always deserves a fair margin; I am not much offended if I see a trim far trimmer than she that wears it; in a word, whatever Christianity or civility will allow, I can afford with London measure. But when I hear a nugiperous gentledame inquire what dress the Queen is in this week, what the nudiustertian fashion of the court, with edge to be in it in all haste, whatever it be; I look at her as the very gizzard of a trifle, the product of a quarter of a cipher, the epitome of nothing, fitter to be kicked, if she were of a kickable substance, than either honored or humored.

To speak moderately, I truly confess it is beyond the ken of my understanding to conceive how those women should have any true grace or valuable virtue that have so little wit as to disfigure themselves with such exotic garbs as not only dismantles their native lovely lustre but transclouts them into gant bar-geese, ill-shapen, shotten shellfish, Egyptian hieroglyphics, or at the best into French flirts of the pastry, which a proper Englishwoman should scorn with her heels; it is no marvel they wear drails on the hinder part of their heads, having nothing as it seems in the fore part but a few squirrels' brains to help them frisk from one ill-favored fashion to another.

> These whim-crowned shes, these fashion-fancying wits,
> Are empty thin-brained shells and fiddling kits.

The very troublers and impoverishers of mankind; I can hardly forbear to commend to the world a saying of a lady living sometime with the Queen of Bohemia; I know not where she found it, but it is pity it should be lost:

The world is full of care, much like unto a bubble,
Women and care, and care and women, and women and
care and trouble.

The verses are even enough for such odd pegmas. I can make myself sick at any time with comparing the dazzling splendor wherewith our gentlewomen were embellished in some former habits, with the gut-foundered goosedom wherewith they are now surcingled and debauched. We have about five or six of them in our colony; if I see any of them accidentally, I cannot cleanse my fancy of them for a month after. I have been a solitary widower almost twelve years, purposed lately to make a step over to my native country for a yoke-fellow; but when I consider how women there have tripe-wifed themselves with their clad-ments, I have no heart to the voyage, lest their nauseous shapes and the sea should work too sorely upon my stomach. I speak sadly; methinks it should break the hearts of Englishmen to see so many goodly Englishwomen imprisoned in French cages, peering out of their hood-holes for some men of mercy to help them with a little wit; and nobody relieves them.

It is a more common than convenient saying that nine tailors make a man; it were well if nineteen could make a woman to her mind; if tailors were men indeed, well furnished but with mere moral principles, they would disdain to be led about like apes by such mimic marmosets. It is a most unworthy thing for men that have bones in them to spend their lives in making fiddle-cases for futilous women's fancies, which are the very pettitoes of infirmity, the giblets of perquisquilian toys. I am so charitable to think that most of that mystery would work the cheerfuller while they live if they might be well discharged of the tiring slavery of mis-tiring women; it is no little labor to be continually putting up Englishwomen into outlandish casks, who, if they be not shifted anew once in a few months, grow too sour for their husbands. What this trade will answer for themselves when God shall take measure of tailors' consciences is beyond my skill to imagine. There was a time when

> The joining of the red rose with the white
> Did set our state into a damask plight.

But now our roses are turned to fleur-de-lis, our carnations to tulips, our gilliflowers to daisies, our city-dames to an indenominable quaemalry of overturcased things. He that makes coats for the moon had need to take measure every noon; and he that makes for women, as often, to keep them from lunacy.

I have often heard divers ladies vent loud feminine complaints of the wearisome varieties and chargeable changes of fashions; I marvel themselves prefer not a bill of redress. I would Essex ladies would lead the chore, for the honor of their county and persons; or rather the thrice honorable ladies of the court, whom it best beseems; who may well presume of a *le roy le veult* ["the King wills it"] from our sober King, a *les seigneurs ont assentus* ["the Lords approve it"] from our prudent Peers, and the like *assentus* ["approval"] from our considerate, I dare not say wife-worn Commons, who I believe had much rather pass one such bill than pay so many tailors' bills as they are forced to do.

Most dear and unparalleled ladies, be pleased to attempt it; as you have the precellency of the women of the world for beauty and feature, so assume the honor to give and not take law from any, in matter of attire; if ye can transact so fair a motion among yourselves unanimously, I dare say they that most renite will least repent. What greater honor can your honors desire than to build a promontory president to all foreign ladies, to deserve so eminently at the hands of all the English gentry present and to come; and to confute the opinion of all the wise men in the world, who never thought it possible for women to do so good a work?

If any man think I have spoken rather merrily than seriously, he is much mistaken; I have written what I write with all the indignation I can, and no more than I ought.

I confess I veered my tongue to this kind of language *de industria* though unwillingly, supposing those I speak to are uncapable of grave and rational arguments. . . .

There is a quadrobulary saying which passes current in the western world: that the Emperor is King of kings; the Spaniard, King of men; the French, King of asses; the King of England, King of devils. By his leave that first brayed the speech, they are pretty wise devils and pretty honest; the worst they do is to keep their kings from devilizing, and themselves from assing: were I a king (a simple supposal) I would not part with one good English devil for two of the Emperor's kings nor three of the Spaniard's men nor four French asses; if I did, I should think myself an ass for my labor. I know nothing that Englishmen want, but true grace and honest pride: let them be well furnished with those two, I fear they would make more asses than Spain can make men, or the Emperor kings. You will say I am now beyond my latchet; but you would not say so, if you knew how high my latchet will stretch, when I hear a lie with a latchet that reaches up to his throat that first forged it.

He is a good king that undoeth not his subjects by any one of his unlimited prerogatives; and they are a good people that undo not their prince by any one of their unbounded liberties, be they the very least. I am sure either may, and I am sure neither would be trusted, how good soever. Stories tell us in effect, though not in terms, that over-risen kings have been the next evils to the world unto fallen angels, and that over-franchised people are devils with smooth snaffles in their mouths. A king that lives by law lives by love; and he that lives above law shall live under hatred, do what he can. Slavery and knavery go as seldom asunder as tyranny and cruelty.

I have a long while thought it very possible, in a time of peace and in some king's reign for disert statesmen to cut an exquisite thread between and quite through kings' prerogatives and subjects' liberties of all sorts, so as Caesar might have had his due and people their share, without such sharp disputes. Good casuists would case it and case it, part it and part it, now it and then it, punctually. Aquinas, Suarez, or Valentia would have done it long ere this, had they not been Popish—I might have said knavish; for, if they be so anywhere, it is in their "Tractates of Privileges." Our common law doth well but it must do better before things do as they should. There are some maxims in law that would be taught to speak a little more mannerly, or else well anti-maximed: we say, the King can do a subject no wrong; why may we not say, the Parliament can do the King no wrong? We say, *Nullum tempus occurrit Regi* ["No occasion opposes the King"] in taking wrong; why may we not say, *Nullum tempus succurrit Regi* ["No occasion assists the King"] in doing wrong? Which I doubt will prove a better canon, if well examined.

Authority must have power to make and keep people honest; people, honesty to obey authority; both, a joint council to keep both safe. Moral laws, royal prerogatives, popular liberties are not of man's making or giving, but God's. Man is but to measure them out by God's rule: which if man's wisdom cannot reach, man's experience must mend. And these essentials must not be ephorized or tribuned by one or a few men's discretion, but lineally sanctioned by supreme councils. In *pro-re-nascent* occurrences (which cannot be foreseen) diets, parliaments, senates or accountable commissions must have power to consult and execute against intersilient dangers and flagitious crimes prohibited by the light of nature; yet it were good if states would let people know so much beforehand, by some safe-woven *manifesto,* that gross delinquents may tell no tales of anchors and buoys, nor palliate their presumptions with pretense of ignorance. I know no difference in these essentials between monarchies, aristocracies or democracies: the rule and reason will be found all one, say Schoolmen and Pretorians what they will. And in all, the best standard to measure prerogatives is the ploughstaff; to measure liberties, the scepter: if the terms were a little altered into loyal prerogatives and royal liberties, then we should be sure to have royal kings and loyal subjects.

Subjects their King, the King his subjects greets,
Whilome the scepter and the ploughstaff meets.

But progenitors have had them for four and twenty
predecessions; that would be spoken in the Norman tongue
or Cimbrian, not in the English or Scottish: when a conqueror turns Christian, Christianity turns conqueror. If they
had had them time out of mind of man, before Adam was
made, it is not a pin to the point in *foro rectae rationis*
["in the forum of right reason"]. Justice and equity were
before time, and will be after it: time hath neither politics
nor ethics, good nor evil in it; it is an empty thing, as empty
as a New English purse, and emptier it cannot be. A man
may break his neck in time, and in a less time than he can
heal it.

6. JONATHAN MITCHELL, 1624–1668

[In the spring of every year the citizens (who by a
law of 1631 were limited to full members of the churches,
so that only one out of about every five adult males had
a vote) or their representatives met in Boston to elect the
governor and other officers and the General Court. Before
the voting, the custom was early devised of having one
of the more distinguished ministers preach an "election
sermon." This would naturally contain a review of the political situation and exhortations for the future.

After 1660 it seemed to those who adhered to the ideals
of the founders that history had turned against them.
Charles II was restored to the throne, and the Puritan
revolution completely collapsed. The government began to
interfere in the domestic affairs of the colonies, stopping
Massachusetts from executing Quakers after it had hanged
four on Boston Common, demanding extension of the
franchise and comformity to the laws of trade, and threatening to impose the Church of England. Meanwhile a succession of disasters—hurricanes, crop-failures, fires, plagues
—afflicted the land. Still worse, affairs of this world so occupied the people that there appeared to be a steady

deterioration in their religious dedication. Hence the election sermons became, year after year, "jeremiads"—interpreting the afflictions as punishments for the communities' violation of the covenant (as Winthrop in the *Model* had predicted), and calling for reformation of manners and a resuscitation of zeal. By constantly invoking the example of the founders, the orators bit by bit worked out a definition of the meaning of orthodox New England as seen in the perspective of events.

Jonathan Mitchell, intellectual leader of the second generation, was born in Halifax, Yorkshire, and brought by his parents to Massachusetts Bay in 1635. Graduated from Harvard in 1647, he was chosen minister at Cambridge, where he married the widow of his great predecessor, Thomas Shepard. He was the tutor and mentor of Increase Mather. He preached this election sermon in 1667; it was printed at Cambridge in 1671.]

NEHEMIAH ON THE WALL

Civil rulers are especially to seek the welfare of the people of God; or to seek the welfare of the people over whom they are rulers, especially when they are the Lord's people. . . .

I. This point shows us what ought to be the general end and rule of all the motions and actions of rulers: the welfare of the people. To that scope Nehemiah bends all his actions and endeavors; and *Finis est mensura mediorum*—the end serves to measure, regulate, direct and limit the means, and show what should be done. That maxim of the Romans was, and is, a principle of right reason: *Salus populi suprema lex* ["the welfare of the people is the supreme law"], and is engraven on the forehead of the law and light of nature. Hence it is owned and confirmed by the scriptures, as we see in the text; and it is easily deducible from the law of God: for that that is indeed the law of nature is a part of the eternal law of God; and the law of God enjoins that in human, civil affairs things be managed according to right reason and equity; and that rulers, as they are for the people, so they are to make it their main business—and the scope of all their actions, laws and motions—to seek the welfare of the people. There is sunlight for this maxim; and it was never doubted nor denied by any that held but to rational and moral principles. Hence this law being supreme, it limits all other laws and considerations. Hence it is impossible that a people or their rulers should be bound by any other law, or custom, or consideration whatsoever, to do anything that is really and evidently contrary to this. If it be indeed contrary or destructive to the welfare of the people (of the community they stand charged with), it is impossible they should be bound in conscience to do it.

This is the compass that rulers are to steer by, and the touchstone of right and wrong in all their motions: what is for or against the public good and the welfare of the people (Rom. 13. 14), that bounds and regulates his whole ministration. What is for the common good—that and that only you are to do; and all that are set in place of rule and government (be they of higher or of lower quality) do stand charged with the welfare of that people, whom they are rulers over.

I know when it comes to particulars, the doubt will still be: what is for the welfare of the people? One will say this is most for the common good, another that. But:

1. It will help much if this principle be settled and acknowledged: that in civil affairs, the consideration of the welfare of the whole is that which shows and determines what is right and weighs down all other considerations whatsoever. Men will say: "We must do what is right, whatsoever comes of it"—*Fiat justitia ruat coelum.* True; but it is most certain it is not right if it be against the welfare of the people. It is impossible that anything should be truly right that is destructive to the common good: for it will constantly hold, *Salus populi suprema lex.*

2. Consider the things wherein the welfare of a people does consist—religion in the first place, and then their safety, or the preservation of their being, both personal and political, and their participation in the rules and fruits of righteousness, equity, order and peace—and that will

help to discover and discern what is for the welfare of the people, or for the common good, and what not. There is need of much prudence and wariness in particular applications and cases; but those general principles will hold: that a people's welfare lies in such things as these, and that rulers are bound in all their motions and actions to seek the welfare of the people, and to do nothing contrary thereunto.

II. Hence see, that difficulties and troubles do not excuse, nor should discourage, rulers from doing the work of their places, which God call them unto, or from seeking the welfare of the people. Such things do not excuse nor should discourage them from taking and accepting the place of rule when called to it. As they did not Nehemiah: though he heard before that their condition was a condition of great affliction and reproach (Neh. 1. 3), yet he voluntarily left the court of Persia to embark with the Jews at Jerusalem, when in so stormy a time as this was: and how is he honored in the Book of God for it? It was a difficult time and task that Moses was sent upon, accompanied also with a deep sense of his own infirmity and unfitness (Exod. 3. 4); he could not but be slow and backward to such a work. But yet when he was over-backward, the Lord grew angry, and chides him into a consent. But (I say) difficulties and troubles should not discourage nor hinder rulers from doing the work of their places when set therein, *i.e.*, from faithful seeking and acting for the welfare of the people, which is (as we have said) the summary work of the ruler's place. . . .

Go on, therefore, in the work of the Lord and in the service of your several places, and be not taken off by trouble, difficulties, oppositions, felt infirmities in yourselves, weaknesses and distempers in persons and things round about you (which will always be). When were there work for patience, faith, fortitude, self-denial, and for the spirit of a soldier, wrestler, etc., if it were not for such things? We must none of us say, of one order or other, "I will serve God in my place, and help build the wall of Jerusalem, if I may do it with ease and tranquility, without trouble, without hazard, without reproaches and ill requitals from men, etc." Christ is little beholden to us if that be all we will do for him: that is too low for the spirit of a good soldier of Christ Jesus (II Cor. 6. 4, 5, 8). Yea, now you look like the ministers of God, when you cheerfully discharge your places, though surrounded and loaden with afflictions, distresses, labors, false reproaches, etc. Now you are dressed like a minister, like a servant of God and of His people in public works: and through such things as these you must go on in your work, as the Apostles then did.

7.   WILLIAM STOUGHTON, 1631–1701

[The son of a founder of Dorchester, William Stoughton graduated from Harvard and went to Oxford. He was a minister in Sussex, but was ejected by the Restoration, whereupon he returned to the Bay in 1662. He preached at Dorchester, but turned (one of the first Harvard graduates to do so) from the pulpit to the law. He held various posts under the old charter, was named lieutenant-governor under the new charter in 1692. As chief justice of the special court which condemned the witches at Salem he earned infamy with posterity, but he is said never to have repented his action. He delivered this election sermon in 1668; it was printed by the little press at Cambridge in 1670.]

NEW ENGLAND'S TRUE INTEREST

And here I shall consider that the words of the text are spoken concerning a people, even the body of a nation; and so my endeavor shall be to apply the truths delivered unto this present assembly, standing before the Lord this day as the body of this people. Such in several respects is the capacity of this solemn congregation; and unto you, as such, my desire is to speak in the name of the Lord. For many a day and year, even from our first beginnings, hath this word of the Lord been verified concerning us in this wilderness: the Lord hath said of New England, "Surely they are my people, children that will not lie." So hath He been our savior. Upon this basis have all the saviorly undertakings of the Lord been founded in the midst of us, and upon this bottom do we unto this day abide.

The solemn work of this day is "foundation-work": not to lay a new foundation, but to continue and strengthen, and beautify and build upon, that which hath been laid. Give me leave therefore, honored and beloved, to awaken, and call upon you, in the name of Him who sends me, with reference unto those foundations that are held forth to us in the text. For if these should be out of course, what could the righteous do? If we should so frustrate and deceive the Lord's expectations that His covenant-interest in us, and the workings of His salvation be made to cease, then all were lost indeed: ruin upon ruin, destruction upon destruction would come, until one stone were not left upon another. . . .

Use I. Of information: to let New England know what that gracious, infinitely wise, holy and awful dispensation of divine providence is, under which the Lord hath set us and continued unto this day. We must look upon ourselves as under a solemn divine probation: it hath been and it is a probation-time, even to this whole people. Under great hopes and singular eminent expectations hath the Lord our God been trying of us, and is yet trying us in the ways of His salvation. There is this one voice of all His providences towards us; they call aloud unto us in this language of a probation-time: today, if this my people will hear my voice; today, if they will come up to the Lord's expectations and answer His promises; today, that is whilst it is a day of salvation, whilst the Lord is yet so wonderfully preserving of us, displaying His banner over us, holding underneath the everlasting arms, and making us to taste so much of His loving kindness and tender mercies every way. Divine expectations frustrated will issue dreadfully, when the Lord shall make us know His breach of promise (Numb. 14. 34).

This we must know, that the Lord's promises and expectations of great things have singled out New England,

and all sorts and ranks of men amongst us, above any nation or people in the world; and this hath been and is a time and season of eminent trial to us. If I should say that the very world or common ordinary professors expect great things from us at this day, there is a great deal of weight in it; if I say that the faithful precious suffering saints of God in all other places that have heard of the Lord's providences towards us do expect and promise great things from us, this is far more; but to mention the Lord's own expectations, this is most of all, these are certainly most solemn and awful. Every expectation of God is most just and righteous. "Are not my ways equal?" saith God (Ezek. 18. 29). Yes, most equal, blessed God: bountiful and rich hast Thou been in all Thy free bestowings; equal and just art Thou in all Thy greatest expectations. If we do but run over the forementioned grounds of divine expectation, it will be sufficient to commit the judgment of this case even to ourselves (Isa. 5. 3).

As for special relation unto God: whom hath the Lord more signally exalted than His people in this wilderness? The name and interest of God, and covenant-relation to Him, it hath been written upon us in capital letters from the beginning. God had His creatures in this wilderness before we came, and His rational creatures too—a multitude of them; but as to sons and children that are covenant-born unto God, are not we the first in such a relation? In this respect we are surely the Lord's first-born in this wilderness. Of the poor natives before we came, we may say (Isa. 63. 19): "They were not called by the Lord's name, He bear not rule over them." But we have been from the beginning, and we are the Lord's.

As for extraction and descent; if we be considered as a posterity, O what parents and predecessors may we, the most of us, look back unto? Through whose loins the Lord hath stretched forth the line of His covenant, measuring of us out, and taking us in to be a peculiar portion to Himself?

As for restipulations and engagements back again to God: what awful public transactions of this kind have there been amongst us? Hath not the eye of the Lord beheld us

laying covenant-engagements upon ourselves? Hath not His
ear heard us solemnly avouching Him, and Him alone, to
be our God and savior? Hath not a great part of the world
been a witness of these things, even of our explicit ownings
of, and covenantings with, the Lord as our God, laying
this as a foundation stone in our building? And of this we
may say, it hath been a special exasperation unto adversaries and ill willers that despised New England hath laid
claim to, and publicly avouched and challenged, a special
interest in God above others.

As for our advantages and privileges in a covenant state:
here time and strength would fail to reckon up what we
have enjoyed of this kind. If any people in the world have
been lifted up to heaven as to advantages and privileges,
we are the people. Name what you will under this head,
and we have had it. We have had Moses and Aaron to lead
us; we have had teachings and instructions, line upon line
and precept upon precept; we have had ordinances and
Gospel dispensations, the choicest of them; we have had
peace and plenty; we have had afflictions and chastise-
ments in measure; we have had the hearts and prayers
and blessing of the Lord's people everywhere; we have
had the eye and hand of God, watching and working every
way for our good; our adversaries have had their rebukes,
we have had our encouragements and a wall of fire round
about us. What could have been done more for us than
hath been done?

And then, in the last place, as to New England's first
ways: what glorious things might here be spoken unto the
praise of free grace, and to justify the Lord's expectations
upon this ground? Surely God hath often spoke concerning
His churches here (as in Jer. 2. 2): "I remember the kindness of thy youth," etc. O what were the open professions
of the Lord's people that first entered this wilderness? How
did our fathers entertain the Gospel and all the pure institutions thereof, and those liberties which they brought
over? What was their communion and fellowship in the
administrations of the kingdom of Jesus Christ? What was
the pitch of their brotherly love, of their zeal for God and
His ways, and against ways destructive of truth and holi-

ness? What was their humility, their mortification, their exemplariness? How much of holiness to the Lord was written upon all their ways and transactions? God sifted a whole nation that he might send choice grain over into this wilderness.

Thus it hath been with us as to grounds of divine expectation. And therefore let us in the fear of God learn this great truth today, and receive the instruction thereof sealed up unto all our souls: That the great God hath taken up great expectations of us, and made great promises to Himself concerning us, and this hath been—and is—New England's day and season of probation.

8. WILLIAM HUBBARD, 1621–1704

[Born in Tenring, Essex, William Hubbard was brought to New England in 1635, to graduate with the first class at Harvard College in 1642. He studied both medicine and theology, was ordained at Ipswich in 1656. He became spokesman for that shadowy party of "moderates" who advocated coming to terms with the government of the Restoration, and was willing to accept a policy of toleration. However, in 1687 he protested, along with John Wise, against Andros's taxation; he lived to become one of the most venerated ministers in the colony, though after his wife died he shocked his congregation by marrying, in 1694, his housekeeper.

When he delivered this election sermon, May 3, 1676, the colonies had been decimated by King Philip's War. Though as a moderate Hubbard advocated caution about resisting England, he still held forth the fundamental Puritan conception of social cohesion articulated in a hierarchy of classes. The full title of the sermon, printed at Boston, is *The Happiness of a People In the Wisdome of their Rulers Directing And in the Obedience of their Brethren Attending.*]

THE HAPPINESS OF A PEOPLE

It was order that gave beauty to this goodly fabric of the world, which before was but a confused chaos, without form and void. Therefore when Job—when he would set out the terribleness of the grave and dismal state of death—he calls it the land of darkness, and the shadow of death without any order (Job 10. 22). For order is as the soul of the universe, the life and health of things natural, the beauty and strength of things artificial.

The better to understand this we may consider what order is. The schools tell us it is: *parium impariumque; sua cuique; tribuens loca, opta disposito*—such a disposition of things in themselves equal and unequal as gives to every one their due and proper place. It suited the wisdom of the infinite and omnipotent creator to make the world of differing parts, which necessarily supposes that there must be differing places for those differing things to be disposed into, which is order. The like is necessary to be observed in the rational and political world, where persons of differing endowments and qualifications need differing stations to be disposed into, the keeping of which is both the beauty and strength of such a society. Naturalists tell us that beauty in the body arises from an exact symmetry or proportion of contrary humors, equally mixed one with another: so doth an orderly and artificial distribution of diverse materials make a comely building, while homogeneous bodies (as the depths of waters in the sea, and heaps of sand on the shore) run into confused heaps, as bodies incapable to maintain an order in themselves. So that it appears: whoever is for a parity in any society will in the issue reduce things into an heap of confusion. That God, who assumes to Himself the title of being the God of glory, is the God of peace or order, and not of confusion (I Cor. 14. 33 compared with verse 40). He is so in His palace of the world as well as in His temple of His church: in both may be observed a sweet subordination of persons and things, each unto other.

Look we into the third heavens, the high and holy place,

as a royal pavilion pitched by the Almighty for the residence of His glory: although it be furnished with inhabitants suitable to the nature of that celestial throne, yet are they not all of one rank and order; there are cherubims as well as seraphims, archangels as well as angels, thrones and dominions as well as principalities and powers. There are also, as in a middle rank, the spirits of just men made perfect: though no unclean thing may enter in, yet have they not attained their perfection in glory, but do yet expect an addition of glory. But in the outward court, as there are diversity of gifts, so there are of places and order: some that are to rule and go before, others that are to be subject and to follow.

If we shall but descend and take notice of the firmament —the pavement of that glorious mansion place, although it be the roof of this lower world—may we not there see one star differing from another in glory? There is placed the sun, the lord and ruler of the day, as well as the moon that rules the night, together with the stars as the common people of that upper region, who yet do immediately veil their glory and withdraw their light when their bridegroom cometh forth of his chamber. In the firmament of the air, may we not see the lofty eagle in his flight far surmounting the little choristers of the valleys? The like disproportion, who observes not amongst those creatures that take their pastime in the deep waters, or that range upon the high mountains, hunting for their prey?

And hath not the same Almighty Creator and Disposer of all things made some of the sons of men as far differing in height of body one from the other, as Saul from the rest of the people? And are not some advanced as high above others in dignity and power as much as the cedars of Lebanon the low shrubs of the valley? It is not then the result of time or chance that some are mounted on horseback while others are left to travel on foot, that some have with the Centurion power to command while others are required to obey. The poor and the rich meet together, the Lord is the maker of them both. The Almighty hath appointed her that sits behind the mill, as well as him that ruleth on the throne. And herein hath He as well consulted the good of human nature as the glory of His own wisdom and power, those of the superior rank but making a supply of what is wanting in the other. Otherwise might not the foolish and ignorant be like to lose themselves in the wilderness if others were not as eyes to them? The fearful and the weak might be destroyed if others more strong and valiant did not protect and defend them. The poor and needy might starve with hunger and cold, were they not fed with the morsels and warmed with the fleece of the wealthy. Is it not found by experience that the greatest part of mankind are but as tools and instruments for others to work by, rather than any proper agents to effect any thing of themselves? In peace, how would most people destroy themselves by slothfulness and security? In war, they would be destroyed by others were it not for the wisdom and courage of the valiant. If the virtue and valor of the good did not interpose by their authority to prevent and save, the vice of the bad would bring mischief enough upon places to ruin both. Else why is it so frequently intimated in the latter end of the Book of Judges that in those days, when there was no king in Israel, but every man was left to do what seemed right in his own eyes, that these and those enormities break forth that violated all laws, and offered violence even unto nature itself? . . .

Thus if order were taken away, soon would confusion follow, and every evil work (James 3. 16). Nothing therefore can be imagined more remote either from right reason or true religion than to think that, because we were all once equal at our birth and shall be again at our death, therefore we should be so in the whole course of our lives. In fine, a body would not be more monstrous and deformed without an head, nor a ship more dangerous at sea without a pilot, nor a flock of sheep more ready to be devoured without a shepherd, than would human society be without an head and leader in time of danger. . . .

In a curious piece of architecture that which first offers itself to the view of the beholder is the beauty of the structure, the proportion that one piece bears to another, wherein the skill of the architect most shows itself. But that which is most admirable in sensitive and rationable beings is that inward principle, seated in some one part, able to guide the whole and influence all the rest of the parts, with an apt and regular motion, for their mutual good and safety. The wisdom of the creation was more seen in the breath of life breathed into the nostrils of Adam, whereby he became a living soul, than in the feature and beauty of the goodly frame of his body formed out of the dust—as the Poet speaks, *Os homini sublime dedit* ["He imparted sublimity to the bone of man"]. . . .

The architect of that curious piece hath placed the head in the forefront, the highest sphere, where are lodged all the senses, as in a watchtower, ready to be improved upon all occasions, for the safety and preservation of the whole. There are placed those that look out at the windows, to foresee evil and danger approaching, accordingly to alarm all the other inferior powers, to take the signal and stand upon their guard for defense of the whole. There also is the seat of the daughters of music, ready to give audience to all reports and messages that come from abroad. If anything should occur or happen nearer home or further off, imparting either fear of evil or hope of good, their work is immediately to dispatch messages through the whole province of nature, to summon all the other members together, to come in and yield the assistance to prevent the mischief feared, or prepare for the reception of the good promised or pretended, as the nature of the case may require.

Thus are all orders wont to be dispatched and issued from the Cinque ports of the senses in and about the head, for the benefit and advantage of the whole body. Very fitly therefore in the body politic are the rulers by way of allusion, called heads. And in case of inability to discharge those functions, such societies may not undeservedly be compared to the Psalmist's idols, that have eyes but see not, and have ears but hear not. Suppose the hands be never so strong for action or the feet never so swift for motion, yet if there be not discretion in the head to discern, or judgment to determine what is meet to be done for the obviating of evil and danger, or procuring of good, it will be impossible to save such a body from ruin and destruction. If the mast be never so well strengthened, and the

tackling never so well bound together, yet if there want a
skillful pilot to steer and guide, especially in a rough and
tempestuous sea, the lame will soon take the prey.

9. JOHN WISE, 1652–1725

[After being almost forgotten for two centuries, John
Wise has recently come to fame because he was the first
(and in the colonial period the only) one to draw into
explicit utterance the democratic tendency inherent in the
Congregational polity.

Perhaps the reason for his uniqueness lies in the fact
that he was the son of an indentured servant: at least, it
is tempting to think so. Somehow he managed to go to
Harvard, graduating in 1673. He was ordained in 1682 at
the Chebacco parish, a corner of Ipswich township. He led
the town in fiery protest against taxes levied in 1687 by
Governor Andros without the consent of any legislature. In
1690 he was chaplain of the disastrous expedition against
Quebec; he helped check the witchcraft panic, supported
inoculation in 1721, and in his last years, in sharp contrast
to others of the ministerial caste, advocated paper money.
We know nothing about his sermons or his theology, but
his writings on polity show him both a man of the people
—using their language and their wit—and a highly developed rationalist.

The effort of the old Puritan interest to keep control over
Massachusetts after the charter of 1692 became progres-
sively difficult because, among other reasons, the Congregational principle of the autonomy of particular churches
prevented any unified organization against the invading
Anglicans and Baptists. In 1705 Cotton Mather and the
ministers in the Boston area proposed a method of central-
ization, to give ministerial "associations" power over the
selection of ministers and the administration of censures.
Nothing came of the scheme in Massachusetts, though a
similar movement in Connecticut achieved through *The
Saybrook Platform* in 1708 a species of "semi-Presbyterial"
order. John Wise attacked Mather's proposal in a humorous

sketch (published in New York in 1713 but written in 1710), *The Churches Quarrel Espoused,* and then addressed himself to a more sober rebuttal in 1717, *Vindication of the Government of New-England Churches.* Since the proposal was long since dead, Wise was arguing not against a pressing danger but from a clear determination to produce out of Congregational theory all the radically democratic potentialities which the founders had striven, by the use of Winthrop's logic, to keep suppressed.

The revolution Wise proposed in New England thinking —he had little effect on his contemporaries, but his position is prophetic—lies in the structure of his book. Where Cotton and Hooker, in their works on polity, cited New Testament precedents and then supported them by reason, Wise compresses into his first section a hasty review of Biblical authority, and then expands his second section into a long argument from unaided natural wisdom. Instead of the precariously balanced unity of early Puritan theory, Wise's account is out-and-out rationality. Though Wise was curiously not invoked in the Revolutionary discussion, still the intellectual line from his second "Demonstration" to the Declaration of Independence is direct. He seized upon the substance of the Congregational covenant, and quietly extricated it from the scholastic metaphysics by which Winthrop, as in the *Speech to the General Court,* had contrived that the covenant should mean the subjection of inferiors to superiors.]

VINDICATION OF THE GOVERNMENT OF NEW ENGLAND CHURCHES

CHAPTER I.

The divine establishment in providence of the forenamed [New England] churches in their order is apparently the royal assent of the supreme monarch of the churches to the grave decisions of reason in favor of man's natural state of being and original freedom. For if we should make a new survey of the constitution before named under the brightest light of nature, there is no greater example of natural wisdom in any settlement on earth, for the present and future security of human beings in all that is most valuable and grand, than in this: that it seems to me as though wise and provident nature, by the dictates of right reason, excited by the moving suggestions of humanity, and awed with the just demands of natural liberty, equity, equality and principles of self-preservation, originally drew up the scheme, and then obtained the royal approbation. And certainly it is agreeable that we attribute it to God, whether we receive it next from reason or revelation, for that each is equally an emanation of His wisdom: (Prov. 20. 27) "The spirit of man is the candle of the Lord, searching all the inward parts of the belly." There be many larger volumes in this dark recess called the belly to be read by that candle God has lit up. And I am very well assured the forenamed constitution is a transcript out of some of their pages: (John 1. 4, 9) "And the life was the light of men, which lighteth every man which cometh into the world." This admirable effect of Christ's creating power in hanging out so many lights to guide man through a dark world is as applicable to the light of reason as to that of revelation, for that the light of reason as a law and rule of right is an effect of Christ's goodness, care and creating power, as well as of revelation—though revelation is nature's law in a fairer and brighter edition. . . .

But in the further and more distinct management of this plea, I shall:

1. Lay before the reader several principles of natural knowledge;

2. Apply or improve them in ecclesiastical affairs;

3. Infer from the premises a demonstration that these churches, if not properly formed, yet are fairly established in their present order by the law of nature.

CHAPTER II.

I shall disclose several principles of natural knowledge, plainly discovering the law of nature, or the true sentiments of natural reason, with respect to man's being and government. And in this essay I shall peculiarly confine the discourse to two heads, *viz.*

I. Of the natural (in distinction to the civil), and then,

II. Of the civil being of man. . . .

I. I shall consider man in a state of natural being, as a freeborn subject under the crown of heaven and owing homage to none but God Himself.

It is certain, civil government in general is a very admirable result of providence and an incomparable benefit to mankind, yet must needs be acknowledged to be the effect of human free compacts and not of divine institution. It is the produce of man's reason, of human and rational combinations, and not from any direct orders of infinite wisdom in any positive law where is drawn up this or that scheme of civil government. Government, says Lord Warrington, is necessary, in that no society of men can subsist without it; and that particular form of government is necessary which best suits the temper and inclination of a people. Nothing can be God's ordinance but what He has particularly declared to be such; there is no particular form of civil government described in God's word, neither does nature prompt it. The government of the Jews was changed five times. Government is not formed by nature, as other births or productions: if it were, it would be the same in all countries, because nature keeps the same method, in the same thing, in all climates. If a commonwealth be changed into a monarchy, is it nature that forms and brings forth the monarch? Or if a royal family be wholly extinct (as in Noah's case, being not heir apparent from descent from Adam), is it nature that must go to work (with the king bees, who themselves alone preserve the royal race in that empire) to breed a monarch before the people can have a king or a government set over them? And thus we must leave kings to resolve which is their best title to their crowns, whether natural right or the constitution of government settled by human compacts, under the direction and conduct of reason.

But to proceed under the head of a state of natural being, I shall more distinctly explain the state of human nature in its original capacity, as man is placed on earth by his maker and clothed with many investitures and immunities which properly belong to man separately considered. As:

1. The prime immunity in man's state is that he is most properly the subject of the law of nature. He is the favorite animal on earth, in that this part of God's image—*viz.* reason—is congenate with his nature, wherein, by a law immutable, instamped upon his frame, God has provided a rule for men in all their actions, obliging each one to the performance of that which is right, not only as to justice but likewise as to all other moral virtues, the which is nothing but the dictate of right reason founded in the soul of man. . . .

That which is to be drawn from man's reason, flowing from the true current of that faculty—when unperverted—may be said to be the law of nature: on which account, the Holy Scriptures declare it written on men's hearts. For being endowed with a soul, you may know from yourself how and what you ought to act: (Rom. 2. 14) "These having not a law, are a law to themselves." So that the meaning is: when we acknowledge the law of nature to be the dictate of right reason, we must mean that the understanding of man is endowed with such a power as to be able, from the contemplation of human condition, to discover a necessity of living agreeably with this law: and likewise to find out some principle by which the precepts of it may be clearly and solidly demonstrated. The way to discover the law of nature in our own state is by a narrow watch and accurate contemplation of our natural condition and propensions. Others say this is the way to find out the law of nature: if a man any ways doubts whether what he is going to do to another man be agreeable to the law of nature, then let him suppose himself to be in that other man's room. And by this rule effectually executed, a man must be a very dull scholar to nature not to make proficiency in the knowledge of her laws.

But more particularly, in pursuing our condition for the discovery of the law of nature, this is very obvious to view, *viz.*

A principle of self-love and self-preservation is very predominant in every man's being;

A sociable disposition;

An affection or love to mankind in general.

And to give such sentiments the force of a law, we must suppose a God who takes care of all mankind, and has thus obliged each one, as a subject of higher principles of being than mere instincts. For that all law, properly considered, supposes a capable subject and a superior power; and the law of God which is binding is published by the dicates of right reason as other ways. "Therefore," says Plutarch, "to follow God and obey reason is the same thing."

But moreover, that God has established the law of nature as the general rule of government is further illustrable from the many sanctions in providence, and from the peace and guilt of conscience in them that either obey or violate the law of nature. But moreover, the foundation of the law of nature with relation to government may be thus discovered: man is a creature extremely desirous of his own preservation; of himself he is plainly exposed to many wants, unable to secure his own safety and maintenance without the assistance of his fellows; and he is also able of returning kindness by the furtherance of mutual good. But yet man is often found to be malicious, insolent and easily provoked, and as powerful in effecting mischief as he is ready in designing it. Now, that such a creature may be preserved, it is necessary that he be sociable—that is, that he be capable and disposed to unite himself to those of his own species, and to regulate himself towards them, that they may have no fair reason to do him harm, but rather incline to promote his interests and secure his rights and concerns. This then is a fundamental law of nature, that every man, as far as in him lies, do maintain a sociableness with others, agreeable with the main end and disposition of human nature in general. For this is very apparent, that reason and society render man the most potent of all creatures. And finally, from the principles of sociableness it follows as a fundamental law of nature that man is not so wedded to his own interest but that he can make the common good the mark of his aim. And hence he becomes capacitated to enter into a civil state by the law of nature; for without this property in nature—*viz.* sociableness, which is for cementing of parts—every government would soon moulder and dissolve.

2. The second great immunity of man is an original liberty instamped upon his rational nature. He that intrudes upon this liberty violates the law of nature. In this discourse I shall waive the consideration of man's moral turpitude, but shall view him physically as a creature which God has made and furnished essentially with many ennobling immunities which render him the most august animal in the world; and still, whatever has happened since his creation, he remains at the upper end of nature, and as such is a creature of a very noble character. For as to his dominion, the whole frame of the lower part of the universe is devoted to his use and at his command; and his liberty under the conduct of right reason is equal with his trust.

Which liberty may be briefly considered—internally, as to his mind; and externally, as to his person:

The internal native liberty of man's nature in general implies a faculty of doing or omitting things according to the direction of his judgment. But in a more special meaning, this liberty does not consist in a loose and ungovernable freedom or in an unbounded license of acting. Such license is disagreeing with the condition and dignity of man, and would make man of a lower and meaner constitution than brute creatures, who in all their liberties are kept under a better and more rational government by their instincts. Therefore as Plutarch says, "Those persons only who live in obedience to reason are worthy to be accounted free; they alone live as they will who have learned what they ought to will." So that the true natural liberty of man, such as really and truly agrees to him, must be understood as he is guided and restrained by the ties of reason and laws of nature; all the rest is brutal, if not worse.

Man's external, personal, natural liberty, antecedent to all human parts or alliances, must also be considered. And so every man must be conceived to be perfectly in his own power and disposal, and not to be controlled by the authority of any other. And thus every man must be acknowledged equal to every man, since all subjection and all command are equally banished on both sides; and considering all men thus at liberty, every man has a prerogative to judge for himself, *viz.* what shall be most for his behoof, happiness and well-being.

3. The third capital immunity belonging to man's nature is an equality amongst men, which is not to be denied by the law of nature till man has resigned himself with all his rights for the sake of a civil state. And then his personal liberty and equality is to be cherished, and preserved to the highest degree as will consist with all just distinctions amongst men of honor, and shall be agreeable with the public good. For man has a high valuation of himself, and the passion seems to lay its first foundation, not in pride, but really in the high and admirable frame and constitution of human nature. The word "Man," says my author, is thought to carry somewhat of dignity in its sound; and we commonly make use of this as the most proper and prevailing argument against a rude insulter, *viz.* "I am not a beast or a dog, but am a man as well as yourself." Since then human nature agrees equally with all persons, and since no one can live a sociable life with another that does not own or respect him as a man, it follows as a command of the law of nature that every man esteem and treat another as one who is naturally his equal, or who is a man as well as he. There be many popular or plausible reasons that greatly illustrate this equality: *viz.* that we all derive our being from one stock, the same common father of [the] human race. On this consideration Boethius checks the pride of the insulting nobility: . . .

> Fondly our first descent we boast;
>   If whence at first our breath we drew,
>   The common springs of life we view,
> The airy notion soon is lost.

> The Almighty made us equal all;
>   But he that slavishly complies

To do the drudgery of vice,
Denies his high original.

And also, that our bodies are composed of matter, frail, brittle, and liable to be destroyed by [a] thousand accidents. We all owe our existence to the same method of propagation. The noblest mortal, in his entrance onto the stage of life, is not distinguished by any pomp or of passage from the lowest of mankind; and our life hastens to the same general mark: death observes no ceremony, but knocks as loud at the barriers of the Court as at the door of the cottage.

This equality being admitted, bears a very great force in maintaining peace and friendship amongst men. For that he who would use the assistance of others, in promoting his own advantage, ought as freely to be at their service when they want his help on the like occasions. "One good turn requires another" is the common proverb; for otherwise he must need esteem others unequal to himself, who constantly demands their aid, and as constantly denies his own. And whoever is of this insolent temper cannot but highly displease those about him, and soon give occasion of the breach of the common peace. It was a manly reproof which Charactacus gave the Romans: *Num si vos omnibus*, etc., "What! because you desire to be masters of all men, does it follow therefore that all men should desire to be your slaves?" For that it is a command of nature's law that no man that has not obtained a particular and special right shall arrogate to himself a larger share than his fellows, but shall admit others to equal privileges with himself. So that the principle of equality in a natural state is peculiarly transgressed by pride, which is when a man without sufficient reason prefers himself to others. And though, as Hensius paraphrases upon Aristotle's *Politics* to this purpose, *viz.* "Nothing is more suitable to nature than that those who excel in understanding and prudence should rule and control those who are less happy in those advantages, etc.," yet we must note that there is room for an answer: that it would be the greatest absurdity to believe that nature actually invests the wise with a sovereignty over the weak, or with a right of forcing them against their wills. For that no sovereignty can be established, unless some human deed or covenant precede. Nor does natural fitness for government make a man presently governor over another: for that, as Ulpian says, "by a natural right all men are born free." And nature having set all men upon a level and made them equals, no servitude or subjection can be conceived without inequality; and this cannot be made without usurpation or force in others, or voluntary compliance in those who resign their freedom and give away their degree of natural being.

II. And thus we come to consider man in a civil state of being: wherein we shall observe the great difference between a natural and political state; for in the latter state many great disproportions appear, or at least many obvious distinctions are soon made amongst men.

Which doctrine is to be laid open under a few heads:

1. Every man considered in a natural state must be allowed to be free and at his own dispose; yet to suit man's inclinations to society—and in a peculiar manner to gratify the necessity he is in of public rule and order—he is impelled to enter into a civil community, and divests himself of his natural freedom and puts himself under government: which amongst other things comprehends the power of life and death over him, together with authority to enjoin him some things to which he has an utter aversion, and to prohibit him other things for which he may have as strong an inclination, so that he may be often, under this authority, obliged to sacrifice his private for the public good. So that, though man is inclined to society, yet he is driven to a combination by great necessity. For that the true and leading cause of forming governments, and yielding up natural liberty and throwing man's equality into a common pile to be new cast by the rules of fellowship, was really and truly to guard themselves against the injuries men were liable to interchangeably. For none so good to man as man, and yet none a greater enemy.

2. So that, the first human subject and original of civil

power is the people. For as they have a power, every man over himself in a natural state, so upon a combination they can and do bequeath this power unto others, and settle it according as their united discretion shall determine. For that this is very plain: that when the subject of sovereign power is quite extinct, that power returns to the people again. And when they are free, they may set up what species of government they please; or, if they rather incline to it, they may subside into a state of natural being, if it be plainly for the best. In the Eastern country of the Mogul, we have some resemblance of the case: for upon the death of an absolute monarch, they live so many days without a civil head; but in that interregnum, those who survive the vacancy are glad to get into a civil state again, and usually they are in a very bloody condition when they return under the covert of a new monarch. This project is to endear the people to a tyranny, from the experience they have so lately had of an anarchy.

3. The formal reason of government is the will of a community, yielded up and surrendered to some other subject, either of one particular person or more, conveyed in the following manner:

Let us conceive in our mind a multitude of men, all naturally free and equal, going about voluntarily to erect themselves into a new commonwealth. Now, their condition being such, to bring themselves into a politic body they must needs enter into divers covenants.

They must interchangeably, each man, covenant to join in one lasting society, that they may be capable to concert the measures of their safety by a public vote.

A vote or decree must then nextly pass to set up some particular species of government over them. And if they are joined in their first compact upon absolute terms to stand to the decision of the first vote concerning the species of government, they all are bound by the majority to acquiesce in that particular form thereby settled, though their own private opinion incline them to some other model.

After a decree has specified the particular form of government, then there will be need of a new covenant, whereby those on whom sovereignty is conferred engage

to take care of the common peace and welfare, and the
subjects on the other hand to yield them faithful obedience.
In which covenant is included that submission and union
of wills by which a state may be conceived to be but one
person. So that the most proper definition of a civil state
is this: a civil state is a compound moral person whose will
(united by those covenants before passed) is the will of
all, to the end it may use and apply the strength and riches
of private persons towards maintaining the common peace,
security and well-being of all. Which may be conceived as
though the whole state was now become but one man, in
which the aforesaid covenants may be supposed, under
God's providence, to be the divine fiat pronounced by God,
"Let us make man."

And by way of resemblance, the aforesaid being may be
thus anatomized:

The sovereign power is the soul infused, giving life and
motion to the whole body.

Subordinate officers are the joints by which the body
moves.

Wealth and riches are the strength.

Equity and laws are the reason.

Councilors the memory.

Salus Populi, or the happiness of the people, is the end
of its being, or main business to be attended and done.

Concord amongst the members and all estates is the
health.

Sedition is sickness, and civil war death.

4. The parts of sovereignty may be considered; so:

As it prescribes the rule of action, it is rightly termed
legislative power.

As it determines the controversies of subjects by the
standard of those rules, so is it justly termed judiciary
power.

As it arms the subjects against foreigners or forbids
hostility, so it's called the power of peace and war.

As it takes in ministers for the discharge of business, so
it is called the right of appointing magistrates. So that all
great officers and public servants must needs owe their
original to the creating power of sovereignty. So that those

whose right it is to create may dissolve the being of those who are created, unless they cast them into an immortal frame. And yet must needs be dissoluble if they justly forfeit their being to their creators.

The chief end of civil communities is that men thus conjoined may be secured against the injuries they are liable to from their own kind. For if every man could secure himself singly, it would be great folly for him to renounce his natural liberty, in which every man is his own king and protector.

The sovereign authority, besides that it inheres in every state as in a common and general subject, so farther, according as it resides in some one person, or in a council (consisting of some select persons or of all the members of a community) as in a proper and particular subject, so it produceth different forms of commonwealths, *viz.* such as are either simple and regular, or mixed.

The forms of a regular state are three only, which forms arise from the proper and particular subject in which the supreme power resides. As:

1. A democracy: which is when the sovereign power is lodged in a council consisting of all the members, and where every member has the privilege of a vote.

This form of government appears in the greatest part of the world to have been the most ancient. For that reason seems to show it to be most probable that when men (being originally in a condition of natural freedom and equality) had thoughts of joining in a civil body, [they] would without question be inclined to administer their common affairs by their common judgment, and so must necessarily, to gratify that inclination, establish a democracy. Neither can it be rationally imagined that fathers of families, being yet free and independent, should in a moment, or little time, take off their long delight in governing their own affairs and devolve all upon some single sovereign commander. For that it seems to have been thought more equitable that what belonged to all should be managed by all, when all had entered by compact into one community. "The original of our government," says Plato (speaking of the Athenian commonwealth), "was taken from the equality of our race. Other states there are, composed of different blood and of unequal lines, the consequences of which are disproportionable sovereignty, tyrannical or oligarchical sway, under which men live in such a manner as to esteem themselves partly lords and partly slaves to each other. But we and our countrymen, being all born brethren of the same mother, do not look upon ourselves to stand under so hard a relation as that of lords and slaves; but the parity of our descent inclines us to keep up the like parity by our laws, and to yield the precedency to nothing but to superior virtue and wisdom."

And moreover, it seems very manifest that most civil communities arose at first from the union of families that were nearly allied in race and blood. And though ancient story make frequent mention of kings, yet it appears that most of them were such that had an influence rather in persuading than in any power of commanding. . . .

A democracy is then erected when a number of free persons do assemble together, in order to enter into a covenant for uniting themselves in a body. And such a preparative assembly hath some appearance already of a democracy: it is a democracy in embryo properly in this respect, that every man hath the privilege freely to deliver his opinion concerning the common affairs. Yet he who dissents from the vote of the majority is not in the least obliged by what they determine, till by a second covenant a popular form be actually established. For not before then can we call it a democratical government, *viz.* till the right of determining all matters relating to the public safety is actually placed in a general assembly of the whole people, or by their own compact and mutual agreement, determine themselves the proper subject for the exercise of sovereign power.

And to complete this state, and render it capable to exert its power to answer the end of a civil state, these conditions are necessary:

That a certain time and place be assigned for assembling.

That when the assembly be orderly met, as to time and

place, that then the vote of the majority must pass for the vote of the whole body.

That magistrates be appointed to exercise the authority of the whole, for the better dispatch of business of every day's occurrence; who also may with more mature diligence search into more important affairs, and if in case any thing happens of greater consequence may report it to the assembly, and be peculiarly serviceable in putting all public decrees into execution—because a large body of people is almost useless in respect of the last service, and of many others as to the more particular application and exercise of power. Therefore it is most agreeable with the law of nature that they institute their officers to act in their name and stead.

2. The second species of regular government is an aristocracy. And this is said then to be constituted when the people or assembly, united by a first covenant and having thereby cast themselves into the first rudiments of a state, do then, by common decree, devolve the sovereign power on a council, consisting of some select members. And these, having accepted of the designation, are then properly invested with sovereign command. And then an aristocracy is formed.

3. The third species of a regular government is a monarchy, which is settled when the sovereign power is conferred on some one worthy person. . . .

An aristocracy is a dangerous constitution in the church of Christ, as it possesses the presbytery of all church power. What has been observed sufficiently evinces it. And not only so but from the nature of the constitution, for it has no more barrier to it—against the ambition, insults and arbitrary measures of men—than an absolute monarchy.

But to abbreviate: it seems most agreeable with the light of nature that if there be any of the regular government settled in the church of God, it must needs be a democracy.

This is a form of government which the light of nature does highly value, and often directs to as most agreeable to the just and natural prerogatives of human beings. This was of great account in the early times of the world. And not only so, but upon the experience of several thousand years, after the world had been tumbled and tossed from one species of government to another, at a great expense of blood and treasure, many of the wise nations of the world have sheltered themselves under it again:—or at least have blendished and balanced their governments with it.

It is certainly a great truth, that man's original liberty, after it is resigned (yet under due restrictions), ought to be cherished in all wise governments; or otherwise a man, in making himself a subject, he alters himself from a free-man into a slave, which to do is repugnant to the law of nature. Also the natural equality of men amongst men must be duly favored, in that government was never established by God or nature to give one man a prerogative to insult over another. Therefore in a civil, as well as in a natural, state of being, a just equality is to be indulged, so far as that every man is bound to honor every man, which is agreeable both with nature and religion: (I Pet. 2. 17) "Honor all men."

The end of all good government is to cultivate humanity and promote the happiness of all, and the good of every man in all his rights, his life, liberty, estate, honor, etc., without injury or abuse done to any. Then certainly it cannot easily be thought that a company of men, that shall enter into a voluntary compact, to hold all power in their own hands, thereby to use and improve their united force, wisdom, riches and strength for the common and particular good of every member, as is the nature of a democracy— I say, it cannot be that this sort of constitution will so readily furnish those in government with an appetite or disposition to prey upon each other, or embezzle the common stock, as some particular persons may be apt to do when set off and entrusted with the same power. And moreover, this appears very natural, that when the aforesaid government or power, settled in all—when they have elected certain capable persons to minister in their affairs, and the said ministers remain accountable to the assembly, these officers must needs be under the influence of many wise cautions from their own thoughts (as well as under confinement by their commission) in their whole administration. And from thence it must needs follow that they will be more apt and inclined to steer right for the main point, *viz.* the peculiar good and benefit of the whole and every particular member fairly and sincerely. And why may not these stand for very rational pleas in church order?

For certainly if Christ has settled any form of power in his church, he has done it for his church's safety and for the benefit of every member. Then he must needs be presumed to have made choice of that government as should least expose his people to hazard, either from the fraud or arbitrary measures of particular men. And it is as plain as daylight, there is no species of government like a democracy to attain this end. There is but about two steps from an aristocracy to a monarchy, and from thence but one to a tyranny. An able standing force and an ill nature *ipso facto* turn an absolute monarch into a tyrant; this is obvious among the Roman Caesars, and through the world. And all these direful transmutations are easier in church affairs (from the different qualities of things) than in civil states. For what is it that cunning and learned men can't make the world swallow as an article of their creed if they are once invested with an uncontrollable power, and are to be the standing orators to mankind in matters of faith and obedience?

10. JONATHAN MAYHEW, 1720-1766

[In order to include Jonathan Mayhew this anthology here reaches beyond the chronological limit set to the other chapters. Mayhew was so advanced a rationalist that he is now regarded as the precursor of Unitarianism. In political doctrine, however, he carried on the development which Wise disclosed, and in his last year was a prominent agitator against the Stamp Act. His most famous sermon was delivered on January 30, 1750, the anniversary of the execution of Charles I in 1649.]

A DISCOURSE CONCERNING UNLIMITED SUBMISSION

If we calmly consider the nature of the thing itself, nothing can well be imagined more directly contrary to common sense than to suppose that millions of people should be subjected to the arbitrary, precarious pleasure of one single man (who has naturally no superiority over them in point of authority), so that their estates and everything that is valuable in life, and even their lives also, shall be absolutely at his disposal, if he happens to be wanton and capricious enough to demand them. What unprejudiced man can think that God made all to be thus subservient to the lawless pleasure and frenzy of one, so that it shall always be a sin to resist him! Nothing but the most plain and express revelation from heaven could make a sober impartial man believe such a monstrous, unaccountable doctrine, and, indeed, the thing itself appears so shocking —so out of all proportion—that it may be questioned whether all the miracles that ever were wrought, could make it credible, that this doctrine really came from God. At present, there is not the least syllable in scripture which gives any countenance to it. The hereditary, indefeasible, divine right of kings, and the doctrine of non-resistance which is built upon the supposition of such a right, are altogether as fabulous and chimerical as transubstantiation or any of the most absurd reveries of ancient or modern visionaries. These notions are fetched neither from divine revelation nor human reason; and if they are derived from neither of those sources, it is not much matter from whence they come, or whither they go. Only it is a pity that such doctrines should be propagated in society, to raise factions and rebellions, as we see they have, in fact, been both in the last and in the present reign.

But then, if unlimited submission and passive obedience to the higher powers, in all possible cases, be not a duty, it will be asked, "How far are we obliged to submit? If we may innocently disobey and resist in some cases, why not in all? Where shall we stop? What is the measure of our duty? This doctrine tends to the total dissolution of civil government; and to introduce such scenes of wild anarchy and confusion, as are more fatal to society than the worst of tyranny."

After this manner, some men object; and, indeed, this is the most plausible thing that can be said in favor of such an absolute submission as they plead for. But the worst (or rather the best) of it is that there is very little strength or solidity in it. For similar difficulties may be raised with respect to almost every duty of natural and revealed religion. To instance only in two, both of which are near akin, and indeed exactly parallel, to the case before us: it is unquestionably the duty of children to submit to their parents, and of servants to their masters. But no one asserts that it is their duty to obey and submit to them in all supposable cases; or universally a sin to resist them. Now does this tend to subvert the just authority of parents and masters? Or to introduce confusion and anarchy into private families? No. How then does the same principle tend to unhinge the government of that larger family, the body politic? We know, in general, that children and servants are obliged to obey their parents and masters respectively. We know also, with equal certainty, that they are not obliged to submit to them in all things, without exception, but may, in some cases reasonably, and therefore innocently, resist them. These principles are acknowledged upon all hands, whatever difficulty there may be in fixing the exact limits of submission. Now there is at least as much difficulty in stating the measure of duty in these two cases as in the case of rulers and subjects. So that this is really no objection, at least no reasonable one, against resistance to the higher powers. Or, if it is one, it will hold equally against resistance in the other cases mentioned.

It is indeed true, that turbulent, vicious-minded men may take occasion from this principle, that their rulers may in some cases be lawfully resisted, to raise factions and disturbances in the state; and to make resistance where resistance is needless and therefore sinful. But is it not equally true that children and servants of turbulent, vicious minds, may take occasion from this principle, that parents and masters may in some cases be lawfully resisted, to resist when resistance is unnecessary and therefore criminal? Is the principle in either case false in itself, merely because it may be abused and applied to legitimate disobedience and resistance in those instances, to which it ought not to be applied? According to this way of arguing, there will be no true principles in the world; for there are none but what may be wrested and perverted to serve bad purposes, either through the weakness or wickedness of men.[1]

[1] We may very safely assert these two things in general, without undermining government: one is, that no civil rulers are to be obeyed when they enjoin things that are inconsistent with the commands of God. All such disobedience is lawful and glorious, particularly if persons refuse to comply with any legal establishment of religion because it is a gross perversion and corruption (as to doctrine, worship and discipline) of a pure and divine religion, brought from heaven to earth by the son of God (the only king and head of the Christian church) and propagated through the world by his inspired apostles. All commands running counter to the declared will of the supreme legislator of heaven and earth, are null and void: and therefore disobedience to them is a duty, not a crime. . . .

Another thing that may be asserted with equal truth and safety is that no government is to be submitted to at the expense of that which is the sole end of all government: the common good and safety of society. Because, to submit in this case, if it should ever happen, would evidently be to set up the means as more valuable, and above, the end: than which there cannot be a greater solecism and contradiction. The only reason of the institution of civil government, and the only rational ground of submission to it, is the common safety and utility. If therefore, in any case, the common safety and utility would not be promoted by submission to government, but the contrary, there is no ground or motive for obedience and submission, but for the contrary.

Whoever considers the nature of civil government must, indeed, be sensible that a great degree of implicit confidence must unavoidably be placed in those that bear rule. This is implied in the very notion of authority's being originally a trust, committed by the people to those who are vested with it, as all just and righteous authority is. All besides, is mere lawless force and usurpation, neither God nor nature having given any man a right of dominion over any society, independently of that society's approbation and consent to be governed by him. Now as all men are fallible, it cannot be

A people, really oppressed to a great degree by their sovereign, cannot well be insensible when they are so oppressed. And such a people (if I may allude to an ancient fable) have, like the hesperian fruit, a dragon for their

supposed that the public affairs of any state should be always administered in the best manner possible, even by persons of the greatest wisdom and integrity. Nor is it sufficient to legitimate disobedience to the higher powers that they are not so administered, or that they are, in some instances, very ill-managed; for upon this principle, it is scarcely supposable that any government at all could be supported, or subsist. Such a principle manifestly tends to the dissolution of government and to throw all things into confusion and anarchy.

But it is equally evident, upon the other hand, that those in authority may abuse their trust and power to such a degree that neither the law of reason nor of religion requires that any obedience or submission should be paid to them but, on the contrary, that they should be totally discarded and the authority which they were before vested with transferred to others, who may exercise it more to those good purposes for which it is given. Nor is this principle, that resistance to the higher powers is in some extraordinary cases justifiable, so liable to abuse as many persons seem to apprehend it. For although there will be always some petulant, querulous men, in every state—men of factious, turbulent and carping dispositions—glad to lay hold of any trifle to justify and legitimate their caballing against their rulers and other seditious practices, yet there are, comparatively speaking, but few men of this contemptible character: it does not appear but that mankind in general have a disposition to be as submissive and passive and tame under government as they ought to be. Witness a great, if not the greatest part of the known world, who are now groaning, but not murmuring, under the heavy yoke of tyranny! While those who govern, do it with any tolerable degree of moderation and justice, and in any good measure act up to their office and character, by being public benefactors, the people will generally be easy and peaceable and be rather inclined to flatter and adore than to insult and resist them. Nor was there ever any general complaint against any administration which lasted long but what there was good reason for. Till people find themselves greatly abused and oppressed by their governors, they are not apt to complain; and whenever they do, in fact, find themselves thus abused and oppressed, they must be stupid not to complain.

To say that subjects in general are not proper judges when their governors oppress them and play the tyrant and when protector and guardian. Nor would they have any reason to mourn if some Hercules should appear to dispatch him. For a nation thus abused to arise unanimously, and to resist their prince, even to the dethroning him, is not criminal, but a reasonable way of vindicating their liberties and just rights; it is making use of the means, and the only means, which God has put into their power, for mutual and self-defense. And it would be highly criminal in them not to make use of this means. It would be stupid tameness and unaccountable folly for whole nations to suffer one unreasonable, ambitious and cruel man to wanton and riot in their misery. And in such a case it would, of the two, be more rational to suppose that they that did not resist, than that they who did, would receive to themselves damnation.

---

they defend their rights, administer justice impartially, and promote the public welfare, is as great treason as ever man uttered: 'tis treason, not against one single man, but the state—against the whole body politic—'tis treason against mankind—'tis treason against common sense—'tis treason against God. And this impious principle lays the foundation for justifying all the tyranny and oppression that ever any prince was guilty of. The people know for what end they set up and maintain their governors; and they are the proper judges when they execute their trust as they ought to do it—when their prince exercises an equitable and paternal authority over them—when from a prince and common father, he exalts himself into a tyrant—when from subjects and children, he degrades them into the class of slaves, plunders them, makes them his prey, and unnaturally sports himself with their lives and fortunes.

CHAPTER THREE

THIS WORLD AND THE NEXT

1. THOMAS SHEPARD, 1605–1649

[Congregational and Independent Puritans developed their conception of the church covenant and the social covenant out of a more fundamental exposition of the covenant as a universal term for describing the innermost personal relationship between the Christian and Jehovah. Also, the covenant became their way of conceiving the relationship of the creator to the created universe.

This "federal theology" was not so much a separate or self-contained system—in doctrinal theology, all Puritans were what we call "Calvinists"—as it was an idiom, taken both from the Old Testament and from contemporaneous legal thinking, for expounding the mystery of the election and perseverance of the saints. In the middle of the eighteenth century the revivalists, led by Jonathan Edwards, subordinated or obliterated this covenant phraseology, invoking a more stark assertion of absolute decree; in the modern rediscovery of the Puritan concept theologians have found not a forgotten system of rhetoric but a theme central to both the Old Testament and to Protestantism. It no longer seems a curious oddity of the Puritan mind, but a serious effort to formulate the connection between finite man and absolute God, even though too many Puritans tended to debase the cosmological vision into a guarantee for personal security.

Such time as New Englanders had for abstract speculation, and most of the doctrinal portions of the sermons, were devoted to the covenant. In detail, it is too technical for brief discussion, but Thomas Shepard's preface to the volume of sermons Peter Bulkeley preached in the frontier outpost of Concord, *The Gospel-Covenant; or the Covenant of Grace Opened* (second edition, London, 1651) gives, as well as any short selection can, the heart of the idea.

The covenant theology was a special way of reading scripture, so that the assembled Bible could be seen as a consistent whole. After Adam failed the Covenant of Works, God voluntarily condescended to treat with man as an equal and to draw up a covenant or contract with His creature, in which He laid down the terms of salvation by which, putting off His arbitrary freedom, He would henceforth abide. This Covenant of Grace did not alter the fact that those only are saved upon whom God sheds His grace, enabling them to believe in Christ; but it made clear why and how certain men are selected, and prescribed the conditions under which they might reach a fair assurance of their own standing. Above all, in the Covenant of Grace, and the covenants of nations and churches that arise out of it, God pledged Himself not to run tyrannically athwart human conceptions of justice. The creator was represented as agreeing to abide by ideas comprehensible to man. The principal result, at least in the original version, was not to diminish the majesty of the creation, but to present the Bible, believed by faith, as wholly and beautifully rational; it contains a consistent doctrine, that of the Covenant of Grace, extending unbroken from Abraham to Boston, which makes it at once the source of doctrine and the fountain of reason.

Shepard's brief exhortation reveals how the Puritan comprehended his own and his country's distresses within the framework of this covenant theory, because the covenant is the intelligible medium between the absolute and undecipherable mystery of God's original purposes and His ultimate performance, between the beginning and end of time.]

THE COVENANT OF GRACE

The blessed God hath evermore delighted to reveal and communicate Himself by way of Covenant. He might have done good to man before his fall, as also since his fall, without binding Himself in the bond of Covenant; Noah, Abraham, and David, Jews, Gentiles, might have had the blessings intended, without any promise or Covenant. But the Lord's heart is so full of love (especially to His own) that it cannot be contained so long within the bounds of secrecy—*viz.* from God's eternal purpose to the actual accomplishment of good things intended—but it must aforehand overflow and break out into the many streams of a blessed Covenant. The Lord can never get near enough to His people, and thinks He can never get them near enough unto Himself, and therefore unites and binds and fastens them close to Himself, and Himself unto them, by the bonds of a Covenant. And therefore when we break our Covenant, and that will not hold us, He takes a faster bond and makes a sure and everlasting Covenant, according to Grace, not according to Works; and that shall hold His people firm unto Himself, and hold Himself close and fast unto them, that He may never depart from us.

Oh! the depth of God's grace herein: that when sinful man deserves never to have the least good word from Him, that He should open His whole heart and purpose to him in a Covenant; that when he deserves nothing else but separation from God, and to be driven up and down the world as a vagabond, or as dried leaves fallen from our God, that yet the Almighty God cannot be content with it, but must make Himself to us, and us to Himself, more sure and near than ever before! And is not this Covenant then (Christian reader) worth thy looking into and searching after? Surely never was there a time wherein the Lord calls His people to more serious searching into the nature of the Covenant than in these days.

For are there not some who cut off the entail to children of those in Covenant, and so lessen and shorten the riches of grace in the Lord's free Covenant, and that in the time of more grace under the Gospel than He was wont to dispense under the Law? Are there not others who preach a new, or rather another Gospel or Covenant—*viz.* that actual remission of sins and reconciliation with God (purchased indeed in redemption by Christ's death) is without, nay, before faith . . . ? Is it not time for the people of God now to pry into the secret of God's Covenant—which He reveals to them that fear Him (Psal. 25. 14)—when, by clipping of it and distinguishing about it, the beautiful countenance of it begins to be changed and transformed by those angels of "new light" [from that] which once it had when it began to be published in the simplicity of it by the Apostles of Christ (II Cor. 11. 3)? Nay, is not the time come wherein the Lord of hosts seems to have a quarrel against all the world, and especially His churches and people, whom He goes on to waste by the sharpest sword that (almost) was ever drawn out? And is it not the duty of all that have the least spark of holy fear and trembling to ask and search diligently what should be the reason of this sore anger and hot displeasure, before they and theirs be consumed in the burning flames of it?

Search the scriptures, and there we shall find the cause, and see God Himself laying His finger upon that which is the sore and the wound of such times: for so it is said (Isa. 24. 1–5), "Behold, the Lord maketh the earth empty and waste, and turns it upside down, and scattereth abroad the inhabitants thereof; and it shall be as with the people, so with the priest; and the land shall be utterly spoiled." Why? "For the earth is defiled under the inhabitants thereof." Why so? "Because they have transgressed the laws, changed the ordinance, and broken the everlasting Covenant." And therefore when the Lord shall have wasted His church, and hath made it as Adnah and Zeboim, when heathen nations shall ask, "Wherefore hath the Lord done all this against this land? What meaneth the heat of His great anger?", the answer is made by the Lord Himself expressly (Deut. 29. 25): *viz.* "Because they have forsaken the Covenant of the Lord God of their fathers." And no wonder, for they that reject the Covenant of Grace, they break the league of peace between God and themselves.

And hence, if acts of hostility in desolating kingdoms, churches, families and persons break out from a long-suffering God, they may easily see the cause, and that the cause and quarrel of God herein is just.

As all good things are conveyed to God's people not barely by common providence but by special Covenant (Isa. 16. 8, 9), so all the evils they meet with in this world (if in them the face of God's anger appears), upon narrow search, will be found to arise from breach of Covenant, more or less. So that if it be the great cause of all the public calamities of the church and people of God, and those calamities are already begun, and God's hand is stretched out still—was there then ever a more seasonable time and hour to study the Covenant, and so see the sin, repent of it, and at last to lay hold of God's rich grace and bowels in it, lest the Lord go on and fulfill the word of His servants, and expose most pleasant lands to the doleful lamentation of a very little remnant, reserved as a few coals in the ashes, when all else is consumed?

As particular persons, when they break their Covenant, the Lord therefore breaks out against them: so, when whole churches forsake their Covenant, the Lord therefore doth sorely visit them. Sins of ignorance the Lord Jesus pities (Heb. 5. 2) and many times winks at, but sins against light He cannot endure (II Pet. 2. 21). Sins against light are great, but sins against the purpose and Covenant, nay God's Covenant, are by many degrees worse, for the soul of man rusheth most violently and strongly against God when it breaks through all the light of the mind and purposes of the will that stand in his way to keep him from sin. And is not this done by breach of Covenant? And therefore no wonder if the Lord makes His people's chain heavy by sore affliction, until they come to consider and behold this sin, and learn more fear (after they are bound to their good behavior) of breaking Covenant with God again.

It is true, the Covenant effectually made can never be really broke, yet externally it may. But suppose God's churches were in greatest peace, and had a blessed rest from all their labors round about them: yet what is the child's position, but his legacy left him, written with the finger of God his father, in the New Covenant, and the blood of Jesus Christ his redeemer, in His last will and testament? What is a Christian's comfort, and where doth it chiefly lie, but in this: that the Lord hath made with him an everlasting Covenant, in all things stablished and sure? Which were the last breathing of the sweet singer of Israel, and the last bubblings up of the joy of his heart (II Sam. 23. 5).

God the Father's eternal purposes are sealed secrets, not immediately seen, and the full and blessed accomplishments of those purposes are not yet experimentally felt. The Covenant is the midst between both God's purposes and performances, by which and in which we come to see the one before the world began, and by a blessed faith (which makes things absent, present) to enjoy the other, which shall be our glory when this world shall be burned up and all things in it shall have an end. For in God's Covenant we see with open face God's secret purpose for time past—God's purposes toward His people being, as it were, nothing else but promises concealed, and God's promises in the Covenant being nothing else but His purposes revealed. As also, in the same Covenant and promises we see performances for [the] future, as if they were accomplishments at present. Where then is a Christian's comfort but in that Covenant, wherein two eternities (as it were) meet together, and whereby he may see accomplishments (made sure to him) of eternal glory, arising from blessed purposes of eternal grace? In a word, wherein he fastens upon God, and hath Him from everlasting to everlasting, comprehended at hand near and obvious in His words of a gracious Covenant?

The Church of God is therefore bound to bless God much for this food in season, and for the holy judicious and learned labors of this aged, experienced and precious servant of Christ Jesus, who hath taken much pains to discover —and that not in words and allegories but in the demonstration and evidence of the Spirit—the great mystery of godliness wrapped up in the Covenant, and hath now fully opened sundry knotty questions concerning the same, which happily have not been brought so fully to light until now. Which cannot but be of singular and seasonable use, to prevent apostasies from the simplicity of the Covenant and Gospel of Christ. The sermons were preached in the remote ends of the earth and, as it were, set under a bushel, a church more remote from the numerous society of others of the saints; if now, therefore, the light be set upon a hill, 'tis where it should stand, and where Christ surely would have it put. The good Lord enlighten the minds of all those who seek for the truth by this and such like helps; and the Lord enlighten the whole world with His glory, even with the glory of His Covenant, grace and love, that His people hereby may be sealed up daily unto all fulness of assurance and peace, in these evil times.

2. PETER BULKELEY, 1583–1659

[The turmoil produced in England by the war, the unchecked rage of sectarian heresy, and the treason of the Independents in going over to toleration, agonized the New England Puritans because the whole insane sequence, as they were bound to consider it, upset the covenantal theory of history. In the midst of his highly scholastic discourse, *The Gospel-Covenant*, Peter Bulkeley paused to deliver a homily on the immediate lesson for both Englands. The passage succinctly reveals the terror New England felt by 1651 at the unaccountable development which left it remote and isolated, instead of making it the leader of an English and so of a world reformation, as Winthrop had dreamed in 1630 when he foresaw it as a city on a hill.

Bulkeley was born in Bedfordshire, took his M.A. at St. John's College, Cambridge, in 1608, and for several years was a Fellow. Inheriting a fortune from his father, he came with his family to Massachusetts in 1635, and later that year was one of the founders of Concord, where he remained as minister.]

THE LESSON OF THE COVENANT, FOR ENGLAND AND NEW ENGLAND

This may serve to be a warning to all such people to whom the Gospel of Christ is come: let them in the fear of God take heed lest they neglect so great salvation, and let them with thankfulness and love entertain the grace which is brought unto them by the revelation of Jesus Christ. If you become despisers, God will work such things among you as whoso heareth them, his ears shall tingle, and your hearts shall ache in the suffering of them much more; for if every transgression and disobedience committed against the law, or against the dim light of nature, do receive a just recompense of reward—if those which are without the law perished in those sins which they committed without the law, and if those which are without the Gospel perish in their ignorance because they know it not—how then shall those escape which have law of grace and Gospel of grace revealed unto them, and do neglect those great things? . . .

And here, O England, my dear native country (whose womb bare me, whose breasts nourished me, and in whose arms I should desire to die), give ear to one of thy children which dearly loveth thee. Be thou exhorted thankfully to accept the grace which is now ready to be revealed unto thee. The way is now preparing: the high mountains, which with their shadows caused darkness, are now alaying low, and the low valleys ready to be exalted, the crooked things to be made straight, that all flesh (that lives within thy borders) may see the salvation of our God. Thy light is now coming, and the glory of the Lord is now rising upon thee. Though darkness hath covered a part of thee hitherto, through the wickedness of those that hated light, yet now the Lord Himself (I trust) will rise upon thee, and the glory of the Lord shall be seen upon thee. Now therefore stir up thyself with thankfulness and joy of heart to embrace the things of thy peace, which shall be brought unto thee. See that thou love the Gospel not in word and in show only but in deed and in truth: and not for novelty's sake but for truth's sake, not because it is a new way but because the grace of God which brings salvation is thereby revealed. Though in respect of order and government all things may become new, yet look not after new substantials, new foundations. Thou hast had the foundation truly laid, by many skillful builders, many years ago: only some have built thereupon hay and stubble, instead of gold and precious stones. Let therefore the roof be new, but let the foundation be the same. Take heed of too much of that "new light" which the world is now gazing upon. Some have reported sad things concerning thee in this respect: so much new light breaking forth that the old zeal is almost extinct by it. Herein take heed. "The old way is the good way": this is now ready to be revealed. The time of grace is coming unto thee: this is the accepted season, now is the day of thy salvation. Oh, be wise to consider it, and walk worthy of it, esteeming the Gospel as thy pearl, thy treasure, thy crown, thy felicity! Thou canst not love it too dearly. Make much of it therefore: otherwise, know the neglect of it will bring heaviest wrath, and thy judgment hastenth, and sleepeth not.

And thou, New England, which art exalted in privileges of the Gospel above many other people, know thou the time of thy visitation, and consider the great things the Lord hath done for thee. The Gospel hath free passage in all places where thou dwellest: oh, that it might be glorified also by thee. Thou enjoyest many faithful witnesses, which have testified unto thee the Gospel of the grace of God. Thou has many bright stars shining in thy firmament, to give thee the "knowledge of salvation from on high, to guide thy feet in the way of peace" (Luke 1. 78, 79). Be not high-minded because of thy privileges, but fear because of thy danger. The more thou hast committed unto thee, the more thou must account for. No people's account will be heavier than thine if thou do not walk worthy of the means of thy salvation. The Lord looks for more from thee than from other people: more zeal for God, more love to His truth, more justice and equity in thy ways. Thou shouldst be a special people, an only people—none like thee in all the earth. Oh, be so, in loving the Gospel and ministers of it, having them "in singular love for their work's sake" (I Thess. 5. 13). Glorify thou the word of the Lord, which hath glorified thee. Take heed lest for neglect of either, God remove thy candlestick out of the midst of thee; lest being now as a city upon an hill, which many seek unto, thou be left like a beacon upon the top of a mountain, desolate and forsaken. If we walk unworthy of the Gospel brought unto us, the greater our mercy hath been in the enjoying of it, the greater will our judgment be for the contempt. Be instructed, and take heed.

3. THOMAS HOOKER, 1586–1647

[The most persistent misunderstanding of the Puritan mind is that which charges it with "fatalism." Modern sensibility supposes that believers in predestination must necessarily give over exertions. In fact, the Puritans combined a trust in God's disposing power with an assurance of victory, and were capable of tremendous performances in order that what was decreed might come to pass. Thomas Hooker's analysis of the true sight of sin uncovers the springs of this titanic energy. Anyone who sees himself as pitilessly as Hooker requires would spend his days and nights trying to lift himself, or seeking to be lifted, out of the mire of depravity. When we consider how intense was the warfare of the spirit and the flesh, and how interminable a campaign the true soldier of Christ undertook when he enrolled in the regiment of the godly, we can perhaps gauge the true sublimity of Puritanism as we find Hooker insisting, and his congregation no doubt agreeing, that the awakened sinner should be grateful to the minister who by his winged sermons had pierced the door of his complacency. He should be, and many were, overjoyed that he was dragged against his natural inclination from the peace and security of a false contentment into the heat and fury of this battle.]

A TRUE SIGHT OF SIN

Wherein this true sight and apprehension of sin properly discovers itself:

I answer, a true sight of sin hath two conditions attending upon it, or it appears in two things: we must see sin (1) clearly; (2) convictingly—what it is in itself and what it is to us, not in the appearance and paint of it, but in the power of it; not to fathom it in the notion and conceit only, but to see it with application.

We must see it clearly in its own nature, its native color and proper hue. It's not every slight conceit, not every general and cursory, confused thought or careless consideration that will serve the turn or do the work here. We are all sinners: it is my infirmity, I cannot help it; my weakness, I cannot be rid of it. No man lives without faults and follies, the best have their failings, "In many things we offend all." But alas! all this wind shakes no corn, it costs more to see sin aright than a few words of course. It's one thing to say sin is thus and thus, another thing to see it to be such; we must look wisely and steadily upon our distempers, look sin in the face and discern it to the full. The want whereof is the cause of our mistaking our estates and not redressing of our hearts and ways: (Gal. 6. 4) "Let a man prove his own work." Before the goldsmith can sever and see the dross asunder from the gold, he must search the very bowels of the metal, and try it by touch, by taste, by hammer and by fire; and then he will be able to speak by proof what it is. So here: we perceive sin in the crowd and by hearsay, when we attend some common and customary expressions taken up by persons in their common converse, and so report what others speak, and yet never knew the truth, what either others or we say; but we do not single out our corruptions and survey the loathsomeness of them, as they come naked in their own natures.

This we ought to do. There is great odds betwixt the knowledge of a traveler, that in his own person hath taken a view of many coasts, passed through many countries and hath there taken up his abode some time, and by experience hath been an eyewitness of the extreme cold and scorching heats, hath surveyed the glory and beauty of the one, the barrenness and meanness of the other—he hath been in the wars, and seen the ruin and desolation wrought there—and another that sits by his fireside and happily reads the story of these in a book, or views the proportion of these in a map. The odds is great, and the difference of their knowledge more than a little: the one saw the country really, the other only in the story; the one hath seen the very place, the other only in the paint of the map drawn. The like difference is there in the right discerning of sin. The one hath surveyed the compass of his whole course, searched the frame of his own heart, and examined the windings and turnings of his own ways. He hath seen what sin is and what it hath done, how it hath made havoc of his peace and comfort, ruinated and laid waste the very principles of reason and nature and morality, and made him a terror to himself. When he hath looked over the loathsome abominations that lie in his bosom, that he is afraid to approach the presence of the Lord to bewail his sins and to crave pardon, lest he could be confounded for them while he is but confessing of them—afraid and ashamed lest any man living should know but the least part of that which he knows by himself, and could count it happy that himself was not, that the remembrance of those hideous evils of his might be no more. Another happily hears the like preached or repeated, reads them writ or recorded in some authors, and is able to remember and relate them. The odds is marvelous great! The one sees the history of sin, the other the nature of it; the one knows the relation of sin as it is mapped out and recorded, the other the poison, as by experience he hath found and proved it. It's one thing to see a disease in the book or in a man's body, another thing to find and feel it in a man's self. There is the report of it, here the malignity and venom of it.

But how shall we see clearly the nature of sin in his naked hue?

This will be discovered, and may be conceived in the

particulars following. Look we at it: first, as it respects God; secondly, as it concerns ourselves.

As it hath reference to God, the vileness of the nature of sin may thus appear:

It would dispossess God of that absolute supremacy which is indeed His prerogative royal, and doth in a peculiar manner appertain to Him, as the diamond of His crown and diadem of His deity; so the Apostle, "He is God over all blessed for ever" (Rom. 9. 5). All from Him and all for Him, He is the absolute first being, the absolute last end, and herein is the crown of His glory. All those attributes of wisdom, goodness, holiness, power, justice, mercy, the shine and concurrency of all these meeting together, is to set out the inconceivable excellency of His glorious name, which exceeds all praise: "Thine is the kingdom, the power and the glory," the right of all and so the rule of all and the glory of all belongs to Him.

Now herein lies the inconceivable heinousness of the hellish nature of sin: it would jostle the Almighty out of the throne of His glorious sovereignty, and indeed be above Him. For the will of man being the chiefest of all His workmanship, all for his body, the body of the soul, the mind to attend upon the will, the will to attend upon God and to make choice of Him and His will, that is next to Him and He only above that: and that should have been His throne and temple or chair of state in which He would have set his sovereignty forever. He did in a special manner intend to meet with man, and to communicate Himself to man in His righteous law, as the rule of His holy and righteous will, by which the will of Adam should have been ruled and guided to Him and made happy in Him; and all creatures should have served God in man, and been happy by or through him, serving of God being happy in him. But when the will went from under the government of his rule, by sin, it would be above God and be happy without Him, for the rule of the law, in each command of it, holds forth a threefold expression of sovereignty from the Lord, and therein the sovereignty of all the rest of His attributes.

1. The powerful supremacy of His just will, as that He

hath right to dispose of all and authority to command all at His pleasure: "What if God will?" (Rom. 9. 22); "My counsel shall stand and I will do all my pleasure" (Isa. 46. 10). And as it's true of what shall be done upon us, so His will hath sovereignty of command in what should be done by us; we are to say, "The will of the Lord be done." David's warrant was to do all God's will (Acts 13. 22), and our saviour himself professeth (John 6. 38) that "he came not to do his own will but the will of Him that sent him." And therefore His wrath and jealousy and judgment will break out in case that be disobeyed.

2. There is also a fullness of wisdom in the law of God revealed to guide and direct us in the way we should walk: (Psal. 19. 7) "The law of God makes wise the simple"; (II Tim. 3. 15) "It's able to make us wise unto salvation."

3. There's a sufficiency of God to content and satisfy us. "Blessed are they who walk in His ways and blessed are they that keep His testimonies" (Psal. 119. 1, 2). "Great prosperity have they that love the law, and nothing shall offend them" (verse 16). And in truth there can be no greater reward for doing well than to be enabled to do well; he that hath attained his last end he cannot go further, he cannot be better.

Now by sin we jostle the law out of its place and the Lord out of His glorious sovereignty, pluck the crown from His head and the scepter out of His hand; and we say and profess by our practice, there is not authority and power there to govern, nor wisdom to guide, nor good to content me, but I will be swayed by mine own will and led by mine own deluded reason and satisfied with my own lusts. This is the guise of every graceless heart in the commission of sin; so Pharaoh: "Who is the Lord? I know not the Lord nor will I let Israel go" (Exod. 5. 2). In the time of their prosperity, see how the Jews turn their backs and shake off the authority of the Lord: "We are lords," say they, "we will come no more at Thee" (Jer. 2. 31), and "Our tongues are our own, who shall be lord over us" (Psal. 12. 4)? So for the wisdom of the world, see how they set light by it as not worth the looking after it: (Jer. 18. 12) "We will walk after our own devices and we will every one do the imagination of his own evil heart." Yea, they set up their own traditions, their own idols and delusions, and lord it over the law: "Making the command of God of none effect" (Matt. 15. 8, 9). So for the goodness of the word: (Job 22. 17; Matt. 3. 14) "It is in vain to serve God and what profit is there that we have kept his ordinances, yea, His commandments are ever grievous." It's a grievous thing to the loose person, he cannot have his pleasures but he must have his guilt and gall with them; it's grievous to the worldling that he cannot lay hold on the world by unjust means but conscience lays hold upon him as breaking the law. Thou that knowest and keepest thy pride and stubbornness and thy distempers, know assuredly thou dost jostle God out of the throne of His glorious sovereignty, and thou dost profess, not God's will but thine own (which is above His) shall rule thee. Thy carnal reason and the folly of thy mind is above the wisdom of the Lord, and that shall guide thee; to please thine own stubborn crooked perverse spirit is a greater good than to please God and enjoy happiness, for this more contents thee. That when thou considerest but thy course, dost thou not wonder that the great and terrible God doth not pash such a poor insolent worm to powder and send thee packing to the pit every moment?

It smites at the essence of the Almighty and the desire of the sinner, in not only that God should not be supreme but that indeed He should not be at all; and therefore it would destroy the being of Jehovah (Psal. 81. 15). Sinners are called the haters of the Lord: (John 15. 24) "They hated both me and my Father." Now he that hates endeavors, if it be possible, the annihilation of the thing hated, and it's most certain, were it in their power, they would pluck God out of Heaven, the light of His truth out of their consciences and the law out of the societies and assemblies where they live, that they might have elbow room to live as they list. Nay, whatever they hate most, and intend and plot more evil against in all the world, they hate God most of all, and intend more evil against Him than against all their enemies besides, because they hate all for His sake. Therefore wicked men are said to destroy the law (Psal. 126, 119). The adulterer loathes that law that condemns uncleanness; the earthworm would destroy that law that forbids covetousness, they are said to hate the light (John 3. 21), to hate the saints and servants of the Lord: (John 15. 18) "The world hates you." He that hates the lantern for the light's sake, he hates the light much more; he that hates the faithful because of the image of God and the grace that appears there, he hates the God of all grace and holiness, most of all. So God to Sennacherib: (Isa. 37. 28) "I know thy going out and thy coming in, and thy rage against me." Oh! it would be their content if there was no God in the world to govern them, no law to curb them, no justice to punish, no truth to trouble them. Learn therefore to see how far your rebellions reach. It is not arguments you gainsay, not the counsel of a minister you reject, the command of a magistrate ye oppose, evidence of rule or reason ye resist, but be it known to you, you fly in the very face of the Almighty. And it is not the gospel of grace ye would have destroyed, but the spirit of grace, the author of grace, the Lord Jesus, the God of all grace that ye hate.

It crosseth the whole course of providence, perverts the work of the creation and defaceth the beautiful frame and that sweet correspondence and orderly usefulness the Lord first implanted in the order of things. The heavens deny their influence, the earth her strength, the corn her nourishment: thank sin for that. Weeds come instead of herbs, cockle and darnel instead of wheat: thank sin for that, (Rom. 8. 22) "The whole creature" (or creation) "groans under vanity"—either cannot do what it would or else misseth of that good and end it intended, breeds nothing but vanity, brings forth nothing but vexation. It crooks all things so as that none can straighten them, makes so many wants that none can supply them (Eccles. 1. 15). This makes crooked servants in a family, no man can rule them, crooked inhabitants in towns, crooked members in congregations; there's no ordering nor joining of them in that comely accord and mutual subjection: "Know," they said, "the adversary sin hath done all this." Man was the mean betwixt God and the creature, to convey all good with all the constancy of it; and therefore when man breaks, heaven and earth breaks all asunder: the conduit being cracked and displaced, there can be no conveyance from the fountain.

In regard of ourselves, see we and consider nakedly the nature of sin, in four particulars:

It's that which makes a separation between God and the soul, breaks that union and communion with God for which we were made, and in the enjoyment of which we should be blessed and happy: (Isa. 59. 1, 2) "God's ear is not heavy that it cannot hear nor His hand that it cannot help, but your iniquities have separated betwixt God and you and your sins have hid His face that He will not hear." For He professeth, (Psal. 5. 4) that He is a God that wills not wickedness, neither shall iniquity dwell with him. "Into the new Jerusalem shall no unclean thing enter, but without shall be dogs" (Rev. 21. 27). The dogs to their kennel, and hogs to their sty and mire; but if an impenitent wretch should come into heaven, the Lord would go out of heaven: Iniquity shall not dwell with sin. That then that deprives me of my greatest good for which I came into the world, and for which I live and labor in the world, and without which I had better never to have been born —nay, that which deprives me of an universal good, a good that hath all good in it—that must needs be an evil, but have all evil in it. But so doth sin deprive me of God as the object of my will, and that wills all good, and therefore it must bring in truth all evil with it. Shame takes away my honor, poverty my wealth, persecution my peace, prison my liberty, death my life, yet a man may still be a happy man, lose his life, and live eternally. But sin takes away my God, and with Him all good goes: prosperity without God will be my poison, honor without Him my bane; nay, the word without God hardens me, my endeavor without Him profits nothing at all for my good. A natural man hath no God in anything, and therefore hath no good.

It brings an incapability in regard of myself to receive good, and an impossibility in regard of God Himself to work my spiritual good, while my sin continues, and I continue impenitent in it. An incapability of a spiritual blessing: "Why transgress ye the commandment of the Lord that ye cannot prosper do what ye can" (II Chron. 24. 20). And he that being often reproved hardens his heart, shall be consumed suddenly and there is no remedy, he that spills the physic that should cure him, the meat that should nourish him, there is no remedy but he must needs die: so that the commission of sin makes not only a separation from God, but obstinate resistance and continuance in it maintains an infinite and everlasting distance between God and the soul. So that so long as the sinful resistance of thy soul continues, God cannot vouchsafe the comforting and guiding presence of His grace, because it's cross to the Covenant of Grace He hath made, which He will not deny, and His oath which He will not alter. So that should the Lord save thee and thy corruption, carry thee and thy proud unbelieving heart to heaven He must nullify the Gospel (Heb. 5. 9): "He's the author of salvation to them that obey Him," and forswear Himself (Heb. 3. 18): "He hath sworn unbelievers shall not enter into His rest"; He must cease to be just and holy, and so to be God. As Saul said to Jonathan concerning David (I Sam. 20. 30, 31), "So long as the son of Jesse lives, thou shalt not be established, nor thy kingdom." So do thou plead against thyself, and with thy own soul: so long as these rebellious distempers continue, grace and peace and the kingdom of Christ can never be established in thy heart. For this obstinate resistance differs nothing from the plagues of the state of the damned, when they come to the highest measure, but that it is not yet total and final, there being some kind of abatement of the measure of it and stoppage of the power of it. Imagine thou sawest the Lord Jesus coming in the clouds, and heardest the last trump blow, "Arise, ye dead, and come to judgment"; imagine thou sawest the Judge of all the world sitting upon the throne, thousands of angels before Him and ten thousands ministering unto Him, the sheep standing on His right hand and the goats at the left; suppose thou heardest that dreadful sentence, and final doom pass from the Lord of life (whose word made heaven and earth, and will shake both) "Depart from me, ye cursed": how would thy heart shake and sink, and die within thee in the thought thereof, wert thou really persuaded it was thy portion? Know, that by thy daily continuance in sin, thou dost to the utmost of thy power execute that sentence upon thy soul. It's thy life, thy labor, the desire of thy heart, and thy daily practice to depart away from the God of all grace and peace, and turn the tombstone of everlasting destruction upon thine own soul.

It's the cause which brings all other evils of punishment into the world and without this they are not evil, but so far as sin is in them. The sting of a trouble, the poison and malignity of a punishment and affliction, the evil of the evil of any judgment, it is the sin that brings it, or attends it: (Jer. 2. 19) "Thine own wickedness shall correct thee, and thy backslidings shall reprove thee, know therefore that it is an evil, and bitter thing that thou hast forsaken the Lord"; (Jer. 4. 18) "Thy ways and doings have procured these things unto thee, therefore it is bitter, and reacheth unto the heart." Take miseries and crosses without sin, they are like to be without a sting, the serpent without poison; ye may take them, and make medicines of them. So Paul (I Cor. 15. 55), he plays with death itself, sports with the grave: "Oh death, where is thy sting? Oh grave, where is thy victory?" The sting of death is sin. All the harmful annoyance in sorrows and punishments, further than either they come from sin or else tend to it, they are rather improvements of what we have than parting with anything we do enjoy; we rather lay out our conveniences than seem to lose them, yea, they increase our crown and do not diminish our comfort. "Blessed are ye when men revile you, and persecute you, and speak all manner of evil of you for my sake, for great is your reward in Heaven" (Matt. 5. 11). There is a blessing in persecutions and reproaches when they be not mingled with the deserts of our sins; yea, our momentary short affliction for a good cause and a good conscience works an excessive exceeding weight of glory. If then sin brings all evils, and makes all evils indeed to us, then is it worse than all those evils.

It brings a curse upon all our comforts, blasts all our blessings, the best of all our endeavors, the use of all the choicest of all God's ordinances: it's so evil and vile, that it makes the use of all good things, and all the most glorious, both ordinances and improvements, evil to us (Hag. 2. 13, 14). When the question was made to the priest, "If one that is unclean by a dead body touch any of the holy things, shall it be unclean?" And he answered, "Yea. So is this people, and so is this nation before me, saith the Lord; and so is every work of their hands, and that which they offer is unclean." If any good thing a wicked man had, or any action he did, might be good, or bring good to him, in reason it was the services and sacrifices wherein he did approach unto God and perform service to Him, and yet "the sacrifice of the wicked is an abomination to the Lord" (Prov. 28. 9 and Tit. 1. 15) "To the pure all things are pure; but to the unbelieving there is nothing pure, but their very consciences are defiled." It is a desperate malignity in the temper of the stomach that should turn our meat and diet into diseases, the best cordials and preservatives into poisons, so that what in reason is appointed to nourish a man should kill him. Such is the venom and malignity of sin, makes the use of the best things become evil, nay, the greatest evil to us many times: (Psal. 109. 7) "Let his prayer be turned into sin." That which is appointed by God to be the choicest means to prevent sin is turned into sin out of the corrupt distemper of these carnal hearts of ours.

Hence then it follows that sin is the greatest evil in the world, or indeed that can be. For, that which separates the soul from God, that which brings all evils of punishment and makes all evils truly evil, and spoils all good things to us, that must needs be the greatest evil. But this is the nature of sin, as hath already appeared.

But that which I will mainly press is, sin is only opposite to God, and cross as much as can be to that infinite goodness and holiness which is in His blessed majesty. It's not the miseries or distresses that men undergo that the Lord distastes them for, or estrangeth Himself from them; He is with Joseph in the prison, with the three children in the furnace, with Lazarus when he lies among the dogs and gathers the crumbs from the rich man's table, yea, with Job upon the dunghill, but He is not able to bear the presence of sin. Yea, of this temper are His dearest servants: the more of God is in them, the more opposite they are to sin wherever they find it. It was that He commended in the church of Ephesus, "That she could not bear those that were wicked" (Rev. 2. 3). As when the stomach is of a pure temper and good strength, the least surfeit or distemper that befalls, it presently distastes and disburdens itself with speed. So David noted to be "a man after God's own heart." He professeth: (Psal. 101. 3, 7) "I hate the work of them that turn aside, he that worketh deceit shall not dwell in my house; he that telleth lies, shall not tarry in my sight." But when the heart becomes like the stomach, so weak it cannot help itself nor be helped by physic, desperate diseases and dissolution of the whole follows, and in reason must be expected. Hence see how God looks at the least connivance or a faint and feeble kind of opposition against sin as that in which He is most highly dishonored; and He follows it with most hideous plagues, as that indulgent carriage of Eli towards the vile behavior of his sons for their grosser evils: (I Sam. 2. 23, 24) "Why do you such things? It's not well, my sons, that I hear such things." It is not well, and is that all? Why, had they either out of ignorance not known their duty or out of some sudden surprisal of a temptation neglected it, it had not been well; but for them so purposely to proceed on in the practice of such gross evils, and for him so faintly to reprove, the Lord looks at it as a great sin thus feebly to oppose sin. And therefore (verse 29) He tells him that he honored his sons above God, and therefore He professeth, "Far be it from me to maintain thy house and comfort, for he that honors me I will honor, and he that despiseth me shall be lightly esteemed" (verse 30). Hence it is the Lord Himself is called "the holy one of Israel," (Hab. 1. 12) "who is of purer eyes than to behold evil, and cannot look upon iniquity"—no, not in such as profess themselves saints, though most dear unto Him; no, nor in His son the Lord Jesus, not in his saints. (Amos 8. 7) The Lord hath sworn by Himself, "I abhor the excellency of Jacob"; whatever their excellencies, their privileges are, if they do not abhor sin, God will abhor them: (Jer. 22. 24) "Though Coniah was as the signet of my right hand, thence would I pluck Him." Nay, He could not endure the appearance of it in the Lord Christ, for when but the reflection of sin (as I may so say) fell upon our savior, even the imputation of our transgressions to him, though none iniquity was ever committed by him, the Father withdrew His comforting presence from him, and let loose His infinite displeasure against him, forcing him to cry out, "My God, my God, why hast thou forsaken me?"

Yea, sin is so evil (that though it be in nature, which is the good creation of God) that there is no good in it, nothing that God will own; but in the evil of punishment it is otherwise, for the torments of the devils, and punishments of the damned in hell, and all the plagues inflicted upon the wicked upon earth, issue from the righteous and revenging justice of the Lord, and He doth own such execution as His proper work: (Isa. 45. 7) "Is there any evil in the city," viz. of punishment, "and the Lord hath not done it? I make peace, I create evil, I the Lord do all these things." It issues from the justice of God that He cannot but reward everyone according to His own ways and works; those are a man's own, the holy one of Israel hath no hand in them. But he is the just executioner of the plagues that are inflicted and suffered for these; and hence our blessed savior becoming our surety, and standing in our room, he endured the pains of the second death, even the fierceness of the fury of an offended God, and yet it was impossible he could commit the least sin, or be tainted with the least corrupt distemper. And it's certain it's better to suffer all plagues without any one sin than to commit the least sin and to be freed from all plagues. Suppose that all miseries and sorrows that ever befell all the wicked in earth and hell should meet together in one soul, as all waters gathered together in one sea; suppose thou heardest the devil's roaring, and sawest hell gaping, and flames of everlasting burnings flashing before thine eyes? It's certain it were better for thee to be cast into those inconceivable torments than to commit the least sin against the Lord. Thou dost not think so now, but thou wilt find it so one day.

4. THOMAS HOOKER, 1586–1647

[In their effort to confront the blinding mystery of salvation directly, to spare themselves and the people nothing, to keep attention from ever being beguiled by flourishes, Puritan preachers and writers cultivated the "plain style." This was by no means a crude or unstudied mode of composition; quite the contrary, behind it lay a thorough training in rhetoric and a strenuous discipline in the liberal arts, particularly grammar and logic. Puritans consciously opposed their stylistic code to the ornate "metaphysical" orations delivered by preachers of the Laudian party, such as those of John Donne or Lancelot Andrewes. In order to avoid temptation, the Puritans constructed their sermons in a logical form, with numbered passages, so that the congregation (many of whom took notes) could follow the progress from the "doctrine" through the sequential "reasons" to the enumerated "uses." But within these paragraphs all the resources of rhetoric, illustration, metaphor, simile, were skillfully employed—as long, that is, as the rhetoric never became an end in itself but was rigorously subordinated to conveying the meaning. Likewise, the grammar and logic used in exposition were not to divert the sermon from being a public exercise in communication, not a college recitation. In these extracts from Hooker, the throbbing pulse, even at this distance, can still be felt. The vigor of such prose transmitted to the people the vigor that became their never ending search of soul and their righteous exertion.]

REPENTANT SINNERS AND THEIR MINISTERS

Doctrine: They whose hearts are pierced by the ministry of the word, they are carried with love and respect to the ministers of it.

Men and brethren, they be words of honor and love, and they spoke them seriously and affectionately. They mocked them before, and they now embrace them; they cared not what terms of reproach they cast upon their persons, they know not now what titles of love and tenderness to put upon them; they now fall at their feet as clients, who flouted them before as enemies. So it was with the jailor; (Acts 16. 30, 31, 34) how kindly doth he Paul and Silas, whom, erewhile he handled so currishly, beyond the bounds of reason and humanity, he entertains them in the best room of his house, who before thought the worst place in the prison too good for them. He bathes their wounded parts which he had whipped and stocked before, fears and trembles before them as his counselors, whom he handled most harshly before as prisoners; he feasts them as his guests whom he had struck as malefactors; the wind was in another door, the man is of another mind, yea, is another man than he was. God had no sooner opened the heart of Lydia to attend the word but her affections were exceedingly enlarged towards the dispensers thereof (Acts 16. 15), so that the cords of her loving invitation led Paul and held him captive; he professed, "She compelled them," *i.e.*, by her loving and affectionate expressions, prevailed with them for a stay. And while Paul had the Galatians under the pangs of the new birth and Christ was now forming in them, they professed they "would have plucked out their eyes" and have given them to the apostle (Gal. 4. 15).

Naaman hath no sooner his leprosy healed, and his heart humbled and cut off from his corruption, but he professed himself and what he had is at the devotion of the prophet, and that not out of compliment but in truth: (II Kings 5. 15) "Take a blessing from thy servant."

Reasons are two:

They see and know more than formerly they did, when happily the crooked counsels of others deceived them, and their own carnal reason cozened and deluded their own souls that they misjudged the men and their doctrine also. As that they did not speak the truth, or else had some crooked and self-seeking ends in what they spoke: as either to gratify other men's humors whom they would please or else to set up their own persons and praise and esteem in the apprehensions of others as singular men and more than of an ordinary frame; and therefore would wind men up to such a high pitch of holiness, and force them to such a singular care to fly the very appearance of all evil, when it's more than needs and more than God requires, and more than any man can do. But now they find by proof and are forced out of their own sense and feeling to acknowledge the truth of what they have spoken and what they have heard, and themselves also to be the faithful ambassadors of the Lord Jesus, and therefore worthy to be believed and attended in their dispensations and honored of all. So Paul: (II Cor. 4. 3) "We hope we are made manifest unto your consciences." Thus the woman of Samaria, when our savior came home to the quick and met with the secrets of her heart, she then fell from her taunting and slighting of our savior to admiring of him: "Come, faith, she beheld the man that told me all that ever I did: is not he the Christ" (John 4. 29)? Look as Nebuchadnezzar said: (Dan. 4.) "Now I know the God of Daniel is the true God, and now I praise the living God." So when they have been in the fire, and God hath had them upon the anvil: now I know what sin is, now I know what the danger is, now I know what necessity there is to part with sin. When the patient hath found the relation and direction of the physician hath proved real, it makes him prize and honor his skill and counsel forever, and forever to have his custom. As the pythonist was compelled from the power of Paul's administration to confess, "These are the servants of the living God which show unto us the way of salvation"; so here.

As they see more and can therefore judge better of the worth of persons and things, so their conscience now hath more scope, and the light of reason hath more liberty, and allowance to express that they know, and nothing now can withstand and hinder. For while men are held captive under the power of their lusts and corruptions of their hearts, in which they live and which for the while they are resolved to follow—though their reason happily do yield it, and their own hearts and consciences cannot but inwardly confess it, the persons are holy, the sins are vile which they condemn and dangers dreadful which they forewarn —yet to profess so much openly to others and to the world were to judge themselves while they would acquit others, and condemn their own courses while they should praise and honor the carriages and persons of others, and therefore darken the evidence of the word by carnal cavils and reproaches, stifle the witness of conscience, and stop its mouth that it cannot speak out. Thus (Rom. 1. 18): "They hold down the truth in unrighteousness." When the truth that is by their judgments assented unto and by their hearts yielded, and therefore should break out and give in testimony to the good ways of God, their corrupt and unrighteous and rebellious hearts hold it prisoner, will not suffer it either to appear unto others or prevail with themselves; as it fared with the scribes and Pharisees when the wonder was wrought by Peter, say they: (Acts 4. 16) "That indeed a notable miracle hath been done by them is manifest to all that dwell in Jerusalem, and we cannot deny it" (q.d. they would have done it if they could) "but that it spread no further, let us charge them straightly that they speak no more in this name." But here when the conscience of a poor sinner is convinced and the heart wounded, and that resistance and gainsaying distemper is taken off and crushed, now conscience is in commission and hath his scope, and the coast is now clear that reason may be heard. Now the broken-hearted sinner will speak plainly: these are the guides that God hath set up, their direction I will attend, these are the dear and faithful servants of the Lord whom I must honor, and with them I would betrust my soul; not with the blind guides and false teachers, who daub with untempered mortar and are not trusty to God nor their own souls, and therefore cannot be to me. Oh, send for such, though in their lifetime they could not endure the sight, abide the presence, nor allow them a good word, reviled their persons and proceedings and professions (yea, that they will confess), but it was directly against their own judgment and knowledge and conscience. Mine own heart often gave my tongue the lie, when I did so speak and so disparage their conversation; otherwise I must have condemned mine own course and conscience also. But the Lord is with them, and the truth is with them, and a blessing will undoubtedly follow them.

Ask why these poor pierced sinners did not go to the scribes, they would tell the truth. Oh, it was they that deceived us, led and drew us to the commission of this hellish wickedness; we cannot call them teachers but murderers; they could never help themselves, therefore not help us.

Instruction: Sound contrition and brokenness of heart brings a strange and a sudden alteration into the world, varies the price and value of things and persons beyond imagination, turns the market upside down, makes the things appear as they be, and the persons to be honored and respected as they are in truth, that look what the truth determines, reason approves, and conscience witnesseth. That account is current in the hearts and apprehensions of those whose hearts have been pierced with godly sorrow for their sins. Because such judge not by outward appearance as it is the guise of men of corrupt minds, but upon experience, that which they have found and felt in their own hearts, what they have seen and judged in their own spirits, they cannot but see so and judge so of others. Those who were mocked as "men full of new wine" are now the precious servants of the Lord; flouted to their faces not long since, now they attend them, honor and reverence them—yea, fall at their very feet. It was before men and drunkards, now men and brethren; the world you see is well amended, but strangely altered. It was said of John Baptist, the forerunner of our savior, and the scope of whose doctrine was mainly to prepare the way for the Lord—it's said of him that Elias is come and hath reformed all, set a new face and frame in the profession of the Gospel: (Matt. 17. 11) "Turned the disobedient to the wisdom of the just men, the hearts of children to the fathers." That though they were so degenerate that Abraham would not own them had he been alive, yet when the ministry of John had hammered and melted them for the work of our savior, they became to be wholly altered, their judgments altered and their carriage also. For in truth, the reason why men see not the loathsomeness of other men's sins, or else have not courage to pass a righteous sentence upon them, it is because they were never convinced to see the plague sore of their own corruptions, never had their hearts affected with the evil of them in their own experience, but their own conscience was misled out of authority, and stifled that it durst not outwardly condemn that which inwardly they could not but approve. They therefore who either do not see their own evil or dare not proceed in open judgment to condemn, they will either not see or not pass a righteous judgment upon others; so Paul intimates to Agrippa: (Acts 26. 8, 9) "Let it not seem strange, oh King, for I myself did think I should do many things against the name of Jesus, which I also did." Q.d.: whilst thou so continuest thou wilt see as I did and do as I did, but after God had entered into combat with him and spoken dreadfully to his soul, see! he is another man and of another mind. He destroyed the churches, now takes care of them; he that hated the name and Gospel of Jesus counts all things dung and dross for the excellent knowledge of Jesus; the world is well amended but it's marvelously altered, and therefore "We have found this man a pestilent fellow" (Acts 24. 5); he hath subdued the state of the world.

Terror: This shows the dreadful and miserable condition of all those who after all the light that hath been let into their minds, conviction into their consciences, horror into their hearts touching the evils that have been committed and come now to be discovered unto them, they loathe the light that hath laid open their evils, distaste those persons and preachers and Christians most, that have dealt most plainly to discover the loathsomeness of their distempers. It shows the irrecoverable corruption of the mind and heart that grows worst under the best means, and cleaves most to its sins under all the choicest means that would pluck their sins from their heart, and their heart from them. They are either fools or madmen that cannot endure the presence of the physician without whose help they could not be cured. This is made an evidence of the estrangement of God's heart from a people, and an immediate forerunner of their ruin: (Isa. 9. 13, 14, 17) "For this people turneth not unto him that smote them, neither do they seek the Lord, therefore the Lord will cut off from Israel head and tail, branch and rush, in one day; therefore the Lord shall have no pity on their young men, nor mercy on their fatherless, for every one is an hypocrite." It takes away all pity in God, all hopes in themselves of any good. After Pharaoh had many qualms and recoilings of spirit by Moses' dealing with him and the miracles which he had wrought for his repentance, and at last sides it with the hellish stiffness of his own stubborn heart, so that he cannot endure the speech or presence of Moses any more, (Exod. 10. 28) "Get thee from me, see my face no more, for the day thou seest my face thou shalt die," God sends Moses no more, but sends His plagues to destroy his first-born. He will not see the face of Moses, he shall feel the fierceness of the wrath of the Lord.

5. JOHN COTTON, 1584–1652

[One respect in which the Puritans seemed a diabolical contradiction in terms to their enemies, and to many modern viewers remain a riddle, was the way they took to heart—and to an astounding degree translated into daily conduct—an observation of John Cotton's:

"There is another combination of virtues strangely mixed in every lively, holy Christian: and that is, diligence in worldly businesses, and yet deadness to the world. Such a mystery as none can read but they that know it."

Recently this complex mentality has been scientifically analyzed by the great sociologist, Max Weber, and after him it is called, for shorthand purposes, "the Protestant ethic." Actually, it is a logical consequence of Puritan theology: man is put into this world, not to spend his life in profitless singing of hymns or in unfruitful monastic contemplation, but to do what the world requires, according to its terms. He must raise children, he must work at his calling. No activity is outside the holy purpose of the overarching covenant. Yet the Christian works not for the gain that may (or may not) result from his labor, but for the glory of God. He remains an ascetic in the world, as much as any hermit outside it. He displays unprecedented energy in wresting the land from the Indians, trading in the seven seas, speculating in lands: "Yet," says Cotton, "his heart is not set upon these things, he can tell what to do with his estate when he hath got it." In New England the phrase to describe this attitude soon became: loving the world with "weaned affections." It was applied not only to one's love of his property, but also to his love for wife, children, parents and country. It was a razor's edge, and the true Puritan was required to walk it. No wonder that some Puritans fell off to one side, becoming visionary idealists, while some fell to the other side, becoming hypocrites. Ultimately, another group gave up the struggle entirely, and became either John Wise or Benjamin Franklin. Yet out of the original ethic both of these, like thousands of men of business, came; they are inexplicable without an understanding of their origin. This is true, above all, in the case of Franklin: he transported the Puritan ethic of Christian industry into a secular context, but it was always the Puritan ethic.

Regarded by his contemporaries as equally a master of the plain style with Hooker, Cotton's writings may not seem to us to have quite so much vehemence; but he was a master at expounding the paradoxes of Puritan theology, and in this passage gave a classic exposition of the business ethic.]

CHRISTIAN CALLING

We are now to speak of living by faith in our outward and temporal life. Now, our outward and temporal life is twofold, which we live in the flesh: it is either a civil or a natural life; for both these lives we live, and they are different the one from the other. Civil life is that whereby we live as members of this or that city or town or commonwealth, in this or that particular vocation and calling.

Natural life I call that by which we do live this bodily life. I mean, by which we live a life of sense, by which we eat and drink, and by which we go through all conditions, from our birth to our grave, by which we live and move and have our being. And now both these a justified person lives by faith.

To begin with the former: A true believing Christian, a justified person, he lives in his vocation by his faith.

Not only my spiritual life but even my civil life in this world, all the life I live, is by the faith of the Son of God: He exempts no life from the agency of His faith; whether he lives as a Christian man, or as a member of this or that church or commonwealth, he doth it all by the faith of the Son of God.

Now, for opening of this point, let me show you what are those several acts of faith which it puts forth about our occasions and vocations, that so we may live in God's sight therein:

First: faith draws the heart of a Christian to live in some warrantable calling. As soon as ever a man begins to look towards God and the ways of His grace, he will not rest till he find out some warrantable calling and employment. An instance you have in the prodigal son, that after he had received and spent his portion in vanity, and when being pinched, he came home to himself, and coming home to his father, the very next thing after confession and repentance of his sin, the very next petition he makes is: "Make me one of thy hired servants." Next after desire of pardon of sin, then "put me into some calling," though it be but of an hired servant, wherein he may bring in God any service. A Christian would no sooner have his sin pardoned than his estate to be settled in some good calling: though not as a mercenary slave, but he would offer it up to God as a free-will offering; he would have his condition and heart settled in God's peace, but his life settled in a good calling, though it be but of a day laborer—"yet make me as one that may do Thee some service." Paul makes it a matter of great thankfulness to God, that He had given him ability and put him in [a] place where he might do Him service (I Tim. 1. 12). And in the Law, they were counted unclean beasts that did not divide the hoof into two (Lev. 11. 3). Therefore the camel, though he chewed the cud, yet because he did not divide the hoof, he was

counted unclean. And God by the beasts did signify to us
sundry sorts of men, who were clean, who not, as you may
see in Peter's vision in Acts 10. It shows you then that it is
only a clean person that walks with a divided hoof, that
sets one foot in his general and the other in his particular
calling. He strikes with both: he serves both God and man,
else he is an unclean beast. If he have no calling but a
general, or if no calling but a particular, he is an unclean
creature. But now, as soon as ever faith purifies the heart,
it makes us clean creatures (Acts 15. 9); and our callings
do interfere one upon another, but both go an end evenly
together. He drives both these plows at once: "As God
hath called every man, so let him walk" (I Cor. 7. 19, 20).
This the clean work of faith, he would have some employment to fill the head and hand with.

Now more particularly, faith doth warily observe the
warrantableness of its calling.

Three things doth faith find in a particular calling:

1. It hath a care that it be a warrantable calling,
wherein we may not only aim at our own, but at the public
good. That is a warrantable calling: "Seek not every man
his own things, but every man the good of his brother"
(I Cor. 10. 24); (Phil. 2. 4) "Seek one another's welfare";
"Faith works all by love" (Gal. 5. 6). And therefore it will
not think it hath a comfortable calling unless it will not
only serve his own turn, but the turn of other men. Bees
will not suffer drones among them; but if they lay up any
thing, it shall be for them that cannot work: he would see
that his calling should tend to public good.

2. Another thing to make a calling warrantable, is, when
God gives a man gifts for it, that he is acquainted with
the mystery of it and hath gifts of body and mind
suitable to it: (Prov. 16. 20) "He that understands a matter shall find good." "He that understands his business
wisely, God leads him on to that calling" (I Cor. 7. 17).
To show you that when God hath called me to a place,
He hath given me some gifts fit for that place, especially
if the place be suitable and fitted to me and my best gifts.
For God would not have a man to receive five talents and

gain but two; He would have his best gifts improved to the best advantage.

3. That which makes a calling warrantable is, when it is attained unto by warrantable and direct means, when a man enterprises not a calling but in the use of such means as he may see God's providence leading him to it. So Amos manifests his calling against the high priest: (Amos 7. 14, 15) "The Lord took me, and said unto me, Go, feed my people." So he had a warrant for it; God's hand led him to it in God's ordinance, and therein he comforted himself, whereas another man that hath taken up such a calling without warrant from God, he deals ingenuously (Zech. 13. 5) and leaves it—to show you that a man ought to attend upon his own warrantable calling. Now faith that hath respect unto the word of God for all its ways, he would see his calling aiming at the public good; he would see gifts for it and an open door for his entrance into it; he would not come unto it by deceit and undermining of others, but he would see the providence and ordinance of God leading him unto it, the counsel of friends, and encouragement of neighbors—this is the first work of faith.

Secondly: another work of faith, about a man's vocation and calling, when faith hath made choice of a warrantable calling, then he depends upon God for the quickening and sharpening of his gifts in that calling, and yet depends not upon his gifts for the going through his calling but upon God that gave him those gifts; yea, he depends on God for the use of them in his calling. Faith saith not, give me such a calling and turn me loose to it; but faith looks up to heaven for skill and ability. Though strong and able, yet it looks at all its abilities but as a dead work, as like braided wares in a shop, as such as will be lost and rust unless God refresh and renew breath in them. And then if God do breathe in his gifts, he depends not upon them for the acting his work but upon God's blessing in the use of his gifts. Though he have never so much skill and strength, he looks at it as a dead work unless God breathe in him; and he looks not at his gifts as breathed only on by God, as able to do the work, unless also he be followed by God's blessing. "Blessed be the Lord my strength, that teacheth my hands to war, and my fingers to fight" (Psal. 144. 1). He had been trained up to skill that way, yet he rests only in God's teaching of him (Psal. 18. 32, 33, 34). "It is the Lord that girds me with strength; he puts strength into his hands, so that a bow of steel is broken with my arms." And therefore it was that when he went against Goliath, though he had before found good success in his combats with the lion and the bear, yet he saith not, I have made my part good enough with them, and so shall I do with this man. No, but this is the voice of faith: "The Lord my God that delivered me out of their hands, He will deliver me out of the hand of this Philistine; He that gave me strength and skill at that time, He is the same, His hand is not shortened. And then what is this Philistine more than one of them" (I Sam. 17. 37)? And so when he comes in Goliath's presence and looks in his face, he tells him he comes to him in the name of the Lord of Hosts; and he comes not only in the Lord's name, but he looks up to Him for skill and strength to help; and therefore saith (verse 40): "The Lord will close thee in my hands, so that by his own strength shall no flesh prevail." "It is in vain," saith faith, "to rise early, and go to bed late, but it is God that gives His beloved rest" (Psal. 127. 1, 2, 3; Prov. 3. 5, 6). The strongest Christian is never more foiled than when he goes forth in strength of gifts received and his own dexterity.

Thirdly: we live by faith in our vocations, in that faith, in serving God, serves men, and in serving men, serves God. The Apostle sweetly describes it in the calling of servants (Eph. 6. 5–8): "Not with eye service as men-pleasers, but as the servants of Christ, doing the will of God from the heart with good will, as unto the Lord, and not unto men, not so much man or only man, but chiefly the Lord," so that this is the work of every Christian man in his calling. Even then when he serves man, he serves the Lord; he doth the work set before him, and he doth it sincerely and faithfully so as he may give account for it; and he doth it heavenly and spiritually: "He uses the world as if he used it not" (I Cor. 7. 31). This is not the thing his heart is set upon; he looks for greater matters

than these things can reach him, he doth not so much look
at the world as at heaven. And therefore—that which follows upon this—he doth it all comfortably, though he meet
with little encouragements from man, though the more
faithful service he doth, the less he is accepted; whereas
an unbelieving heart would be discontented that he can
find no acceptance, but all he doth is taken in the worst
part. But now if faith be working and stirring, he will say:
"I pass very little to be judged by you, or by man's judgment" (I Cor. 4. 3). I pass little what you say or what you
do; God knows what I have done, and so his spirit is satisfied; (I Thess. 2. 7) "We were tender over you, as a nurse
over her child." We wrought not for wages nor for the
praise of you; if so, we had not been the servants of Christ.
A man therefore that serves Christ in serving of men, he
doth his work sincerely as in God's presence, and as one
that hath an heavenly business in hand, and therefore comfortably as knowing God approves of his way and work.

Fourthly: another act of faith about a man's vocation is
this: It encourageth a man in his calling to the most home-
liest and difficultest and most dangerous things his calling
can lead and expose himself to. If faith apprehend this or
that to be the way of my calling, it encourages me to it,
though it be never so homely and difficult and dangerous.
Take you a carnal, proud heart, and if his calling lead him
to some homely business, he can by no means embrace it;
such homely employments a carnal heart knows not how
to submit unto. But now faith having put us into a calling,
if it require some homely employment, it encourageth us
to it. He considers, "It is my calling," and therefore he goes
about it freely; and though never so homely, he doth it as
a work of his calling: (Luke 15. 19) "Make me one of thy
hired servants." A man of his rank and breeding was not
wonted to hired servile work, but the same faith that made
him desirous to be in a calling made him stoop to any work
his calling led him to; there is no work too hard or too
homely for him, for faith is conscious that it hath done the
most base drudgery for Satan. No lust of pride or what
else so insolent but our base hearts could be content to
serve the Devil and nature in it; and therefore what

drudgery can be too homely for me to do for God? (Phil.
2. 5, 7) "Let the same mind be in you that was in Christ
Jesus, he made himself of no reputation." He stood not
upon it that he was born of God and equal to the Most
High; but he made himself a servant, and of no reputation,
and so to serve God and save men; and when his Father
called him to it, he stooped to a very low employment,
rose up from supper and girded himself with a towel and
washed his disciples' feet (John 13). They thought it was
a service too homely for him to do, but he tells them that
even they ought thus to serve one another. So faith is ready
to embrace any homely service his calling leads him to,
which a carnal heart would blush to be seen in; a faithful
heart is never squeamish in this case, for repentance will
make a man revenge himself upon himself in respect of the
many homely services he hath done for Satan; and so faith
encourageth us to the most difficult and homely businesses.
(Ezra 10. 4) "It is a great thing thou art now about, yet
arise and be doing, for the matter belongs to thee." Yea,
and though sometimes the work be more dangerous, yet if
a man be called to it, faith dares not shrink. It was an hard
point that Herod was put upon: either now he must be
profane or discover his hypocrisy. Now therefore, John dis-
chargeth his conscience; and though it was dangerous for
him to be so plain, yet faith encourageth him to it. If it
appear to be his calling, faith doth not pick and choose as
carnal reason will do.

Fifthly: another act of faith by which a Christian man
lives in his vocation is that faith casts all the failings and
burthens of his calling upon the Lord; that is the proper
work of faith; it rolls and casts all upon Him.

Now there are three sorts of burthens that befall a man
in his calling:

1. Care about the success of it; and for this faith casts
its care upon God: (I Pet. 5. 7; Prov. 16. 3) "Commit
thy works unto the Lord, and thy thoughts shall be established"; (Psal. 55. 22, 24) "Cast thy burthen upon the
Lord, and He will deliver thee." Faith will commend that
wholly to God.

2. A second burthen is fear of danger that my befall us

therein from the hand of man: (Luke 13. 31, 32) Some bids Christ go out of the country for Herod will kill him; what saith Christ to that? "Go tell that fox I must work today and tomorrow." He casts that upon God and his calling; God hath set me a time, and while that time lasts, my calling will bear me out, and when that time is out, then I shall be perfect.

3. Another burthen is the burthen of injuries which befalls a man in his calling. I have not hastened that evil day, Lord thou knowest; he had not wronged himself nor others in his calling, and therefore all the injuries that befall him in his calling, he desires the Lord to take it into His hands.

Sixthly: faith hath another act about a man's vocation, and that is, it takes all successes that befall him in his calling with moderation; he equally bears good and evil successes as God shall dispense them to him. Faith frames the heart to moderation; be they good or evil, it rests satisfied in God's gracious dispensation: "I have learned in what estate soever I am, therewith to be content" (Phil. 4. 11, 12). This he had learned to do: if God prosper him, he had learned not to be puffed up; and if he should be exposed to want, he could do it without murmuring. It is the same act of unbelief that makes a man murmur in crosses which puffs him up in prosperity. Now faith is like a poise: it keeps the heart in an equal frame; whether matters fall out well or ill, faith takes them much what alike; faith moderates the frame of a man's spirit on both sides.

Seventhly: the last work which faith puts forth about a man's calling is this: faith with boldness resigns up his calling into the hands of God or man; whenever God calls a man to lay down his calling when his work is finished, herein the sons of God far exceed the sons of men. Another man when his calling comes to be removed from him, he is much ashamed and much afraid; but if a Christian man be to forgo his calling, he lays it down with comfort and boldness in the sight of God and man.

First, in the sight of God: (II Tim. 4. 7) "I have fought the fight, I have kept the faith and finished my course, and therefore, henceforth is laid up for me a crown of righteousness, which God according to His righteous word and promise will give him as a reward for his sincere and faithful walking." He looks up to God and resigns up his calling into His hand; he tells Timothy the day of his departure is at hand; and now, this is matter of strong consolation to him, faith believing, that God put him into his calling and hath been helpful to him hitherto. And now grown nigh to the period of his calling, here was his comfort, that he had not thrown himself out of his work; but God calls him to leave it, and so he leaves it, in the same hand from whom he received it. A man that in his calling hath sought himself and never looked farther than himself, he never comes to lay down his calling, but he thinks it is to his utter undoing. A swine that never did good office to his owner till he comes to lie on the hurdle, he then cries out; but a sheep, who hath many times before yielded profit, though you take him and cut his throat, yet he is as a lamb dumb before the shearer. So a carnal man that never served any man but himself, call him to distress in it and he murmurs and cries out at it; but take you a Christian man that is wonted to serve God in serving of men, when he hath been faithful and useful in his calling, he never lays it down but with some measure of freedom and boldness of spirit. As it was with the three princes in the furnace, they would live and die in God's service, and therefore God marvelously assisted them in their worst hours; the soul knows whom it hath lived upon. This is the life of faith in the upshot of a man's calling: he lays it down in confidence of God's acceptance; and for man, he hath this boldness in his dealings with men—he boldly challenges all the sons of men of any injury done to them, and he freely offers them restitution and recompense if any such there should be. It was the comfort of Samuel when he was grown old and the people were earnest for a king (I Sam. 12. 3), he saith unto them, "Behold, here am I before you this day, bear witness against me this day, whose ox or ass have I taken?" He makes an open challenge to them all; and they answered, "Thou hast done us no wrong." This is the comfort of a Christian: when he comes to lay down his calling, he cannot only with comfort look God in the face but all the sons of men. There is never a Christian that lives by faith in his calling but he is able to challenge all the world for any wrong done to them; we have wronged and defrauded no man (Acts 20. 26; II Cor. 12). We have done most there, where we are least accepted; that is the happiness of a Christian: those who have been the most weary of him have had the least cause.

Use 1. From hence you see a just reproof of the infidelity found in them that live without a calling: they either want faith or the exercise of faith. If thou beest a man that lives without a calling, though thou hast two thousands to spend, yet if thou hast no calling tending to public good, thou art an unclean beast. If men walk without a cloven hoof, they are unclean; and hast thou a calling and art never so diligent in it, it is but dead work if thou want faith. It likewise reproves such Christians as consider not what gifts they have for this and that calling; he pleads for himself, his wife and children, further than himself he respects no calling; and this is want of faith in a Christian's calling. Or if men rest in the strength of their own gifts for the performing of their callings and will serve God in some things and themselves and theirs in other some, or if we can tell how to be eye-servants, it is but a dead work for want of faith. Or if thou lose thyself, and thy heart is carnal and not heavenly-minded, thou mayest have faith; but that is but a dead work. And if thou cast not all thy care and burthen upon God, thou wilt be very dead when ill successes fall out. But had we faith, it would support us in our worst successes; and if better successes come, if faith be wanting, our vain heart will be lifted up; and if Christians be confounded before God and men when they are to resign up their callings, it is a sign that either they have no faith, or it puts not forth life and courage into them; and if it so fall out, know that the root of it springs from an unbelieving heart.

Use 2. It is an use of instruction to every Christian soul that desires to walk by faith in his calling: if thou wouldst live a lively life and have thy soul and body to prosper in thy calling, labor then to get into a good calling and therein live to the good of others. Take up no calling but that thou hast understanding in, and never take it unless thou mayest have it by lawful and just means. And when thou hast it, serve God in thy calling, and do it with cheerfulness and faithfulness and an heavenly mind. And in difficulties and dangers, cast thy cares and fears upon God, and see if he will not bear them for thee; and frame thy heart to this heavenly moderation in all successes to sanctify God's name. And if the hour and power of darkness come, that thou beest to resign up thy calling, let it be enough that conscience may witness to thee that thou hast not sought thyself nor this world, but hast wrought the Lord's works. Thou mayest then have comfort in it, both before God and men.

Use 3. It is a word of consolation to every such soul as hath been acquainted with this life of faith in his calling: be thy calling never so mean and homely and never so hardly accepted, yet, if thou hast lived by faith in thy calling, it was a lively work in the sight of God; and so it will be rewarded when thy change shall come. Many a Christian is apt to be discouraged and dismayed if crosses befall him in his calling. But be not afraid; let this cheer up thy spirit—that whatever thy calling was, yet thou camest into it honestly and hast lived in it faithfully; your course was lively and spiritual, and therefore you may with courage look up for recompense from Christ.

6. INCREASE MATHER, 1639–1723

[The dominating figure among the second generation, Increase Mather was born in Dorchester, where his father, Richard, was minister. He received his B.A. from Harvard, then went to England, studied at Trinity College, Dublin, where he received his M.A. in 1658. When the Restoration closed the avenues of advancement, he returned to Boston, married the daughter of John Cotton, and in 1664 was installed as minister of the Second Church. He became the nonresident president of Harvard College in 1685, and in 1688 was sent as agent of the colony to London; he successfully negotiated the new charter from William and

Mary, and returned in 1692 with the governor and a slate of magistrates nominated by himself. In 1701 he was forced to resign from Harvard, and his influence declined, while Solomon Stoddard became the leader in the western half of the province. Still, he remained a commanding figure in Boston, fighting beside his son, Cotton, to maintain the principles of the founders, and also, in 1721, for inoculation. He was a voluminous writer, the length of his bibliography being surpassed only by Cotton Mather's, and a lifelong exponent of the plain style.

This selection is from *A Discourse Concerning the Uncertainty of the Times of Men,* a sermon delivered at Harvard College in 1697 after two undergraduates, skating on Fresh Pond, broke through the ice and were drowned. It brings us still further into what for the Puritan was the problem of human existence: life, as it is normally lived, is a chronicle of accidents and blunders, afflictions, and hopes defeated. Yet it is not a tale told by an idiot; there is indeed sound and fury, but behind the surface futility stand the ranks of eternal verities.]

MAN KNOWS NOT HIS TIME

The doctrine at present before us is:

That for the most part the miserable children of men know not their time.

There are three things for us here briefly to inquire into: (1) What times they are which men know not? (2) How it does appear that they are ignorant thereof? (3) The reason why they are kept in ignorance of their time.

Question 1. What times are they which men know not?

Answer 1. Time is sometimes put for the proper season for action, for the fittest season for a man to effect what he is undertaking. The seventy Greek interpreters translate the words *kairon autou*. There is a season, a fit time for men to go to work in. If they take hold of that nick of opportunity, they will prosper and succeed in their endeavors. It is a great part of wisdom to know that season. Hence it is said, "A wise man's heart discerneth both time and judgment" (Eccles. 8. 5), but few have that wisdom or knowledge. Therefore it is added in the next verse, "Because to every purpose there is time and judgment, therefore the misery of man is great upon him." The meaning is, because men discern not the proper time for them to effect what they purpose, their misery is great. If they would attempt such a thing just at such a time, they would make themselves and others happy; but missing that opportunity, great misery comes upon them. So it is as to civil affairs very frequently: men discern not the proper only season for them to obtain what they desire. Yea, and so it is as to spirituals. Men are not aware of the proper season wherein they may obtain good for their souls. There is a price put into their hands to get wisdom, but they have no heart to know and improve it. There is a day of grace in which if men seek to God for mercy they shall find it: (Isa. 55. 6) "Seek ye the Lord while He may be found." The most of them that have such a day know it not until their finding time is past. Thus it was with Israel of old: (Jer. 8. 7) "The stork in the heaven knows her appointed times; the turtle and the crane and the swallow observe the time of their coming; but my people know not the judgment of the Lord." They discerned not the judgments, that is the dispensations, of God. They had a summer of prosperity but did not improve it. There was a winter of adversity coming on them, but they knew it not, nor did they use the proper only means to prevent it. So the Jews when Christ was amongst them had a blessed time if they had known it; but they knew not the things of their peace, in the day of their peace; they knew not the time of their visitation.

2. A man knows not what changes shall attend him whilst in this world.

Changes of providence are in the scripture called "times." It is said that the acts of David and "the times that went over him" and over Israel, and over all the kingdoms of the countries, were written by Samuel and Nathan the prophet, and in the book of Gad the seer, meaning the changes of providence which they were subject unto (I Chron. 29. 30). A man knows not whether he shall see good or evil days for the time to come; he knoweth what his past days have been, but does not know what they shall be for the time to come. It may be he is now in prosperity: he has friends, children, relations, which he takes delight in, he has health, an estate, and esteem in the world; he does not know that he shall have any of these things for the future. Indeed, men in prosperity are apt to think (as they would have it) that they shall always, or for a long time, be so; but very often they find themselves greatly mistaken. The Psalmist confesseth that it was so with him: (Psal. 30. 6, 7) "In my prosperity I said, I shall never be moved; Lord, by Thy favor, Thou hast made my mountain to stand strong: Thou didst hide Thy face, and I was troubled." His enemies were all subdued, his mountain, that is his kingdom, especially his royal palace in Mount Sion was become exceeding strong, that now he thought all dangers were over; but Absalom's unexpected rebellion involved him and the whole land in trouble. The good people in Josiah's time promised themselves great happiness for many a year under the government of such a king as he was: (Lam. 4. 20) "Of whom we said under his shadow we shall live." But his sudden death made a sad change in all the public affairs.

A man knows not what afflictions shall come upon him whilst on the earth. This is true concerning particular persons: they may know in general that afflictions shall attend them in an evil sinful world, but what those afflictions in particular shall be they know not. Thus the Apostle speaks: (Acts 20. 22, 23) "I go bound in spirit to Jerusalem, not knowing what things shall befall me there, save that the holy spirit witnesseth in every city, saying, that bonds and afflictions abide me." So that he knew in general that he should meet with affliction, but not in special what the affliction would be. So is it true concerning a people, that they know not what times or changes may pass over them. Little was it thought that whilst Hoshea (who was the best of all the nineteen kings that had ruled over the ten tribes) was reigning, a powerful foreign enemy should invade the land and make them all slaves. Little did the Jews think that when Josiah was but thirty-nine years old, he should

die before that year was out, and they never see good day
more after his death. And as men know not what their
changes and afflictions must be, so neither when they shall
come upon them. Whether it will be a long or a short time
before those changes overtake them: (Mark 13. 35) "You
know not when the master of the house comes, at even, or
at midnight, or at the cock crowing, or in the morning."
Thus a man knoweth not whether the sharpest afflictions
which are reserved for him shall come upon him in his
youth or in his middle age or in his old age, though for
the most part men's greatest afflictions overtake them in
their old age. Nor can any man know whether his afflictions will soon be over or continue for a longer time. Thus,
the Lord's people knew that their captivity in Babylon
should last for seventy years and no longer; but that knowledge was by divine revelation. As for some other persecutions they knew not how long they would continue: (Psal.
74. 9) "There is no more a prophet, neither is there any
that knows how long." Those words seem to respect the
persecution under Antiochus, when there was no prophet.

3. A man knows not the time of his death. Often it is so,
that when death falls upon a man, he thinks no more of it
than the fishes think of the net before they are caught in
it, or than the birds think of the snare before they are taken
in it, as Solomon here speaks. It useth to be said (and it is
a plain, weighty known truth) that nothing is more certain
then that every man shall die, and nothing more uncertain
than the time when. Old Isaac said: (Gen. 27. 2) "Behold,
I know not the day of my death." Though he lived above
twenty years after he spoke those words, he did not know
that he should live a day longer. A man cannot know how
long himself or another shall live. It is true that Hezekiah
was ascertained that he should not die before fifteen years
were expired. And the prophet Jeremiah knew that Han-
aniah should not live a year to an end: (Jer. 28. 16) "This
year thou shalt die, because thou hast taught rebellion
against the Lord." But those were extraordinary cases. It
is not a usual thing for a man to know beforehand how
many months or years he shall live in this world. Nor may
he desire to know it, but he ought to leave that with God.

Although David prayed, saying, "Lord, make me to know my end, and the number of my days, what it is" (Psal. 39. 4). His meaning is, not that he might know just how many days he should live, but that he might be made duly sensible of his own frailty and mortality, and lead his life accordingly. Oftentimes death is nearest to men when they least think of it; especially it is so with ungodly men. We have an instance of it in Agag: he came before Samuel, delicately, and said, "Surely the bitterness of death is past" (I Sam. 15. 32). Little did he think that within a few hours he should be cut in pieces. When Haman boasted of his being the chief favorite at court, and that the queen had invited no one but the king and himself to a banquet, he little thought of the destruction which was then preparing for him. When Belshazzar was in the beginning of the night drinking and making merry with his profane companions, he little thought that he should be a dead man before morning; but "that night was Belshazzar slain" (Dan. 5. 30). The rich fool in the Gospel dream'd of a long life and merry: he said to his soul, eat, drink and be merry, thou hast goods laid up for many years. But God said: "This night thy soul shall be required of thee"; he must appear immediately before the dreadful tribunal (Luke 12. 20). Thus we see what time it is which men know not.

The second thing to be inquired into is, how it does appear that men know not their time?

Answer 1. It is evident, in that all future contingencies are known to God only. Hence Christ said to the disciples, "It is not for you to know the times and the seasons which the Father has put in His own power" (Acts 1. 7). Future times and contingent events, the knowledge and disposal of them, has God reserved to Himself. There are future things which happen necessarily, that a man may know them long before they come to pass: "God has appointed lights in the heaven to be for signs and seasons" (Gen. 1. 14). These move regularly and unfailably according to that order which the creator has established. Therefore a man may know infallibly how many hours or minutes such a day or night will be, long before the time comes; he may know when there will be an eclipse of the sun or of the moon twenty, or an hundred, years before it comes to pass. But for contingent things, which have no necessary dependence on the constituted order of nature but upon the mere pleasure and providence of God, they are not known except unto God, or to them unto whom He shall reveal them. The Lord challengeth this as His prerogative. The idols whom the heathen worshiped, could not make known future contingencies: (Isa. 41. 22, 23) "Let them show us what shall happen, or declare us things for to come, show the things that are to come hereafter, that we may know they are God's." To do this was past their skill. The devil knows many future things which men are ignorant of: he could foretell Saul's ruin and David's coming to the kingdom. Nevertheless, there are many future events which he has no knowledge of. Therefore he often deludes those that inquire of him with deceitful and uncertain answers. But as for men, they are ignorant of future things, which most nearly concern themselves or their own families. No man knows so much as who shall be his heir or enjoy the estate which he has labored for: (Psal. 39. 6) "Surely every man walks in a vain show: he heapeth up riches, and knows not who shall gather them." He knows not whether one of his relations or a mere stranger shall possess that estate which he has taken so much pains, and disquieted himself so much, for the obtaining of it. This meditation made Solomon out of love with this world. He knew as much as any man, and yet he confesseth that he did not know whether the man that should come after him and enjoy all that he had labored for would be a wise man or a fool (Eccles. 2. 18, 19). And he says, "A man knows not that which shall be; for who can tell him when it shall be" (Eccles. 8. 7)? He knows neither what nor when it shall be. And again he saith, "A man cannot tell what shall be; and what shall be after him who can tell him" (Eccles. 10. 14)? This is to be understood concerning contingent events, such as the particular afflictions which are to befall a man, or the time, place or manner of his death.

2. The times of men are ordered according to the decree of God. There is nothing comes to pass in the earth, but

what was first determined by a wise decree in heaven: (Acts 15. 18) "Known unto God are all His works from the beginning of the world." God knows what He has to do. The Apostle speaks there concerning the conversion of the Gentiles; this did God foreknow and decree from the beginning of the world, yea from all eternity. The like is to be said concerning every thing which happens in the world: not a sparrow falls to the ground without His providence, and therefore not without His decree, the one being an infallible effect of the other. He has decreed when and where every man that comes into the world shall be born, and where he shall live, in what country, and in what town; yea, and in what house too: (Acts 17. 26) "He has determined the times before appointed, and the bounds of their habitation." He has decreed when every man shall die: (Eccles. 3. 2) "There is a time to be born and a time to die." That is to say, a time decreed and appointed by God when every man shall be born, and when he shall die. Nor shall any man live a day longer than the time which the Lord has appointed for him: (Job 14. 5) "His days are determined, the number of his months are with Thee, Thou hast appointed his bounds that he cannot pass." All the circumstances attending every man's death, the place and manner of it, whether he shall die by sickness or by any other accident, all is determined in heaven before it comes to pass on the earth. Now the decrees of God are secret things, until the event or some divine revelation shall discover them: (Deut. 29. 29) "Secret things belong unto the Lord our God." His divine decrees are those secret things which Himself alone knows: (Rom. 11. 34) "For who hath known the mind of the Lord? or, who has been his counselor?"

3. The conversations of men generally make it manifest that they know not their time. They do many things which they would not do, and they neglect many things which they would certainly practice, if they knew what times are near them: (Matt. 24. 43) "If the good man of the house had known in what watch the thief would come, he would have watched, and would not have suffered his house to be broken up." Thus men live in a careless neglect

of God, and of their own souls and salvation, but if they
knew that death will come stealing suddenly upon them,
they would watch and pray. Did they know that before
the next week, they shall be in another world, they would
live after another manner than now they do. Most commonly persons are light and vain in their spirits when heavy
tidings is near to them. Did they know what sad news they
shall hear shortly, they would be in a more solemn frame of
spirit: (Isa. 5. 12) "The harp, and the viol, the tabret, and
the pipe, and wine, are in their feasts: but they regard not
the work of the Lord, neither consider the operation of
His hands." Had they known what work God intended to
make with them speedily, they would have minded something else besides their sensual pleasures and delights.

We proceed to inquire 3: Whence it is that men know
not their time?

Answer: It is from God. He will have them to be kept in
ignorance and uncertainties about their time. And for this
wise and holy ends:

1. That so His children might live by faith, that so they
might live a life of holy dependence upon God continually.
They must not know their times, that so they might trust
in the Lord at all times. God would not have His children
to be anxiously solicitous about future events, but to leave
themselves and theirs with their heavenly Father, to dispose of all their concernments, as He in His infinite wisdom
and faithfulness shall see good.

2. That their obedience may be tried; that they may
follow the Lord, as it were blindfold, whithersoever He
shall lead them, though they do not see one step of their
way before them, as Abraham did: (Heb. 11. 8) "When
he was called to go out into a place which he should after
receive for an inheritance, he obeyed; and went out, not
knowing whither he went." We must follow God, though
we know not what He will do with us, or how He will
dispose of us as to our temporal concerns, submitting ourselves, yea, our lives and all, entirely to the will of God in
everything. That saying ought to be often in our mouths,
"If the Lord will," and we shall live, and do this or that
(James 4. 15).

3. Men must not know their time, that so they may be ever watchful: (Matt. 25. 13) "Watch therefore, for you know neither the day nor the hour wherein the son of man comes." The generality of men, if they had it revealed to them (as Hezekiah) that they should certainly live so many years, they would in the meantime be careless about their souls and the world to come. We see that notwithstanding they are uncertain how short their time may be, they are regardless about their future eternal estate. How much more would they be so, if they knew that death and judgment were not far off from them?

4. As to some, they are kept in ignorance of their times that so they may with the more comfort and composure of spirit follow the work which they are called unto; that they may with diligence and cheerfulness attend the duties of their general and particular calling, which they could not do if they knew what evil times and things are appointed for them. The terror of what is coming on them would be so dismal to them that they could not enjoy themselves nor take comfort in anything they enjoy. As the Apostle speaks to the covetous Jews: (James 5. 1). "Go to now, you rich men, weep and howl for your miseries that shall come upon you." So there are many in the world that would spend their days in weeping and howling, did they but know what is coming on them and theirs. When the prophet Elisha had it revealed to him, that sad things were coming on the land, by reason of a bloody neighbor nation, which would break in upon them and exercise barbarous cruelties, the holy man wept at the foreknowledge of it: (II Kings 8. 11) "The man of God wept." So there would be nothing but weeping in many families, weeping in many towns, and in some whole countries, did men but know their times. Therefore they must be kept in ignorance thereof until the things come upon them.

7. URIAN OAKES, 1631–1681

[By now it becomes clear that for Puritan theology, or rather for the ordinary Puritan way of life, the central problem was finite man dealing with infinite God. How and where, behind the apparently designless universe, does the design take hold? After the ordeal of founding the colonies, after the confusions and then the débâcle of the Puritan revolution in England, after the trials and afflictions of New England, and after the slaughter of King Philip's War, how could New England solve the problem of problems, the intelligibility of divine providence within the riot of history?

To this issue Urian Oakes addressed himself at Cambridge on September 10, 1677, the occasion being an election of officers for the Artillery Company. He took as his text that most challenging of statements against all maintainers of design in the moral universe, Ecclesiastes 9. 11: "I returned, and saw under the sun, that the race is not to the swift, nor the battle to the strong, neither yet bread to the wise, nor yet riches to men of understanding, nor yet favor to men of skill: but time and chance happeneth to them all." Like a true Puritan, Oakes accepted the challenge; whether or not you think he answered it, you must admit he did not flinch.

Born in England, Urian Oakes was brought to Cambridge, Massachusetts Bay, by his family. He graduated from Harvard in 1649, and went to Puritan England in 1654, but was ejected from his pulpit in 1662; he struggled to remain in England as a Dissenter, but happily returned to Cambridge to become minister in 1671. For the last five years of his life he was also president of Harvard College. He had genuine wit, was an excellent Latinist, and his few surviving sermons are among the best of New England literary achievements.]

THE SOVEREIGN EFFICACY
OF DIVINE PROVIDENCE

Doctrine: That the successes and events of undertakings and affairs are not determined infallibly by the greatest sufficiency of men or second causes, but by the counsel and providence of God ordering and governing time and chance according to His own good pleasure.

I have endeavored to comprise and grasp the substance of Solomon's intendment in this doctrinal conclusion, and shall explicate and demonstrate the truth of it (as God shall help) in the following propositions:

Proposition 1. Second causes may have a sufficiency in their kind, to produce these and those effects: an hability, a congruous disposition or an aptness, yea, a kind of sufficiency in order to the putting forth this and that act, and the giving existence to these and those effects. Not indeed an absolute and universal sufficiency (which can be affirmed of none but Him that is all sufficient and omnipotent) but a limited sufficiency, or a sufficiency in their kind and order: the sun, to shine; the fire, to burn that which is combustible; the rational creature, to act or effect this or that in a way of counsel and with freedom of will; the swift, to run; the strong and valiant and well-instructed soldier, to fight well; the wise man, to get his bread to gather riches, to gain acceptance among those with whom he hath to do. This is no more than to say that created agents and second causes may have the active power and virtue of causes, all that is requisite on their parts in order to the production of their peculiar and appropriate effects, all that sufficiency that dependent beings and second causes are capable of. And indeed, it belongs to the infinite wisdom and goodness of God to furnish His creatures with sufficient ability for the operations and effects He hath made them for. And so He did at first, when He made everything good in its kind; and whatever defect there is now in this respect, it is the fruit and punishment of sin. Though God is able to give being to things in an immediate way, yet it is His pleasure in the course of His providence to use means, and to produce many things by the mediation and agency of second causes, and so gives causal virtue and ability to these and those things in order to the producing of such and such effects. It is a good observation, that the Lord is pleased, not through any defect of power in Himself, but out of the abundance of His goodness to communicate causal power and virtue to His creatures, and to honor them with that dignity that they may be His instruments, by which He will produce these and those effects: whereby He takes them, as it were, into partnership and fellowship with Himself in the way of His providential efficiency, that they may be under-workers to, yea co-workers with, Himself. Hence He gives them an aptitude and sufficiency in their kind in order to their respective operations and effects, though some have a greater aptitude and sufficiency than others. But without some degree of such sufficiency, nothing can deserve the name of a cause, the very essence whereof consists in its power, virtue and ability to produce an effect. A cause cannot be a cause without an active power, or sufficiency to give being to this or that effect.

Proposition 2. The successes and events of affairs and undertakings do ordinarily depend in some respects upon the sufficiency of second causes.

I do not say in the observation; nor is it the meaning of Solomon that successes and events of affairs and undertakings do not depend at all, in an ordinary course, on the sufficiency of second causes. For this were to deny and destroy their causality, and to make nothing of their efficiency. Second causes have their peculiar influence into their effects, and contribute something to their existence; and to assert the contrary, were to say that causes are no causes, and to speak a flat contradiction. This would be to suppose that the Lord hath set up an order and course in nature in vain, and given to second causes a sufficiency in their kind, for action, to no purpose, and to deny the ordinary providence of God, which is that whereby the Lord observes the order which He hath set, and that course of nature which is originally of His own appointment, whereby one thing depends upon and receives being from another. Though the Lord is pleased sometimes, upon great and important occasions, to leave the ordinary road of providence and act beyond and above the usual, stated course of things, and not to concur with and shine upon the endeavors of created agents, so as to crown them with that success which according to an ordinary course of providence might be rationally expected, yet it is not to be imagined that He should ordinarily dispense with the course and methods of His ordinary providence. For why

then should it be called ordinary? God who is the lord of
hosts, the great leader, commander and ruler of nature,
not only permits but also effectually commands and causes
His whole militia, ordinarily, to move and act according to
their natures and natural properties respectively, without
countermanding them or turning them out of their way.
For (as I remember one argues) He will not show such a
dislike to His own workmanship, as ordinarily to cross the
order and alter the course He hath set in the world. Therefore the meaning of the text is not that swiftness conduces
nothing to the winning of the race, or strength to the
winning of the battle, or wisdom and understanding to the
getting of bread and riches, or prudence, art, or skill, to
the getting of favor and good will of princes or people;
nor, that the race is never to the swift, or the battle never
to the strong; no, nor yet that the race is not more frequently to the swift, and the battle usually to the strong.
For the Lord doth most ordinarily award success unto
causes of greatest sufficiency rather than disappointment
and defeat. Otherwise, it would be a very heartless, if not
a foolish thing (in the eye of reason) to use means or to
think to get the race by swiftness, or bread by labor and
diligence, or favor by dextrous and prudent behavior, or
learning by study and industry, or to win the battle by
good conduct and courage and numbers of men. Yea, then
wisdom would not be better than folly, nor strength more
desirable than weakness, nor diligence more beneficial and
available than idleness and sitting still. This therefore is
evident, that the issues and events of undertakings do in
some respect, ordinarily, depend upon the sufficiency of
second causes, insomuch as the greatest probability of success (according to an ordinary providence, and in the eye
of reason) is ordinarily on the side of causes that are most
sufficient in their kind of efficiency.

Proposition 3. Second causes, though of greatest sufficiency in their kind, have not the certain determination of
successes and events in their own hands, but may be
frustrated and disappointed.

Though the successes and events of undertakings ordinarily depend upon the sufficiency of second causes, yet

they are not infallibly determined thereby. Created agents have not events in their own hands, but may be disappointed; they cannot warrant the events of their undertakings or success of their counsels and endeavors, but may be defeated of their hopes and expectations. Thus no man hath the absolute command of the issue and success of his own undertakings. He may be sure of this or that event, if the Lord promise it to him, or reveal it to be His pleasure to give such success to such endeavors; but he cannot be secured of it from or by any sufficiency of his own. He may, as a wise man, foresee and say what in an ordinary course of providence is rationally to be expected, but cannot warrant the success of his undertakings, or carve out what event he pleases, to himself. His prudence and providence and diligence and sufficiency for action cannot assure him of the event, or determine the success on his side. And there is that demonstration of it, that created agents of the greatest sufficiency are sometimes disappointed. Two things I would say here:

1. Agents of greatest sufficiency are subject to disappointment, as well (I do not say as much, or as ordinarily and often, but as well) as agents of less sufficiency. The ablest men in any kind may miss of the success they expect as well as weaker men. That men of great sufficiency in this or that way may be defeated of their ends and hopes, Solomon from his own experience assures us in the text. And who is it that upon his own observation cannot set his seal to what he asserts? He gives five instances:

1. The race is not to the swift; not profitable, or successful to him always, but sometimes pernicious and destructive. Many a good runner runs himself into mischief and ruin. Thus Asahel, that is said to be as light of foot as a wild roe, ran after Abner so fast that he lost his life in that overhasty pursuit (II Sam. 2. 18–23). There are times when men that are swift would run from danger and cannot; they have neither power to run, nor success in attempting it (Jer. 46. 6). Sometimes the flight perisheth from the swift, and he that is swift of foot or that rideth the horse, though it be at full speed, cannot deliver himself (Amos 2. 14, 15). It is not absolutely in the power of the

swiftest man to escape danger or win the prize by running.

2. The battle is not to the strong. There is *in Bello Alea*, the chance of war, as they used to speak. There is, as it were, a kind of lottery, a great uncertainty in war. Great armies are sometimes defeated by small and inconsiderable forces: the great host of Midian, by Gideon's three hundred men; the garrison of the Philistines by Jonathan and his armor-bearer. This hath often been observed in the world. Sometimes strong and valiant men are overthrown by those that are in strength far inferior to them, great Goliath by little David. Well might David say, (Psal. 33. 16, 17) "There is no king saved by the multitude of an host: a mighty man is not delivered by much strength. A horse is a vain thing for safety: neither shall he deliver any by his great strength." There are times when "the mighty ones are beaten down" (Jer. 46. 5), and "The mighty cannot deliver himself, or the strong strengthen himself; but the courageous among the mighty is put to flight" (Amos 2. 14, 16). Sometimes the strong melt like water at approaching danger, and the stouthearted are spoiled and sleep their sleep, and the men of might cannot find their hands, to make the least defense or resistance (Psal. 76. 5).

3. Bread is not to the wise. Wise men are not able to get their livelihood, but have much ado to make a shift to get a bare subsistence in the world; and, it may be, are forced to beg for it, or be beholden to the charity of others. There have been strange instances of very wise and worthy persons that have been reduced to such a condition. Some of you know the famous story, *Date Obolum*, or (as others have it) *Panem Belisario* ["Bread for Belisarius"]. David was put to beg his bread of Nabal (I Sam. 25), and Paul was often in hunger and thirst (II Cor. 11. 27).

4. Riches are not to men of understanding. Sometimes indeed, wise men get estates and gather riches, and one would think they should be best accomplish'd for it; and yet it so falls out that some understanding men cannot thrive in the world and grow rich, notwithstanding all their endeavors. So it is that many men of great understanding and rational forecastings and contrivances to gather wealth, though they lay out their parts and their hearts this way,

and would be rich, yet they cannot, but are strangely defeated. You read of the poor wise man (Eccles. 9. 15). Many men of great understandings are too wise and of too great spirits to labor after wealth; or if they do, their designs are unsuccessful.

5. Favor is not to men of skill. Many very wise and knowing and skillful men, and experienced in affairs, and prudent also in their deportment, yet cannot get or keep the favor of princes or people. Some expositors on the place instance in Joseph, that was envied and hated and sold by his brethren, and also lost the favor of Potiphar (though he managed the affairs of his house prudently and prosperously, and deserved well at his hands), and was cast into prison by him. David, that was hated and persecuted by Saul; Daniel, that was cast into the lions' den, though an excellent spirit was found in him, and great prudence and faithfulness in managing the affairs of the empire: and before that, though he had been in great favor and esteem in Nebuchadnezzar's time, yet afterwards, in the reign of Belshazzar, he lived obscure and, as it were, buried at court (as Mr. Cartwright gathers from Dan. 5. 11, 12, 13). Many wise and learned and ingenious men cannot get the favor of men or keep it when they have. The poor wise man delivered the city, and yet no man remembered that same poor man (Eccles. 9. 15). Belisarius (whom I mentioned before) was a most prudent, experienced, faithful general under the Emperor Justinian, that had won him many battles, reduced many cities and countries to his obedience and proved himself for a most loyal, and worthy subject; and yet after all his services, even in that Emperor's time, was, through envy, falsely accused, for ought appears by the story, had his eyes put out, and was forced to stand daily in the temple of Sophia, where he held out his wooden dish, begging his bread, and using those words, "Give a little bread to Belisarius, whom his virtue and valor hath raised, and envy depressed and cast down again." Other scripture testimonies and instances, besides those in the text, might be produced, if it were needful. But every observing man's experience may furnish him with demonstrations of His truth, that agents of greatest sufficiency

among men are subject to disappointments, as well as those of less sufficiency.

2. Agents of little or no sufficiency succeed sometimes in their undertakings, when those of greater sufficiency miscarry and meet with disappointment. There is many times one event to both, as Solomon speaks (Eccles. 9. 2), when the ablest agents are frustrated as well as the weakest; and there is sometimes a better event to weaker agents and instruments; they prosper in their way, when abler men are disappointed. The race is sometimes to the slow, and the swift lose the prize. The battle is sometimes to the weak, and the strong are put to flight, as we have many instances both in scripture and common history. Weak and simple people have bread enough sometimes, when wise men are in want of their daily bread. Nabal had good store, when David was hard put to it. Men of shallow heads grow rich and get great estates, when men of understanding can thrive at no hand. Solomon tells us of the poor wise man, and our savior in that parable (Luke 12. 16, 20) tells us of a rich fool. It is ordinarily seen in the world, that the thriving men in estates are none of the most understanding and judicious. Many a man hath this world-craft, that yet is a man of no deep or solid understanding. So, many weak, worthless, ignorant, empty persons find favor with princes and people, when men of skill and learning and great worth are neglected and despised. This is an evil under the sun, and an error that proceeds from the ruler, a great miscarriage in government, that "folly is set in great dignity" (fools are favored and advanced) "and the rich" (*i.e.*, men of rich endowments for wisdom and piety) "sit in low places" (*i.e.*, are depressed and discountenanced). "Servants are upon horses," men of poor servile spirits and conditions are set up and honored, and princes (*i.e.*, men of great worth) "walking as servants upon the earth" (Eccles. 10. 5, 6, 7). So that it appears plainly that success doth not always wait upon the counsels and actions of persons of great sufficiency, but they may suffer disappointment when others are prosperous. Which demonstrates that the issues and events of undertakings and affairs are not determined infallibly by

the qualifications and accomplishments of created agents and second causes.

Proposition 4. The defeat and disappointment of agents of great sufficiency in their kind is from the happening of time and chance unto them.

Some read it (and the original will bear it) "because" or "for" time and chance happeneth to them all. For explication:

1. By time, understand not barely the duration or spate of time, which hath no such determining influence into human affairs, but time so and so circumstanced. Time is sometimes as much as a special season or opportunity, when there is a concurrence of helps, means, and advantages for the furthering the designs and undertakings of men. By time, sometimes we are to understand such a nick or juncture of time, wherein there is a coincidence of difficulties, disadvantages, and hindrances to the effecting of any business. And this seems the meaning of Solomon in the text: "An adverse or evil time" (Eccles. 9. 12). Sometimes the times favor the enterprises of men, sometimes they frown upon them. At one time, wise and good men stand up for the defense of their country and liberties thereof, and prosper in it; the times favor them, there is a concurrence of all manner of furtherances and advantages. At another time, they may endeavor it and the times frown upon them, the spirit and humor of the people is degenerated, and they swim against the stream and are lost in the attempt. And we say, such a man was worthy of better times, had been a brave man if he had lived in better times, his worth had been more known and prized, and he would have had better success. So when the time of judgment upon a people is come, then wrath ariseth against them without remedy; and then the strong man may fight for the defense of such a country, and the wise man endeavor to deliver the city, but all in vain: they shall miscarry in the undertaking. Aben Ezra (as Mercer tells us) refers this to the conjunctions, and aspects of the stars, by which he apprehended these inferior things were governed. We are sure there are certain periods and revolutions of time, respecting the prosperity or adversity of nations, countries, cities,

churches, families, persons. As time is set to all the successes, so to all the defeats and disappointments of men; and when this time comes, no sufficiency of man can withstand disappointments.

2. By chance, understand contingent and casual events. Many things fall out between the cup and the lip, or otherwise than [men] expect or imagine, or can possibly foresee. Some event chops in and interposeth unexpectedly, to cross a man's designs and defeat his hopes and rational expectations. When Saul and his men were compassing David and his men, and ready to take them, then comes a messenger to Saul, saying, "Haste and come: for the Philistines have invaded the land" (I Sam. 23. 27). When Haman had plotted the ruin of the Jews and brought his design near to an issue, then the king cannot sleep, but calls for the book of the records of the chronicles, and they read to him of the good service of Mordecai in discovering the treason that was plotted against his person; and one thing falls in after another, to defeat Haman's cruel design and ruin the whole fabric of his strong built and almost perfected contrivance. In this sense, time and chance happens to men of greatest sufficiency, which they cannot either foresee (Eccles. 9. 12) or prevent, or help themselves against them when they come upon them. And hereby their counsels and undertakings are defeated and ruined sometimes.

Proposition 5. Time and chance which happens to men in the way of their undertakings is effectually ordered and governed by the Lord. God is the Lord of time, and orderer and governor of all contingencies. Time and chance that further or hinder the designs of men are under the rule and management of the Lord. His counsel sets the times, appoints the chances; His providence dispenses the times and frames the chances that befall men. The Lord hath in His own power the dispensation of times (Eph. 1. 10); "The times and seasons He hath put in His own power" (Acts 1. 7). He hath such a dominion over the times that He changeth times and seasons, according to His own pleasure. "My times," saith David, (Psal. 31. 15) "are in thy hands." He means the state and condition of his times, his prosperities and adversities, his successes and disappointments, and universally, whatever should befall him in the times that should pass over him. Moreover, all the chances that happen to men, as the scripture but now mentioned shows, are in the hand of God: "My times," *i.e.*, the chances of my times. No contingency or emergency or accident so casual but it is ordered and governed by the Lord. The arrow that was shot at a venture and smote Ahab through the joints of his harness was directed at him by the hand of God. So in that case of manslaughter and killing a man casually, as if a man be hewing wood and his hand fetcheth a stroke with the axe to cut down a tree, and the head slippeth from the helve and lighteth upon his neighbor, that he die (Deut. 19. 5). God is said in that case, to deliver that man that is slain "into His hand" (Exod. 21. 13); God ordereth that sad event. All casualties in the world are guided by the steady hand of the great God. "Thou," saith David, (Psal. 16. 5) "maintainest my lot." The Lord makes and disposes the lot or chance of every man, whatever it is. He hath appointed all times and chances in His eternal counsel, and in time executes accordingly, in the course of His providence.

Proposition 6. The great God hath the absolute and infallible determination of the successes and events of all the operations and undertakings of created agents and second causes in His own power. His counsel and sovereign will appoints what they shall be, and His providence (which is not determined by any second cause, but is the determiner of them all) executes accordingly. And it must needs be so, if you consider these two particulars:

1. God is the absolute first cause and supreme Lord of all. "Of Him, and to Him, and through Him are all things" (Rom. 11. 36). He that understands anything of God indeed knows this to be a truth. Here we might be large, as they that are acquainted with the doctrine of creation and providence, in conservation and gubernation of all things, will readily apprehend; for here we might show you:

1. That God is the absolute first cause of all the causal power and virtue that is in creatures. He gives them power to act, furnisheth them with a sufficiency for their opera-

tions. He gives swiftness to the runner; skill, and strength, and courage, to the soldier.

2. That He supports and continues the active power of the creature. He continues swiftness, wisdom, strength, courage, as He pleaseth. If He withdraw, all is gone: the swift is lame or slow-footed, the strong is weak and timorous, the wise is foolish and besotted, the man of skill is a mere bungler at anything.

3. That He doth by a previous influx excite and stir up and actuate the active power of the creature, and set all the wheels going. For the most operative, active created virtue is not a pure act, but hath some potentiality mixed with it; and therefore cannot put forth itself into action unless it be set going by the first cause. And the creature cannot be the absolute first cause of any physical action. "In Him we live, and move" (Acts 17. 28).

Again, 4. That He determines and applies second causes to the objects of their actions. When they stand, as it were, *in Bivio*, as it is said of Nebuchadnezzar when he was marching with his army, he "stood at the parting of the way, at the head of the two ways, to use divination," as doubting which way he had best to march, whether to Jerusalem or some other way (Ezek. 21. 21, 22). Then the Lord casts the scale and the lot, and determines them this way and not another. He doth not only stir up second causes to act at large, and set them going, and leave it to their own inclination whither they shall go and what they shall do, but He leads them forth and determines them to this or that object.

5. That He coöperates, and works jointly with second causes in producing their effects. As He predetermines second causes, so He concurs with them in their operations. And this predetermination and concurse is so necessary, that there can be no real effect produced by the creature without it. And it is a truth also, that when God improves second causes for the production of any effect, He so concurs with them that He doth withal most immediately, intimously, and without dependence upon these causes by which He acts, produce the entity or *esse* of the effect. If this be considered, it will appear that created agents are,

as it were, God's instruments that act as they are acted by Him and cannot move of themselves. The busy, bustling, proud Assyrian was so (Isa. 10. 15).

6. That all the *ataxia*, disorder, irregularity, moral evil that is found in the actions of rational agents is by His permission. If it were not the pleasure of God to permit it, no sin should be in the world nor in the actions of men. Though there is no legal permission or allowance of it (for the law of God forbids it), yet there is a providential permission of it. God could have kept it out of His world.

7. That He limits and sets bounds to the actions of second causes: what they shall do, and how far they shall proceed in this or that way. He set bounds to Satan when he had commission to afflict Job. He limits and restrains the eruptions of the wrath and rage of the church's adversaries (Psal. 76. 10). He sets bounds to the sinful actions of men: He regulates and governs all the actions of second causes as to time, place, degrees, and all manner of circumstances. He is not the author, but He is the orderer of sin itself.

8. That He serves Himself and His own ends of all second causes. He makes them all, in all their operations, subservient to His own designs and that not only natural but rational agents that act by counsel. And not only such of them as are His professed willing servants; many serve God's ends beside their intentions and against their wills. I will do this and that, saith God, by the Assyrian: "Howbeit He meaneth not so" (Isa. 10. 6, 7). Wicked men and devils do God's will against their own will and beside their intentions. "Ye thought evil against me," saith Joseph to his brethren, "but God meant it for good" (Gen. 50. 20). God elicits what good He pleases out of the actions of His creatures. Whatever this or that agent proposeth to himself, yet God always attaineth His ends. He serves Himself of the very sins of His creatures, and brings good out of them. He makes that which is not *bonum honestum* to be *bonum conducibile;* and though sin is not good, yet, as God orders the matter, it is good, in order to many holy ends, that sin should be in the world, as Austin observes.

9. That He useth means in themselves unfit, and im-

proves agents of themselves insufficient, to bring about His own purposes and produce marvelous effects. Yea, and it is as easy with Him to do anything by weak and insufficient as by the ablest and most accomplished instruments. "There is no restraint to the Lord to save by many, or by few" (I Sam. 14. 6). "It is nothing with Him to help, whether with many or with them that have no power." (II Chron. 14. 11). Despicable instruments, sometimes, do great things in His hand.

10. That He renders the aptest means ineffectual, and the undertakings of the most sufficient agents unsuccessful, when He pleases. He hath a negative voice upon all the counsels and endeavors and active power of the creature. He can stop the sun in its course and cause it to withdraw its shining; He can give check to the fire, that it shall not burn, and to the hungry lions, that they shall not devour; and He can order it so, that the men of might shall "sleep their sleep and not find their hands." He can break the ranks of the most orderly soldiers, take away courage from the stoutest hearts, send a panic fear into a mighty host, and defeat the counsels of the wisest leaders and conductors. He can blow upon and blast the likeliest undertakings of the ablest men. In a word: the Lord being the absolute first cause and supreme governor of all His creatures and all their actions, though He hath set an order among His creatures—this shall be the cause of that effect, etc.—yet He Himself is not tied to that order but interrupts the course of it when He pleases. The Lord reserves a liberty to Himself to interpose and to umpire matters of success and event, contrary to the law and common rule of second causes. And though He ordinarily concurreth with second causes according to the law given and order set, yet sometimes there is in His providence a variation and digression. Though He hath given creatures power to act, and man to act as a cause by counsel, and hath furnished him with active abilities, yet He hath not made any creature master of events, but reserves the disposal of issues and events to Himself. Herein the absolute sovereignty and dominion of God appears.

2. Otherwise, the Lord might possibly suffer real dis-

appointment, and be defeated of His ends in some instances. He might be cross'd in his designs if any of His creatures could do what they will without absolute dependence upon Him. He could not be sure of His ends, and what He designs in the world, if He had not command of all events that may further or hinder them. If there were any active power in creatures that He cannot control, or any one event that is out of His reach and absolutely in the creature's power, exempted from His providential command, it would be possible that He might be defeated of His ends, and so far unhappy, as to His voluntary happiness, which results from His having His pleasure done in the world and compassing all His ends in the works of creation and providence. God hath made all things, ruleth all things, and manageth all things, according to the counsel of His will, in a way of subserviency to Himself and His own occasions, which He could not do universally and infrustrably if He had not the absolute and infallible determination of all events in His own hand. "But His counsel shall stand, and He will do all His pleasure" (Isa. 46. 10). Thus much for the explication, and confirmation of the doctrine.

Use I. Of instruction, in these particulars:

1. We see what a poor dependent, nothing-creature proud man is, depending absolutely upon God for his being, actions, and the success of them. Men of greatest sufficiency cannot get their own bread or bring anything to effect in their own strength. Let their abilities be what they will (swiftness, for the race; strength, for the battle; wisdom, for getting their bread, etc.), yet they shall stand them in no stead without the concurrence and blessing of God. Man saith, he will do this and that; but he must ask God leave first. He saith, "Today or tomorrow I will go to such a place, and buy and sell, and get gain," whereas he knows not what shall be; but it shall certainly be as the Lord will. The way of man is not in himself; it is not in man that walketh to direct his steps, nor perform anything that he purposeth, without divine concurrence or permission. He hath not the success of any of his actions in his own power, nor doth he know that anything he doth shall pros-

per. One would wonder, poor dependent man should be
so proud! Any little thing lifts him up. When the soldier on
such occasions as these is in his bravery, in his military
garb dressed up for the purpose, with his buff coat, his
scarf, his rich belt, his arms, a good horse under him—
O what a goodly creature is he in his own eyes! And what
wonders can he do in his own conceit! And yet he hath as
absolute need of God's assistance, if he go forth to battle,
as any naked, unarmed man. He cannot move a step, or
fetch his next breath, or bring his hand to his mouth, or leap
over a straw, or do anything, without help from God, "in
whose hand his breath is, and whose are all his ways"
(Dan. 5. 23). It's strange to see how the hearts of men are
lifted up with nothing! O cease ye from man, for wherein
is he to be accounted of?

2. We see that there is, and there is not chance in the
world. Chance there is, in respect of second causes (so
some things fall out κατα Ευγκυριαν as our savior speaks
[Luke 10. 31]), but no chance as to the first cause. That
piece of atheism and heathenism ascribing things to fortune
and chance is hardly rooted out of the minds of men that
are or should be better instructed and informed. The Philistines, when they were plagued, could not tell whether God
had done it or a mere chance happened to them (I Sam.
6. 9). They understood not that what was a chance to
them was ordered by the providence of God. Truth is,
chance is something that falls out beside the scope, intention and foresight of man, the reason and cause whereof
may be hid from him, and so it excludes the counsel of
men; but it doth not exclude the counsel and providence
of God, but is ordered and governed thereby. And it is so
far from being chance to God, that there is as much (if
not more) of the wisdom, and will and power of God appearing in matters of chance and contingency as in any
other events.

3. We see here something of the power, and greatness,
and glory of God appearing in His efficiency, whereby He
works all in all. As He is Himself independent, so all things
have an absolute dependence on Him. He gives success or
causeth disappointment as He pleaseth. So that men are

wholly beholden to Him for all the good they enjoy: for victory, for bread, for riches, for favor and acceptance, for all. Nothing comes to pass without His permission, if it be moral evil; without His concurse and coöperation, yea, predetermination, if it be moral or physical good, or penal evil. In Him we live and move and have our being. The counsels of the ablest statesmen, how rational soever, shall not prosper without Him; ministers, how sufficient soever, pious, learned, industrious, zealous, shall convert no man, edify no man, comfort and establish no man, without Him (I Cor. 3. 6, 7). Though scholars study hard, they shall make no proficiency without the blessing of God. The merchant may trade and project rationally, and yet shall not grow rich upon it, unless God give him success. It is God that maketh Zebulun rejoice in his going out, and Issachar in his tents, that crowns the labors of seamen, merchants and husbandmen with success. "Except the Lord build the house" (Psal. 127, 1). Training days, artillery days, though of great use and very necessary, yet are all in vain unless the Lord bless. He must instruct and teach and accomplish you; otherwise the help of your expert officers and your own endeavors to learn war, will signify nothing. And when valiant soldiers come to fight, whatever skill and strength and courage and conduct and advantages they have, yet they will be worsted if the Lord do not give success. We should learn hence to admire the power and greatness of God. It is a lamentable thing that He that doth all is thought to do nothing! He can work without means, by insufficient means, and blast the ablest instruments— and yet is little minded in the world. God gives forth a challenge to idols: "Do good"—if you can—"or do evil" (Isa. 41. 23). It is God's prerogative to do good or evil— i.e., not the evil of sin (which argues defect and impotency, and comes not within the compass of omnipotency to do it), but of punishment. God only can give good or award bad success, and reward or correct and punish His creatures that way. "Who is he that saith" (what man or angel?) "and it cometh to pass, when the Lord commandeth it not" (Lam. 3. 37)? O see and adore the greatness of God in this respect! He works all in all. . . .

First, whatever your own sufficiency may be, yet acknowledge God thankfully, as if you had been wholly insufficient: for your sufficiency is of God, and He could have disappointed notwithstanding. The ground of our unthankfulness for all good issues and events of affairs and undertakings is because we do not see the good hand of God dispensing all to us. We make too little of God and too much of ourselves, either by thinking we deserve better than God hath done for us (hence a proud heart is never thankful to God or man), or by thinking we have done all, or more than we have done, toward the getting of this or that mercy. We put ourselves too much in the place of God, as if it were in our power to make our endeavors successful and to give good effect and issue to them, according to our desire. We get up into God's throne, and usurp upon His prerogative and assume that which is peculiar to Him, when we presume we can bring anything to pass or do anything successfully in our own strength. If we make ourselves the only and absolute first causes of our good success, no marvel we make ourselves the last end also, and deny God the glory. O, do not ascribe good success to your own wit and parts and policy and industry, and say: "My nimbleness hath won the race, my conduct and courage hath won the battle, my wisdom hath gotten me this bread, my understanding hath heaped up this wealth, my dexterity and skill and complaisance and agreeable conversation hath procured me the favor of rulers or people, my parts or study hath given me this learning." Say not with the vaporing Assyrian: "By the strength of my hand I have done it, and by my wisdom; for I am prudent" (Isa. 10. 13). Let not this be so much as the secret language of your hearts. Say not, as Nebuchadnezzar: "This is great Babylon, which I have built," and so derogate from God that works all in all: lest He turn you a-grazing, as He did him, with the beasts of the field, and teach you better manners by some severe correction. Do not sacrifice to your own nets, and burn incense to your drags, as if by them your portion were fat and meat plenteous (Hab. 1. 16), but ascribe all to God.

There is that deep wickedness in the hearts of men, that

if they get anything by any fraud and crafty fetches and overreaching of their brethren, in a sinful way, they will be too ready to attribute that to the providence and blessing of God, and say, it was God's providence that cast it in upon them, when they have been craftily and sinfully designing it and bringing it about; but when they have gotten anything honestly, by their wisdom and prudence and industry, they are too ready to forget providence and ascribe all to themselves. See the evil of this, and remember that no people in the world have greater cause of thankfulness than we have to God, who hath governed time and chance on our behalf marvelously. O, bless Him for good success, not only when you cannot but acknowledge your own insufficiency, but also when you have apprehensions of the greatest sufficiency of second causes. And "Blessed forever be the Lord, who hath pleasure in the prosperity of His servants" (Psal. 35. 27).

Secondly, acknowledge God also in all your frustrations and disappointments, so as to resent His disposals and dispensations towards you in a gracious manner. We have met with many disappointments in the late war, and in other respects. We should see God in all. When He blasts our corn, defeats our soldiers, frowns upon our merchants, and we are disappointed—now acknowledge the hand of God, ordering time, and chance according to His good pleasure. Justify God in all, and bear such frustrations patiently. When you have done your duty, be quiet, though the event doth not answer your endeavors and hopes. Take heed of quarreling at God's disappointments. Do you know whom you have to do with? "I was dumb, I opened not my mouth, because Thou didst it" (Psal. 89. 9). If we look at faulty instruments, or at mere chance only, we shall be apt to murmur. . . . And if we look at disappointments as our bad fortune and chance only, looking no further, we shall be apt to fret and quarrel. But if we do indeed see God ordering our lot for us, it may and ought to silence us. When magistrates have done their duty, according to the law of God and of the country, and endeavored faithfully to give check and stop to the inundation of profaneness and heresy, and yet the bad genius of the times and de-generous humor of the people, and this or that emergency happens, that frustrates the success of their counsels and endeavors, truly they may sit down and mourn indeed; but yet humbly submit to the all-disposing providence of God. When ministers have labored faithfully, and yet Israel is not gathered, and their labors seem to be in vain, not successful in converting sinners, they may weep in secret indeed; but yet patiently bear the unsuccessfulness of their ministry from the hand of God. When soldiers have showed themselves valiant and faithful, and done what they can, and yet are worsted, they must acknowledge God's hand in it, and that "the battle is the Lord's" (I Sam. 17. 47), who governeth the war and determines the victory on what side He pleaseth. All men have briars and thorns springing up in the way of their callings, as well as husbandmen, and meet with difficulties and crosses therein. Get the spirit David had (II Sam. 15. 25, 26), and so acknowledge God in everything, as to submit humbly to His disposals, even when they are adverse and cross to your desires and expectations.

Thirdly, be always prepared for disappointments. Do not promise yourselves success from the sufficiency of second causes; God may determine otherwise. . . . Events are not in the creature's power. The Lord sometimes disappoints men of greatest sufficiency, overrules and controls their counsels and endeavors, and blasts them strangely. Time and chance happens to them. If Adam had stood, though he would not have had the determination of events and successes in his own hand, yet God would have determined them for him according to his heart's desire, and he should never have been disappointed. But since the fall, as no man hath power to determine events (which is God's prerogative), so it is just with God that every man should meet with crosses and disappointments; and this is the fruit of the curse, under which all natural men lie.

And as for the people of God, though they are delivered from the curse of the law, in the formality of it, so that nothing befalls them as a curse, how cross soever it be, yet they are not yet absolutely delivered from the matter of the curse, as appears by the afflictions they meet with, and death itself. And indeed it makes sometimes for the glory of God, to disappoint men of greatest abilities. When men do not see and own God, but attribute success to the sufficiency of instruments, it's time for God to maintain His own right, . . . and show that He gives or denies success, according to His own good pleasure. God is much seen in controlling the ablest agents, and blasting their enterprises: yea, more, many times, than in backing them and blessing their endeavors in an ordinary course of providence. Herein the wisdom of God is much seen. It is best, sometimes, it should be so, with respect to God's interest and glory. His power also appears in giving check to the ablest instruments, and turning all their designs another way than they intended. His mercy also to His people is seen herein: for it is best for them, in some cases, to be defeated and disappointed. His justice also appears herein, in His correcting and punishing the self-confident, sinful creature with unexpected disappointments.

So that it is our wisdom to look for changes and chances, some occurrences and emergencies that may blast our undertakings, that faith and prayer may be kept going, and lest if such frustrations befall us unexpectedly, we either fly out against God, or faint and sink in discouragements. At the first going out of our forces, in the beginning of the war, what great apprehensions were there of speedy success and ending of the war—that it was but going and appearing, and the enemy would be faced down as if the first news from our soldiers should be, *venimus, vidimus, vicimus* ["we came, we saw, we conquered"]. And several times after, great probability of concluding that unhappy war: and yet all disappointed, contrary to expectation. When there is therefore greatest probability of success, yet remember there may be disappointment, and provide for it, that you may not be surprised thereby. This may be good counsel to men of projecting heads, that are wont to be very confident that they see their way far before them, but they do not know what time and chance may happen. This may check the confidence of man, and teach us not to promise ourselves great things, or build upon this or that event or enjoyment for time to come. Labor to be prepared and provided for disappointments.

8. SAMUEL SEWALL, 1652–1730

[Sewall's father came to New England in 1634, returned to England (where Samuel was born), and brought the family back to America after the Restoration. Samuel Sewall thus graduated from Harvard College in 1671, but after his marriage to Hannah Hull, daughter of the wealthiest man in the colony, he found himself so engrossed in worldly affairs that he gave up the effort to become a clergyman. He held offices under the old charter, was sent to England as a colleague negotiator with Increase Mather in 1688, and as member of the Council under the new charter was a judge at the special court in Salem, in 1692. He continued to serve as judge, and from 1718 to 1728 was chief justice of the colony.

Like many serious Puritans, dedicated to deciphering the often baffling history of the Covenant of Grace, Sewall occupied his leisure with an examination of Biblical prophecies; in 1697 he published in Boston *Phaenomena quaedam Apocalyptica ad Aspectum Novi Orbis configurata*, which is an attempt, amid a staggering array of pedantry, to calculate the place of America in the future drama of history. Suddenly reminded of Plum Island, off Newbury, where his father owned land and where he himself had played as a boy, portly Judge Sewall finds himself carried away into this prose poem on the earthly, the sensuous, delicacies of the land he, good Puritan as he resolutely was, had learned to love with a fervor as passionate as that which he held in reserve for the heavenly kingdom. It is not too much to say that this cry of the heart signalizes a point at which the English Puritan had, hardly with conscious knowledge, become an American, rooted in the American soil.]

PHAENOMENA

Captain John Smith, in his *History* published *anno* 1624, affirms that he found New England well inhabited with a goodly, strong and well-proportioned people. And the proverb is, "Show me the man and not the meat." And if men can be contented with the food and raiment intended in I Tim. 6. 8, they need not fear subsisting where ash, chestnut, hazel, oak and walnut do naturally and plentifully grow. But for this, let Mr. Morden be consulted, to whom New England is beholden for the fair character given them in his *Geography*. It is remarkable that Mr. Parker, who was a successful schoolmaster at Newbury in Barkshire in the happy days of Dr. Twisse, was much about this time preaching and proving at Ipswich in Essex that the passengers came over upon good grounds, and that God would multiply them as He did the children of Israel. His text was Exod. 1. 7. As Mr. Nicholas Noyes, who was an auditor and is yet living, lately informed me, Mr. Parker was at this time (1634) principally concerned in beginning Newbury, where the learned and ingenious Mr. Benjamin Woodbridge, Dr. Twisse's successor, had part of his education under his uncle Parker. Mary Brown (now Godfry) the first-born of Newbury is yet alive, and is become the mother and grandmother of many children. And so many have been born after her in the town that they make two assemblies, wherein God is solemnly worshiped every Sabbath day.

And as long as Plum Island shall faithfully keep the commanded post, notwithstanding all the hectoring words and hard blows of the proud and boisterous ocean; as long as any salmon or sturgeon shall swim in the streams of Merrimac, or any perch or pickerel in Crane Pond; as long as the sea-fowl shall know the time of their coming, and not neglect seasonably to visit the places of their acquaintance; as long as any cattle shall be fed with the grass growing in the meadows which do humbly bow down themselves before Turkey Hill; as long as any sheep shall walk upon Old Town Hill, and shall from thence pleasantly look down upon the river Parker and the fruitful marshes lying beneath; as long as any free and harmless doves shall find a white oak or other tree within the township to perch or feed or build a careless nest upon, and shall voluntarily present themselves to perform the office of gleaners after barley harvest; as long as nature shall not grow old and dote, but shall constantly remember to give the rows of Indian corn their education by pairs: so long shall Christians be born there, and being first made meet, shall from thence be translated, to be made partakers of the Inheritance of the saints in light.

9. COTTON MATHER, 1663–1728

[To modern taste, Cotton Mather repeatedly embodies the more unlovely aspects of the Puritan character; however, he is a highly complex being, sometimes heroic, and not to be summed up in a formula. As historian and preacher of jeremiads he looks backward, striving to keep unchanged the pattern of the founders; at the same time, as scientist welcoming Newton, as advocate of inoculation, as a prose master who could turn from the archaic pedantries of the *Magnalia* to a fluency in the newer, more colloquial, manner, he looks forward to the American Enlightenment.

After a decade or so of the new charter, Mather realized that though the clergy kept some influence in terms of prestige, they could no longer expect to control a government that owed its being to the crown and not to a covenant of the saints. Also sensitively aware that in England and in Germany Protestantism was abandoning the whole conception of political revolution, Mather endeavored to redirect New England Puritanism toward a similar renovation of piety, into pure Pietism, in which charity, simple conviction, and the religious regulation of daily life would take the place of the covenant, abstruse theology, and the conquest of power. In this effort he produced in 1710 *Bonifacius*, generally known by its running title, *Essays to Do Good*.

Its effect on American Protestantism, outside as well as inside New England, was pervasive for over a century. Benjamin Franklin was the foremost to testify to its influence, even upon himself. It marks the end of primitive Puritanism because it turned the religious energy from concentration upon social organization and the purely personal conscience toward a generalized concern with good works and social leadership. Behind the reformulation was still a hope that control might be achieved, but not now by legislation or by compulsion: the new engine would be moral example and the unofficial mobilization of pious conformity.

Accepting the fact that the structure of society had become secularized, Mather prescribed rules for Christian conduct to all the specialized callings—magistrates, doctors, schoolmasters, farmers, ladies, lawyers—not assuming that they were knit, as Winthrop had demanded, into one fabric of mutual dependence, but exhorting them all to assume as part of their status the responsibility of making the moral best of their situations. By trying to form the righteous into "societies" instead of into a society, Mather would subject the unrighteous to an ostracism more formidable than any pronounced by the General Court. The section on the Christian's duty toward his "neighborhood" succinctly marks the transformation that was wrought in the Puritan code between the time of Winthrop and John Cotton and the eighteenth century.]

BONIFACIUS

Methinks, this excellent zeal should be carried into our Neighborhood. Neighbors! you stand related unto one another. And you should be full of devices that all the neighbors may have cause to be glad of your being in the neighborhood. We read: "The righteous is more excellent than his neighbor." But we shall scarce own him so, except he be more excellent *as* a neighbor. He must excel in the duties of good neighborhood. Let that man be better than his neighbor who labors to be a better neighbor, to do most good unto his neighbor.

And here first: the poor people that lie wounded must have wine and oil poured into their wounds. It was a charming stroke in the character which a modern prince had given to him: "To be in distress is to deserve his favor." O good neighbor, put on that princely, that more than royal quality! See who in the neighborhood may deserve thy favor. We are told: "This is pure religion and undefiled" (a jewel that neither is counterfeit nor has any flaws in it), "to visit the fatherless and widows in their affliction." The orphans and widows, and so all the children of affliction in the neighborhood, must be visited and relieved with all agreeable kindness.

Neighbors—be concerned that the orphans and widows in your neighborhood may be well provided for. They meet with grievous difficulties, with unknown temptations. While their next relatives were yet living, they were, perhaps, but meanly provided for. What must they now be in their more solitary condition? Their condition should be considered, and the result of the consideration should be: "I delivered the orphan that had no helper, and I caused the heart of the widow to sing for joy."

By consequence, all the afflicted in the neighborhood are to be thought upon. Sirs, would it be too much for you at least once in a week to think: "What neighbor is reduced into a pinching and painful poverty? Or in any degree impoverished with heavy losses?" Think: "What neighbor is languishing with sickness, especially if sick with sore maladies and of some continuance?" Think: "What neighbor is heartbroken with sad bereavements, bereaved of desirable relatives?" And think: "What neighbor has a soul buffeted and hurried with violent assaults of the wicked one?" But then think: "What shall be done for such neighbors?"

First: you will pity them. The evangelical precept is: "Have compassion one of another—be pitiful." It was of old, and ever will be, the just expectation: "To him that is afflicted, pity should be shown." And let our pity to them flame out in our prayer for them. It were a very lovely practice for you, in the daily prayer of your closet every evening, to think: "What miserable object have I seen to-day that I may do well now to mention for the mercies of the Lord?"

But this is not all. 'Tis possible, 'tis probable, you may do well to visit them: and when you visit them, comfort them. Carry them some good word which may raise a gladness in an heart stooping with heaviness.

And lastly: give them all the assistances that may answer their occasions. Assist them with advice to them, assist them with address to others for them. And if it be needful, be-stow your alms upon them: "Deal thy bread to the hungry; bring to thy house the poor that are cast out; when thou seest the naked, cover him." At least Nazianzen's charity, I pray: *Si nihil habes, da lacrymulam*—"If you have noth-ing else to bestow upon the miserable, bestow a tear or two upon their miseries." This little is better than noth-ing. . . .

In moving for the devices of good neighborhood, a prin-cipal motion which I have to make is that you consult the spiritual interests of your neighborhood as well as the temporal. Be concerned lest the deceitfulness of sin undo any of the neighbors. If there be any idle persons among them, I beseech you, cure them of their idleness. Don't nourish 'em and harden 'em in that, but find employment for them. Find 'em work; set 'em to work; keep 'em to work. Then, as much of your other bounty to them as you please.

If any children in the neighborhood are under no edu-cation don't allow 'em to continue so. Let care be taken that they may be better educated, and be taught to read, and be taught their catechism and the truths and ways of their only savior.

One more: if any in the neighborhood are taking to bad courses—lovingly and faithfully admonish them. If any in the neighborhood are enemies to their own welfare or fam-ilies—prudently dispense your admonitions unto them. If there are any prayerless families, never leave off entreating and exhorting of them till you have persuaded them to set up the worship of God. If there be any service of God or of His people to which anyone may need to be excited,

give him a tender excitation. Whatever snare you see anyone in, be so kind as to tell him of his danger to be en-
snared, and save him from it. By putting of good books
into the hands of your neighbors, and gaining of them a
promise to read the books—who can tell what good you
may do unto them! It is possible you may in this way, with
ingenuity and with efficacy, administer those reproofs
which you may owe unto such neighbors as are to be reproved for their miscarriages. The books will balk nothing
that is to be said on the subjects that you would have the
neighbors advised upon.

Finally: if there be any base houses, which threaten to
debauch and poison and confound the neighborhood, let
your charity to your neighbors make you do all you can for
the suppression of them.

That my proposal to do good in the neighborhood and
as a neighbor may be more fully formed and followed, I
will conclude it with minding you that a world of self-denial
is to be exercised in the execution of it. You must be armed
against selfishness, all selfish and squinting intentions in
your generous resolutions. You shall see how my demands
will grow upon you.

First: you must not think of making the good you do a
pouring of water into a pump to draw out something for
yourselves. This might be the meaning of our savior's direction: "Lend, hoping for nothing again." To lend a thing,
properly is to hope that we shall receive it again. But this
probably refers to the Ερανισμθ, or collation usual among
the ancients, whereof we find many monuments and mentions in antiquity. If any man by burnings or shipwrecks
or other disasters had lost his estate, his friends did use to
lend him considerable sums of money, to be repaid not at
a certain day but when he should find himself able to repay it without inconvenience. Now, they were so cunning
that they would rarely lend upon such disasters unto any
but such as they had hope would recover out of their present impoverishment, and not only repay them their money
but also requite their kindness, if ever there should be
need of it. The thing required by our savior is: "Do good
unto such as you are never like to be the better for."

But then, there is yet an higher thing to be demanded. That is: "Do good unto those neighbors who have done hurt unto you." So says our savior: "Love your enemies; bless them that curse you; do good to them that hate you, and pray for them which despitefully use you and persecute you." Yea, if an injury have been done you, improve it as a provocation to do a benefit unto him who did the injury. This is noble! It will bring marvelous consolations! Another method might make you even with your forward neighbors: this will set you above them all. It were nobly done if, in the close of the day when you are alone before the Lord, you make a particular prayer for the pardon and prosperity of any person from whom you may have suffered any abuse in the day. And it would be nobly done if, at last calling over the catalogue of such as have been abusive to you, you may be able to say (the only intention that can justify your doing anything like to keeping a catalogue of them!): "There is not one of these but I have done him, or watched to do him, a kindness." Among the Jews themselves there were the Hasideans, one of whose institutions it was to make this daily prayer unto God: *Remitte et condona omnibus qui vexant nos* ["Forgive all who trouble and harass us"]. Christians—go beyond them! Yea, Justin Martyr tells us, in primitive times they did so: "Praying for their enemies."

But I won't stop here. There is yet an higher thing to be demanded. That is: do good unto those neighbors who will speak ill of you after you have done it. So says our savior: "Ye shall be the children of the highest: he is kind unto the unthankful and unto the evil." You will every day find, I can tell you, monsters of ingratitude. Yea, if you distinguish any person with doing for him something more than you have done for others, it will be well if that very person do not at some time or other hurt you wonderfully. Oh! the wisdom of divine providence in ordering this thing! Sirs, it is that you may do good on a divine principle: good merely for the sake of good! "Lord, increase our faith!"

And God forbid that a Christian faith should not come up to a Jewish! There is a memorable passage in the Jewish records. There was a gentleman of whose bounty many people every day received reliefs and succors. One day he asked: "Well, what do our people say today?" They told him: "Why, the people partook of your kindnesses and services, and then they blessed you very fervently." "Did they so?" said he, "Then I shall have no great reward for this day." Another day he asked: "Well, and what say our people now?" They told him: "Alas, good sir, the people enjoyed your kindnesses today, and when all was done, they did nothing but rail at you." "Indeed!" said he, "Now for this day I am sure that God will give me a good and great reward."

Though vile constructions and harsh invectives be never so much the present reward of doing the best offices for the neighborhood, yet, my dear Boniface, be victorious over all discouragements. "Thy work shall be well rewarded," saith the Lord.

If your opportunities to do good reach no further, yet I will offer you a consolation, which one has elegantly thus expressed: "He that praises God only on a ten-stringed instrument, with his authority extending but unto his family and his example but unto his neighborhood, may have as thankful an heart here, and as high a place in the celestial choir hereafter, as the greatest monarch that praiseth God upon a ten-thousand-stringed instrument, upon the loud sounding organ having as many millions of pipes as there be people under him."

10.   SOLOMON STODDARD, 1643–1729

[Born to a leading mercantile family of Boston, Solomon Stoddard graduated from Harvard in 1662 and in 1669 was called to the remote frontier fortress of Northampton. In a few years he became "Pope Stoddard," ecclesiastical autocrat of the whole Connecticut Valley, his empire extending to Saybrook and New Haven. He abolished the covenant entirely, both institutional and theoretical, took or drove all the town into the church, and ruled it by sheer force of personality. Between 1700 and 1710 Increase and Cotton Mather waged with him a bitter pamphlet war over his "Presbyterian" innovations (even as, in 1705, Cotton Mather was attempting to work a few of them into eastern Massachusetts, and so exciting the wrath of John Wise). The battle ended formally as a draw, but in reality it was a defeat for the Mathers, since the ecclesiastical independence of the west was won.

In the course of this debate, the Mathers repeatedly invoked the example of the founders, intending to crush Stoddard under the scandal of having deviated from their sacred norm. Finally exasperated, Stoddard several times replied with such a blast as is here reprinted. Even more than Cotton Mather's turn to social pietism, Stoddard's radicalism marks, in one sense, the end of the Puritan era. However, though Stoddard was anything but a liberal, he was a magnificent individual; he now made explicit that deep-seated reliance on the self which was from the beginning a hidden but irresistible thrust of the Puritan theology. This spirit of sublime self-reliance in the struggle for realizing the Christian life Stoddard bequeathed to his grandson and successor, Jonathan Edwards, who was joined to him as colleague in 1727. In 1740 Edwards led New England to a reassertion of the primitive passion, but not within the framework of the ancestral covenant: instead, he employed new and revolutionary conceptions of science and psychology.]

CONCERNING ANCESTORS

As the renown of those Reformers is a bulwark against those errors that were exploded by them, so we find ourselves embarrassed by their mistakes from proceeding in the work of reformation, as if it were criminal not to mistake with them.

It may possibly be a fault and an aggravation of a fault to depart from the ways of our fathers; but it may also be a virtue and an eminent act of obedience to depart from them in some things. Men are wont to make a great noise, that we are bringing in of innovations and depart from the old way. But it is beyond me to find out wherein the iniquity does lie. We may see cause to alter some practices of our fathers without despising of them, without priding ourselves on our own wisdom, without apostasy, without abusing the advantages that God has given us, without a spirit of compliance with corrupt men, without inclinations to superstition, without making disturbance in the church of God. And there is no reason that it should be turned as a reproach upon us.

Surely it is commendable for us to examine the practices of our fathers; we have no sufficient reason to take practices upon trust from them. Let them have as high a character as belongs to them, yet we may not look upon their principles as oracles. Nathan himself missed it in his conjecture about building the house of God. He that believes principles because they affirm them makes idols of them. And it would be no humility but baseness of spirit for us to judge ourselves uncapable to examine the principles that have been handed down to us. If we be any ways fit to open the mysteries of the Gospel, we are capable to judge of these matters; and it would ill become us so to indulge ourselves in ease as to neglect the examination of received principles. If the practices of our fathers in any particulars were mistakes, it is fit they should be rejected; if they be not, they will bear examination. If we be forbidden to examine their practices, that will cut off all hopes of reformation. . . .

The mistakes of one generation many times become the calamity of succeeding generations. The present generation are not only unhappy by reason of the darkness of their own minds, but the errors of those who have gone before them have been a foundation of a great deal of misery. Posterity is very prone to espouse the principles of ancestors, and from an inordinate veneration of them to apprehend a sacredness in their opinions, and don't give themselves the trouble to make an impartial examination of them—as if it were a transgression to call them into question, and bordered upon irreligion to be wavering about them. And the carnal interests of many persons has no small influence upon them, to prevail with them to engage violently in the vindication of them.

And if any particular persons have been led by God into the understanding of those mistakes, and have made their differing sentiments public, it has proved an occasion of much sorrow; and many people have fallen into parties, whereby a spirit of love has been quenched and great heats have risen, from whence have proceeded censures and reproaches, and sometimes separation and persecution.

CHAPTER FOUR

PERSONAL NARRATIVE

1. THOMAS SHEPARD, 1605-1649

[In recounting the history of an individual, whether of another or of himself, the Puritan faced the same antinomy he confronted when writing the history of a people. On the one hand, he had to tell everything, for who could say, since whatever happens from day to day comes out of the providence of God, that the slightest event was without portentous significance? Yet on the other hand, a life story had to be an example—an *exemplum*—whether for good or evil; it had to be organized into a drama, in which the ultimate meaning would emerge out of a welter of fact.

Furthermore, the achievement of form amid detail was made still more complex because few persons were any more led, as was Paul on the road to Damascus, to a dramatic climax of revelation so emphatic that their lives were formed into a rising and falling action. The grace of God, as most men experience it, is elusive; though certainty is written in the tables of divine election, and though the true saint will persevere no matter what sins he falls into, still the sins of the best of men are terribly visible, while the book remains inaccessible to mortals. The creature lives inwardly a life of incessant fluctuation, ecstatically elated this day, depressed into despair the next. The science of biography required clinical skill in narrating these surgings and sinkings, all the time striving to keep the line of the story clear.

If this was a difficult task when recounting the career of some ultimately victorious Christian, what about one's self? The result of the nagging question was that almost every Puritan kept a diary, not so much because he was infatuated with himself but because he needed a strict account of God's dealings with him, so that at any moment, and above all at the moment of death, he could review the long transaction. Or if he himself could not get the benefit of the final reckoning, then his children could; they might find help in their own affairs by studying those of their parent.

In this spirit, and for edification of his children, Thomas Shepard told his story. We may incidentally perceive in it the seeds of that peculiar form of self-reliance—that tacit assurance that in the end of all every man is responsible for his own salvation or damnation—that we have seen blossom in the assertion of Solomon Stoddard.]

AUTOBIOGRAPHY

The first two years I spent in Cambridge was in studying and in my neglect of God and private prayer, which I had sometime used. I did not regard the Lord at all unless it were at some fits. The third year wherein I was sophister, I began to be foolish and proud and to show myself in the public Schools, and there to be a disputer about things which now I see I did not know then at all, but only prated about them. Toward the end of this year, when I was most vile (after I had been next unto the gates of death by the smallpox the year before), the Lord began to call me home to the fellowship of His grace, which was in this manner:

I do remember that I had many good affections (but blind and inconstant) oft cast into me since my father's sickness, by the spirit of God wrestling with me, and hence I would pray in secret. Hence when I was at Cambridge, I heard old Dr. Chadderton, the master of the College when I came; the first year I was there to hear him upon a sacrament day, my heart was much affected, but I did break loose from the Lord again. Half a year after, I heard Mr. Dickinson commonplace in the chapel upon those words, "I will not destroy it for ten's sake" (Gen. 19), and then again was much affected. But I shook this off also, and fell from God to loose and lewd company, to lust and pride and gaming and bowling and drinking; and yet the Lord left me not, but a godly scholar walking with me, fell to discourse about the misery of every man out of Christ, *viz.* that whatever they did was sin. This did much affect me. And at another time, when I did light in godly company, I heard them discourse about the wrath of God and the terror of it, and how intolerable it was, which they did present by fire: how intolerable the torment of that was for a time, what then would eternity be? This did much awaken me, and I began to pray again. But then by loose company, I came to dispute in the Schools and there to join loose scholars of other colleges, and was fearfully left of God and fell to drink with them. I drank so much one day that I was dead drunk, and that upon a Saturday night, and so was carried from the place I had drunk at and did feast at unto a scholar's chamber, one Basset of Christ's College, and knew not where I was until I awakened late on that Sabbath, and sick with my beastly carriage. When I awakened, I went from him in shame and confusion, and went out into the fields, and there spent that Sabbath lying hid in the cornfields, where the Lord, who might justly have cut me off in the midst of my sin, did meet me with much sadness of heart and troubled my soul for this and other my sins, which then I had cause and leisure to think of. Now when I was worst, He began to be best unto me, and made me resolve to set upon a course of daily meditation about the evil of my sin and my own ways; yet although I was troubled for this sin, I did not know my sinful nature all this while. . . .

At this time I cannot omit the goodness of God, as to myself so to all the country, in delivering us from the Pequot furies. These Indians were the stoutest, proudest and most successful in their wars of all the Indians; their chief sachem was Sasakus, a proud, cruel, unhappy and headstrong prince, who, not willing to be guided by the persuasions of his fellow, an aged sachem Momanattuck, nor fearing the revenge of the English, having first sucked the blood of Captain Stone and Mr. Oldam, found it so sweet, and his proceedings for one whole winter so successful, that having besieged and killed about four men that kept Seabrook fort, he adventured to fall upon the English up the river at Weathersfield, where he slew nine or ten men, women, and children, at unawares, and took two maids prisoners, carrying them away captive to the Pequot country. Hereupon, those upon the river first gathered about seventy men and sent them into Pequot country, to make that the seat of war and to revenge the death of those innocents whom they barbarously and most unnaturally slew. These men marched two days and nights from the way of the Narragansett unto Pequot, being guided by those Indians then the ancient enemies of the Pequots. They intended to assault Sasakus' fort; but falling short of it the second night, the providence of God guided them to another nearer, full of stout men and their best soldiers, being as it were cooped up there to the number of three or four hundred in all, for the divine slaughter by the hand of the English. These therefore, being all night making merry and singing the death of the English the next day, toward break of the day being very heavy with sleep, the English drew near within the sight of the fort, very weary with travail and want of sleep, at which time five hundred Narragansetts fled for fear and only two of the company stood to it to conduct them to the fort and the door and entrance thereof. The English being come to it, awakened the fort with a peal of muskets directed into the midst of their wigwams; after this, some undertaking to compass the fort without, some adventured into the fort upon the very faces of the enemy standing ready with their arrows ready bent to shoot whoever should adventure. But the English, casting by their pieces, took their swords in their hands (the Lord doubling their strength and courage), and fell upon the Indians, where a hot fight continued about the space of an hour. At last, by the direction of one Captain Mason, their wigwams were set on fire, which, being dry and contiguous one to another, was most dreadful to the Indians: some burning, some bleeding to death by the sword, some resisting till they were cut off, some flying were beat down by the men without, until the Lord had utterly consumed the whole company, except four or five girls they took prisoners and dealt with them at Seabrook as they dealt with ours at Weathersfield. 'Tis verily thought, scarce one man escaped, unless one or two to carry forth tidings of the lamentable end of their fellows. Of the English, not one man was killed but one by the musket of an Englishman (as was conceived). Some were wounded much, but all recovered and restored again. . . .

But the Lord hath not been wont to let me live long without some affliction or other, and yet ever mixt with some mercy; and therefore April the second, 1646, as He gave me another son, John, so He took away my most dear, precious, meek and loving wife, in childbed, after three weeks' lying in, having left behind her two hopeful branches, my dear children, Samuel and John. This affliction was very heavy to me, for in it the Lord seemed to withdraw His tender care for me and mine, which He graciously manifested by my dear wife: also refused to hear prayer when I did think He would have hearkened and let me see His beauty in the land of the living, in restoring of her to health again: also in taking her away in the prime time of her life when she might have lived to have glorified the Lord long: also in threatening me to proceed in rooting out my family, and that He would not stop, having begun here as in Eli for not being zealous enough against the sins of his sin. I saw that if I had profited by former afflictions of this nature, I should not have had this scourge; but I am the Lord's and He may do with me what He will. He did teach me to prize a little grace gained by a cross as a sufficient recompense for all outward losses; but this loss was very great: she was a woman of incomparable meekness of spirit, toward myself especially, and very loving; of great prudence to take care for and order my family affairs, being neither too lavish nor sordid in anything, so that I knew not what was under her hands. She had an excellency to reprove for sin and discerned the evils of men; she loved God's people dearly, and studious to profit by their fellowship, and therefore loved their company. She loved God's word exceedingly, and hence was glad she could read my notes, which she had to muse on every week. She had a spirit of prayer

beyond ordinary of her time and experience; she was fit
to die long before she did die, even after the death of her
first-born, which was a great affliction to her: but her work
not being done then, she lived almost nine years with me,
and was the comfort of my life to me, and the last sacrament
before her lying in seemed to be full of Christ and thereby
fitted for heaven. She did oft say she should not outlive this
child; when her fever first began (by taking some cold),
she told me so, that we should love exceedingly together
because we should not live long together. Her fever took
away her sleep, want of sleep wrought much distemper
in her head, and filled it with fantasies and distractions
but without raging; the night before she died, she had
about six hours unquiet sleep, but that so cooled and settled
her head that when she knew none else so as to speak to
them, yet she knew Jesus Christ and could speak to him.
Therefore, as soon as she awakened out of sleep, she broke
out into a most heavenly heartbreaking prayer after Christ,
her dear redeemer, for the sparing of life, and so continued
praying until the last hour of her death; "Lord, though I
unworthy, Lord, one word, one word," etc., and so gave
up the ghost. Thus God hath visited and scourged me for
my sins, and sought to wean me from this world; but I have
ever found it a difficult thing to profit ever but a little by
the sorest and sharpest afflictions.

2. INCREASE MATHER, 1639–1723

[The masterpiece of Puritan analytical autobiography
is John Bunyan's *Grace Abounding*, but the archetype of
Puritan biography is *Pilgrim's Progress*: each specific Christian was simply a variant of the representative Christian,
and the life of each was a pilgrimage. The body of Cotton
Mather's *Magnalia* is a collection of these pilgrimages; un-
fortunately space prevents including them in this volume,
but the finest of the New England biographies is undoubtedly Increase Mather's *The Life and Death of that
Reverend Man in God, Mr. Richard Mather*, published at
Cambridge in 1670. The title indicates that it is something

more than just the story of his parent; as Increase says, he undertook the task because "it would be a service not only honorable to my father, but acceptable and honorable to the name of God."]

RICHARD MATHER

Being, as hath been related, settled in the ministry at Toxteth, he resolved to change his single condition, and accordingly he became a suitor to Mrs. Katherine Hoult, daughter to Edmund Hoult, Esq., of Bury in Lancashire. She had (and that deservedly) the repute of a very godly and prudent maid. The motion for several years met with obstructions, by reason of her father's not being affected towards non-conformable Puritans. But at last he gave his consent that Mr. Mather should marry his daughter; the match therefore was consummated September 29, 1624. God made her to become a rich blessing to him, continuing them together for the space of above thirty years. By her, God gave him six sons, four whereof (*viz*. Samuel, Timothy, Nathaniel and Joseph) were born in England, and two (*viz*. Eleazar and Increase) in New England.

After his marriage he removed his habitation three miles from Toxteth, to Much Woolton, having there purchased an house of his own; yet he was wont constantly, summer and winter, to preach the word at Toxteth upon the Lord's days. During his abode there, he was abundant in labors in the Gospel, for every Lord's day he preached twice at Toxteth, and once in a fortnight, on the third day of the week, he kept a lecture at the town of Prescot. Also, faithful and powerful preaching being then rare in those parts, he did frequently preach upon "holy days" (as they are called), being often thereunto desired by godly Christians of other parishes in that country. And this he did, not as thinking that there was any in holiness in those times (or in any other day besides the Lord's day) beyond what belongs to every day, but because then there would be an opportunity of great assemblies. And it is good casting the net where there is much fish: for which cause it might be that the apostles preached mostly in populous towns and cities, and also (which suiteth with what we are speaking) on the Jewish Sabbaths, after their abrogation as to any religious tie upon conscience for their observation.

Yea, and besides all this, he often preached at funerals. It is true that Cartwright, Sherwood, Hildersham, and many other renowned non-conformists have scrupled preaching funeral sermons; also, in some reformed churches that the practice is wholly omitted—yea, and decrees of councils have sometimes been against it. But that hath been chiefly upon account of that custom of praising the dead upon such occasions, and that many times untruly, which custom (as many learned men have observed) is ethnical, having its rise from the funeral orations of the heathen. Publicola made an excellent oration in praise of Brutus, which the people were so taken with that it became a custom that famous men, dying, should be so praised; and when (as Plutarch saith in the life of Camillus) the women amongst the Romans parted with their golden ornaments for the public good, the Senate decreed that it should be lawful to make funeral orations for them also. *Hinc mortuos laudandi mos fluxit quem nos hodiè servamus* (Polydore Virgil, *De Inventoribus Rerum.* liber 3, caput 10). ["Hence the custom of praising the dead, to which we are enslaved."] Nor indeed was this rite practiced in the church before the apostasy began. . . . Thus did he preach the word, being instant in season and out of season, reproving, rebuking, exhorting, with all long-suffering and doctrine. . . .

After that he had thus painfully and faithfully spent fifteen years in the work of the ministry, He that holds the stars in His right hand had more work for him to do elsewhere. And therefore the rage of Satan and wrath of men must be suffered to break forth, until this choice instrument had his mouth stopped in unrighteousness. The lecture which he kept at Prescot caused him to be much taken notice of, and so was the more unto the adversaries of the truth an object of envy. *Magnam famam et magnam quietem eodem tempore nemo potest acquirere* (Quintillian). ["No one can acquire a great fame and a great quiet at the same time."] Wherefore, complaints being made against him for non-conformity to the ceremonies, he was by the prelates suspended. This was in August, *anno* 1633.

Under this suspension he continued until November following. But then, by means of the intercession of some gentlemen in Lancashire, and by the influence of Simon Byby (a near alliance of the bishop's), he was restored again to his public ministry. After his restoration he more fully searched into, and also in his ministry handled, the points of church discipline. And God gave him in those days not only to see, but also to instruct others in the substance of the Congregational way, which came to pass by his much reading of the holy scriptures, and his being very conversant in the writings of Cartwright, Parker, Baynes and Ames. But this restored liberty continued not long. For *anno* 1634, Bishop Neal (he who was sometimes by King James pleasantly admonished of his preaching Popery, because by his carriage he taught the people to pray for a blessing upon his dead predecessor), being now become Archbishop of York, sent his visitors in Lancashire. . . . These visitors being come into the country, . . . kept their courts at Wigan, where, amongst many other unrighteous proceedings, and having Mr. Mather convened before them, they passed a sentence of suspension against him, merely for his non-conformity to the inventions of men in the worship of God.

It was marvelous to see how God was with him, causing a spirit of courage and glory to rest upon him, and filling him with wisdom when he stood before those judges, who were not willing that he should speak for himself or declare the reasons which convinced his conscience of the unlawfulness of that conformity which they required. Concerning the Lord's presence with him at that time, himself doth in a manuscript left in his study thus express it: "In the passages of that day, I have this to bless the name of God for, that the terror of their threatening words, of their pursuivants and of the rest of their pomp, did not so terrify my mind but that I could stand before them without being daunted in the least measure, but answered for myself such words of truth and soberness as the Lord put into my mouth, not being afraid of their faces at all: which supporting and comforting presence of the Lord I count not much less mercy than if I had been altogether preserved out of their hands."

Being thus silenced from public preaching the word, means was again used by Mr. Mather's friends to obtain his liberty, but all in vain. The visitor asked how long he had been a minister? Answer was made, that he had been in the ministry fifteen years. And, said he, how often hath he worn the surplice? Answer was returned, that he had never worn it. "What!" said the visitor, swearing as he spake it, "Preach fifteen years and never wear a surplice? It had been better for him that he had gotten seven bastards!" This was a visitor's judgment. . . .

Wherefore the case being thus, he betook himself to a private life; and no hope being left of enjoying liberty again in his native land, foreseeing also (*sapiens divinat*) ["a wise man foresees"] the approaching calamities of England, he meditated a removal into New England. . . .

During the time of his pilgrimage in New England he underwent not so many changes as before that he had done. For he never removed his habitation out of Dorchester, albeit he had once serious thoughts that way, by reason that his old people in Toxteth, after that the hierarchy was deposed in England, sent to him, desiring his return to them; but Dorchester was in no wise willing to forgo their interest in him, therefore he left them not. Nevertheless, he did in New England (as in a wilderness might be expected) experience many trials of his faith and patience. That which, of outward afflictions, did most aggrieve him was the death of his dear wife, who had been for so many years the greatest outward comfort and blessing which he did enjoy. Which affliction was the more grievous in that she, being a woman of singular prudence for the management of affairs, had taken off from her husband all secular cares, so that he wholly devoted himself to his study and to sacred employments. After he had continued in the state of widowhood a year and half, he again changed his condition, and was married to the pious widow of that deservedly famous man of God, Mr. John Cotton;

and her did God make a blessing and a comfort to him during the remainder of his days.

Old age now being come upon him, he was sensible of the infirmities thereof, being in his latter years something thick of hearing. Also (as it was with great Zanchius), the sight of one of his eyes failed seven years before his death. Yet God gave him health of body and vigor of spirit in a wonderful measure, so as that in fifty years together, he was not by sickness detained so much as one Lord's day from public labors. Which continued health (as to natural causes) proceeded partly from his strong constitution of body, and partly from his accustoming himself to a plain and wholesome diet. *Bona diata est potior quovis Hippocrate.* ["Good diet is better than any Hippocrates."] He never made use of any physician, nor was he ever in all his life sick of any acute disease. Only the two last years of his life he was sorely afflicted with that disease which some have called *flagellum studiosorum* ["the flail of the studious"], *viz.* the stone, which at last brought him to an end of all his labors and sorrows.

Concerning the time and manner of his sickness and death, thus it was: there being some differences in Boston, counsel from neighbor churches was by some desired, to direct them in the Lord what should be done; accordingly the churches sent their messengers, and Dorchester Church, amongst others, sent Mr. Mather, their aged teacher, who assembled in Boston, April 13, 1669. He was, because of his age, gravity, grace and wisdom wherewith the Lord had endowed and adorned him, chosen the moderator in that reverend assembly. For divers days after his being thus in consultation, he enjoyed his health as formerly, or rather better than for some time of late. But as Luther when assembled in a synod was surprised with a violent fit of stone, whence he was forced to return home, his friends having little hopes of his life, so it was with this holy man. For April 16, 1669, he was in the night, being then in his son's [*i.e.*, Increase Mather's] house in Boston, taken exceeding ill through a total stoppage of his urine. The next morning he therefore returned home to Dorchester. Great was the favor of God towards him, that he should be found about such a blessed work as then he was engaged in, for the Lord found him sincerely and earnestly endeavoring to be a peacemaker. . . .

Now as usually providence so ordereth, that they who have been speaking all their lives long shall not say much when they come to die. Blessed Hooker, in his last sickness, when friends would have had him answered to some inquiries which might have made for their edification after he was gone, he referred them wholly to the things which he had taught them in his health, because then he had enough to do to grapple with his own bodily weakness. Neither did this good man speak much in his last sickness, either to friends or to his children. Only his son, who is now teacher of a church in Boston, coming to visit his father, and perceiving the symptoms of death to be upon him, said unto him, "Sir, if there be any special thing which you would recommend unto me to do, in case the Lord should spare me upon the earth after you are in heaven, I would entreat you to express it." At the which, his father making a little pause, and lifting up his eyes and hands to heaven, replied, "A special thing which I would commend to you is care concerning the rising generation in this country, that they be brought under the government of Christ in his church; and that when grown up and qualified, they have baptism for their children. . . ."

His bodily pains continued upon him until April 22, when in the morning his son aforementioned, coming to visit him, asked his father if he knew him; to whom he replied that he did, but was not able to speak any more to him. Whereupon his son saying, "Now you will speedily be in the joy of your Lord," his father lifted up his hands, but could not speak. Not long after, his son again spoke to him, saying, "You will quickly see Jesus Christ, and that will make amends for all your pains and sorrows." At which words, his father again lifted up his hands; but after that he took notice of no person or thing, but continuing speechless until about 10 P.M., he quietly breathed forth his last. Thus did that light, that had been shining in the church above fifty years, expire.

As he was a man faithful and fearing God above many,

so the Lord showed great faithfulness unto him, both in making him serviceable unto the last—yea, and continuing the vigor of his spirit and power of his ministry. Few men, though young, are known to preach with such vigor as he did but ten days before his death. Also, the Lord was faithful and gracious to him, in respect of his children. It was a special token of divine favor unto some of the ancients that their sons after them succeeded in the ministry: so was it with the fathers of Gregory Nazianzen, Gregory Nyssen, Basil, Hilary, etc. And the Lord cheered the heart of this, his servant in his old age, by giving him to see most of his sons employed in the ministry many years before their precious father's decease. He left four sons in that work: one of whom, *viz.* Mr. Eleazar Mather, late pastor of the church at Northampton in New England, went to his rest about three months after his father, with him to sound forth the praises of God among the spirits of just men made perfect. The other three are yet surviving: *viz.* Mr. Samuel Mather, teacher of a church in Dublin; Mr. Nathaniel Mather, late minister of Barnstable in Devon, and since in Rotterdam in Holland; and Increase Mather of Boston in New England. . . .

His way of preaching was plain, aiming to shoot his arrows not over his people's heads but into their hearts and consciences. Whence he studiously avoided obscure phrases, exotic words or an unnecessary citation of Latin sentences, which some men addict themselves to the use of. Mr. Dod was wont to say that "so much Latin was so much flesh in a sermon." So did this humble man look upon the affectation of such things in a popular auditory to savor of carnal wisdom. The Lord gave him an excellent faculty in making abstruse things plain, that in handling the deepest mysteries he would accommodate himself to vulgar capacities, that even the meanest might learn something. He knew how to express καινὰ κοινῶς κὰι κοινὰ καινῶς ["strange things familiarly and familiar things unusually."] He would often use that saying, *Artis est celare artem.* ["The art is to conceal the art."] And much approved that of Austin: "If," said he, "I preach learnedly, then only the learned and not the unlearned can understand and profit by me; but if I preach plainly, then learned and unlearned both can understand; so I profit all." He was mighty in the scriptures: whence Mr. Hooker would say of him, "My brother Mather is a mighty man." Also, his usual way of delivery was very powerful, awakening and zealous: especially in his younger years, there being few men of so great strength of body as he, which together with his natural fervor of spirit, being sanctified, made his ministry the more powerful. And the Lord went forth with his labors to the conversion of many, both in England and in New England.

Yet, though his way of preaching was plain and zealous, it was moreover substantial and very judicious. Even in his beginning times, Mr. Gillebrand (a famous minister in Lancashire, and the more famous, for that though he did exceedingly stammer in his ordinary discourse, he would pray and preach as fluently as any man), once having heard him preach, asked what his name might be. And answer being made that his name was Mather, "Nay," said Mr. Gillebrand, "call him matter, for, believe it, this man hath substance in him." Yea, such was his solidity of judgment that some who were his opposites yet did therefore greatly respect and honor him. Doctor Parr (then Bishop of the Isle of Man), having heard Mr. Mather was silenced, lamented it, saying, "If Mr. Mather be silenced, I am sorry for it, for he was a solid man, and the church of God hath then a great loss. . . ."

It might be said of him, as was said of that blessed martyr, that he was "sparing in his diet, sparing in his speech, and most sparing of all of his time." He was very diligent both as to duties of general and particular calling —which are indeed the two pillars upon which religion stands.

As to his general calling: he was much in prayer, especially in his study, where he ofttimes spent whole days with God in suing for a blessing upon himself and children, and upon the people to whom he was related, and upon the whole country where he lived. The requests which upon such occasions he put up to God in Jesus Christ, and also how his heart was moved to believe that God heard him, he left (many of them) in writing amongst his private papers. I suppose that so himself might have recourse unto those experiences in a time of darkness and temptation; also, that his sons after him might see by their father's example, what it is to walk before God.

Now what a loss is it to the world when such a righteous man is taken away! Well might Philo and Jerome weep bitterly when they heard of the death of any such men, because it portended evil to the places where they had lived and served God. As he was much in prayer, so he was very frequent in hearing the word. It was his manner to attend several lectures in neighbor congregations, until his disease made him unable to ride. Yea, and usually, even to his old age, . . . he took notes from those whom he heard, professing that he found profit in it.

As to his particular calling, he was even from his youth a hard student. Yea, his mind was so intent upon his work and studies that the very morning before he died he importuned those friends that watched with him to help him into his study. They urging that he was not able to go so far, he desired them to help him and try, which they did; but ere he was come to the door of his lodging-room, "I see," saith he, "I am not able, yet I have not been in my study several days, and is it not a lamentable thing that I should lose so much time?"

After his entrance upon the ministry, he was not only in England (as hath been said) but in New England abundant in labors, for except when he had an assistant with him (which was seldom), he preached twice every Lord's day, and a lecture once a fortnight, besides many occasional sermons both in public and in private. Also, he was much exercised in answering many practical cases of conscience, and in polemical, especially disciplinary, discourses. . . .

Notwithstanding those rare gifts and graces wherewith the Lord had adorned him, he was exceeding low and little in his own eyes. Some have thought that his greatest error was that he did not magnify his office, as he might and sometimes should have done. If a man must err, it is good erring on that hand. "Humble enough, and good enough," was the frequent saying of a great divine. And

another observeth, "That every man hath just as much and
no more truth in him, as he hath humility." Austin, being
asked which was the most excellent grace, answered,
"Humility"; and which was the next, answered, "Humility"; and which was the third, replied again, "Humility."
That indeed is comprehensively all, being of great price in
the sight of God. And if so, Mr. Mather was a man of much
real worth.

3. SAMUEL SEWALL, 1652–1730

[Sewall's *Diary* records the impact upon one man, who
lived through and felt all its reverberations, of the transi-
tion from the religious-centered New England of the seventeenth century to the business-directed society of the
eighteenth. More than that, it is also the revelation of a
character, full of crotchets and vanities, but also capable
of the tremendous nobility of repenting his part in the court
that hanged the witches, and so asking his pastor to read
from the pulpit his confession of January 14, 1697. The
modern reader is naturally most delighted with the courtship of Madame Winthrop, but it should be noted that not
all the humor in Sewall's record is unconscious. He knew
what a ridiculous figure he cut; yet three years before his
death, upon the passing of a classmate, he was able to see
himself in solemn humility.]

DIARY

January 13 [1677]. Giving my chickens meat, it came to
my mind that I gave them nothing save Indian corn and
water, and yet they ate it and thrived very well; and that
that food was necessary for them, how mean soever: which
much affected me, and convinced [me] what need I stood
in of spiritual food, and that I should not nauseate daily
duties of prayer, etc.

November 6 [1692]. Joseph threw a knob of brass and
hit his sister Betty on the forehead, so as to make it bleed

and swell; for which, and his playing at prayer time and eating when return thanks, I whipped him pretty smartly. When I first went in (called by his grandmother), he sought to shadow and hide himself from me behind the head of the cradle: which gave me the sorrowful remembrance of Adam's carriage.

January 13 [1696]. When I came in, past 7 at night, my wife met me in the entry and told me Betty had surprised them. I was surprised with the abruptness of the relation. It seems Betty Sewall had given some signs of dejection and sorrow, but a little after dinner she burst out into an amazing cry, which caused all the family to cry too. Her mother asked the reason. She gave none; at last said she was afraid she should go to hell, her sins were not pardoned. She was first wounded by my reading a sermon of Mr. Norton's, about the 5th of January (text, John 7. 34): "Ye shall seek me and shall not find me." And those words in the sermon (John 8. 21): "Ye shall seek me and shall die in your sins," ran in her mind and terrified her greatly. . . . Her mother asked her whether she prayed. She answered yes, but feared her prayers were not heard, because her sins not pardoned. Mr. Willard, though sent for timelier, yet not being told of the message, . . . he came not till after I came home. He discoursed with Betty, who could not give a distinct account but was confused, as his phrase was, and as [he] had experienced in himself. Mr. Willard prayed excellently. The Lord bring light and comfort out of this dark and dreadful cloud, and grant that Christ's being formed in my dear child may be the issue of these painful pangs!

December 26 [1696]. We bury our little daughter. . . . Note: 'twas wholly dry, and I went at noon to see in what order things were set, and there I was entertained with a view of, and converse with, the coffins of my dear father Hull, mother Hull, cousin Quinsey, and my six children; for the little posthumous was now took up and set in upon that that stands on John's, so are three, one upon another twice, on the bench at the end. My mother's lies on a lower bench, at the end, with her head to her husband's head; and I ordered little Sarah to be set on her grandmother's feet. 'Twas an awful yet pleasing treat; having said, "The Lord knows who shall be brought hither next," I came away.

January 14 [1697]. Copy of the bill I put up on the fast day, giving it to Mr. Willard as he passed by, and standing up at the reading of it and bowing when finished, in the afternoon:

"Samuel Sewall, sensible of the reiterated strokes of God upon himself and family, and being sensible that as to the guilt contracted upon the opening of the late Commission of Oyer and Terminer at Salem (to which the order for this day relates), he is upon many accounts more concerned than any that he knows of, desires to take the blame and shame of it; asking pardon of men, and especially desiring prayers that God, who has an unlimited authority, would pardon that sin and all other his sins, personal and relative: and according to His infinite benignity and sovereignty, not visit the sin of him or of any other upon himself or any of his, nor upon the land: but that He would powerfully defend him against all temptations to sin, for the future, and vouchsafe him the efficacious, saving conduct of His word and spirit."

October 1 [1697]. Jeremiah Belcher's sons came for us to go to the island. My wife, through indisposition, could not go, but I carried Samuel, Hannah, Elisa, Joseph, Mary and Jane Tappan. I prevailed with Mr. Willard to go; he carried Simon, Elizabeth, William, Margaret, and Elisa Tyng. Had a very comfortable passage thither and home again, though against tide. Had first, butter, honey, curds and cream. For dinner, very good roast lamb, turkey, fowls, apple pie. After dinner, sung the 121st Psalm. Note: a glass of spirits my wife sent stood upon a joint-stool which, Simon Willard jogging, it fell down and broke all to shivers; I said 'twas a lively emblem of our fragility and mortality.

January 14 [1701]. Having been certified last night, about 10 o'clock, of the death of my dear mother at Newbury, Samuel and I set out with John Sewall, the messenger, for that place. . . . Nathaniel Bricket taking in hand to fill the grave, I said:

"Forbear a little, and suffer me to say that amidst our

bereaving sorrows we have the comfort of beholding this saint put into the rightful possession of that happiness of living desired, and dying lamented. She lived commendably four and fifty years with her dear husband, and my dear father; and she could not well brook the being divided from him at her death, which is the cause of our taking leave of her in this place. She was a true and constant lover of God's word, worship, and saints; and she always, with a patient cheerfulness, submitted to the divine decree of providing bread for herself and others in the sweat of her brows. And now her infinitely gracious and bountiful master has promoted her to the honor of higher employments, fully and absolutely discharged from all manner of toil and sweat. My honored and beloved friends and neighbors! My dear mother never thought much of doing the most frequent and homely offices of love for me, and lavished away many thousands of words upon me before I could return one word in answer. And therefore I ask and hope that none will be offended that I have now ventured to speak one word in her behalf, when she herself is become speechless."

Made a motion with my hand for the filling of the grave. Note: I could hardly speak for passion and tears.

January 24 [1704]. Took 24^s in my pocket, and gave my wife the rest of my cash, £4/3/8, and tell her she shall now keep the cash; if I want, I will borrow of her. She has a better faculty than I at managing affairs. I will assist her, and will endeavor to live upon my salary; will see what it will do. The Lord give His blessing.

April 11 [1712]. I saw six swallows together, flying and chippering very rapturously.

December 23 [1714]. Dr. Cotton Mather preaches excellently from Psalms 37, "Trust in the Lord," only spake of the sun being in the center of our system. I think it inconvenient to assert such problems.

[Sewall's first wife died in 1717; after an unsuccessful courtship of the widow Denison, he married Abigail Tilley in 1719, who, however, died in the night of May 26, 1720, as Sewall says, "to our great astonishment, especially mine."]

September 30 [1720]. Mr. Colman's lecture. Daughter Sewall acquaints Madam Winthrop that if she pleased to be within at 3 P.M., I would wait on her. She answered she would be at home.

October 1. Saturday. I dine at Mr. Stoddard's; from thence I went to Madam Winthrop's just at 3. Spake to her, saying my loving wife died so soon and suddenly, 'twas hardly convenient for me to think of marrying again; however, I came to this resolution, that I would not make my court to any person without first consulting with her. Had a pleasant discourse about 7 (seven) single persons sitting in the fore-seat September 29, *viz.* Madam Rebecca Dudley, Katherine Winthrop, Bridget Usher, Deliverance Legg, Rebecca Lloyd, Lydia Colman, Elizabeth Bellingham. She propounded one and another for me; but none would do; said Mrs. Lloyd was about her age.

October 3. 2. Waited on Madam Winthrop again; 'twas a little while before she came in. Her daughter Noyes being there alone with me, I said I hoped my waiting on her mother would not be disagreeable to her. She answered she should not be against that that might be for her comfort. I saluted her, and told her I perceived I must shortly wish her a good time (her mother had told me she was with child and within a month or two of her time). By and by in came Mr. Airs, chaplain of the Castle, and hanged up his hat, which I was a little startled at, it seeming as if he was to lodge there. At last Madam Winthrop came too. After a considerable time I went up to her and said if it might not be inconvenient, I desired to speak with her. She assented, and spake of going into another room; but Mr. Airs and Mrs. Noyes presently rose up and went out, leaving us there alone. Then I ushered in discourse from the names in the fore-seat; at last I prayed that Katherine [Mrs. Winthrop] might be the person assigned for me. She instantly took it up in the way of denial, as if she had catched at an opportunity to do it, saying she could not do it before she was asked. Said that was her mind unless she should change it, which she believed she should not; could not leave her children. I expressed my sorrow that she should do it so speedily, prayed her consideration, and asked her when I should wait on her again. She setting no time, I mentioned that day sennight. Gave her Mr. Willard's *Fountain*, opened with the little print and verses, saying I hoped if we did well read that book, we should meet together hereafter, if we did not now. She took the book and put it in her pocket. Took leave.

October 5. Midweek. I dined with the Court; from thence went and visited Cousin Jonathan's wife, lying in with her little Betty. Gave the nurse 2ˢ. Although I had appointed to wait upon her, Madam Winthrop, next Monday, yet I went from my cousin Sewall's thither about 3 P.M. The nurse told me Madam dined abroad at her daughter Noyes's, they were to go out together. I asked for the maid, who was not within. Gave Katee a penny and a kiss, and came away. Accompanied my son and daughter Cooper in their remove to their new house. Went to tell Joseph, and Mr. Belcher saw me by the South Meeting-house though 'twas duskish, and said I had been at house-warming (he had been at our house). Invited me to drink a glass of wine at his house at 7, and eat part of the pasty provided for the commissioners' voyage to Casco Bay. His Excellency, Madam Belcher, Solomon Stoddard, Col. Fitch, Mr. D. Oliver, Mr. Anthony Stoddard, Mr. Welsteed, Mr. White, Mr. Belcher sat down. At coming home gave us of the cake and gingerbread to carry away. 'Twas about ten before we got home; Mr. Oliver and I waited on the governor to his gate; and then Mr. Oliver would wait on me home.

October 6th. Lecture day. Mr. Cutler, president of the Connecticut college, preached in Dr. Cotton Mather's turn. He made an excellent discourse from Heb. 11. 14: "For they that say such things, declare plainly that they seek a country." Brother Odlin, Son Sewall of Brookline, and Mary Hirst dine with me. I asked Mary of Madam Lord, Mr. Oliver and wife, and bid her present my service to them. A little after 6 P.M. I went to Madam Winthrop's. She was not within. I gave Sarah Chickering the maid 2ˢ,

Juno, who brought in wood, 1^s. Afterward the nurse came in; I gave her 18^d, having no other small bill. After a while Dr. Noyes came in with his mother, and quickly after his wife came in; they sat talking, I think, till eight o'clock. I said I feared I might be some interruption to their business; Dr. Noyes replied pleasantly he feared they might be an interruption to me, and went away. Madam seemed to harp upon the same string. Must take care of her children; could not leave that house and neighborhood where she had dwelt so long. I told her she might do her children as much or more good by bestowing what she laid out in housekeeping, upon them. Said her son would be of age the 7th of August. I said it might be inconvenient for her to dwell with her daughter-in-law, who must be mistress of the house. I gave her a piece of Mr. Belcher's cake and gingerbread wrapped up in a clean sheet of paper; told her of her father's kindness to me when treasurer, and I constable. My daughter Judith was gone from me and I was more lonesome—might help to forward one another in our journey to Canaan. Mr. Eyre came within the door; I saluted him, asked how Mr. Clark did, and he went away. I took leave about 9 o'clock. I told [her] I came now to refresh her memory as to Monday night; said she had not forgot it. In discourse with her, I asked leave to speak with her sister; I meant to gain Madam Mico's favor to persuade her sister. She seemed surprised and displeased, and said she was in the same condition.

October 7th. Friday. I gather the quinces. Gave Mr. Jonathan Simson and Mrs. Fifield, each of them, a funeral sermon.

Cousin Abiel Hobart comes to us. Mr. Short, having received his £40, returns home.

Mr. Cooper visits me, thanks me for my cheese.

October 8. Mr. Short returns not till this day.

October 9. Mr. Sewall preaches very well from Acts 2. 24 of the resurrection of Christ. One woman taken into church; one child baptized.

October 10th. Examine Mr. Briggs his account; said they could not find Mr. Whittemore. Mr. Willard offered to answer for him. But I showed the necessity of his being here;

and appointed Wednesday, 10 o'clock; and ordered notice to be given to the auditors, to pray their assistance.

In the evening I visited Madam Winthrop, who treated me with a great deal of courtesy; wine, marmalade. I gave her a *News-Letter* about the Thanksgiving proposals, for sake of the verses for David Jeffries. She tells me Dr. Increase Mather visited her this day, in Mr. Hutchinson's coach.

It seems Dr. Cotton Mather's chimney fell afire yesterday, so as to interrupt the Assembly A.M. Mr. Cutler ceased preaching ¼ of an hour.

October 11th. I writ a few lines to Madam Winthrop to this purpose: "Madam, These wait on you with Mr. Mayhew's sermon, and account of the state of the Indians on Martha's Vineyard. I thank you for your unmerited favors of yesterday; and hope to have the happiness of waiting on you tomorrow before eight o'clock after noon. I pray God to keep you, and give you a joyful entrance upon the two hundred and twenty-ninth year of Christopher Columbus his discovery; and take leave, who am, Madam, your humble servant. S.S."

Sent this by Deacon Green, who delivered it to Sarah Chickering, her mistress not being at home.

October 12. Give Mr. Whittemore and Willard their oath to Dr. Mather's inventory. Visit Mr. Cooper. Go to the meeting at the Widow Emon's; Mr. Manly prayed, I read half Mr. Henry's 12th chapter of *The Lord's Supper*. Sung 1, 2, 3, 4, 5, 10, and 12th verses of the 30th Psalm. Brother Franklin concluded with prayer. At Madam Winthrop's steps I took leave of Capt. Hill, etc.

Mrs. Anne Cotton came to door ('twas before 8), said Madam Winthrop was within, directed me into the little room, where she was full of work behind a stand; Mrs. Cotton came in and stood. Madam Winthrop pointed to her to set me a chair. Madam Winthrop's countenance was much changed from what 'twas on Monday, looked dark and lowering. At last the work (black stuff or silk) was taken away; I got my chair in place, had some converse, but very cold and indifferent to what 'twas before. Asked her to acquit me of rudeness if I drew off her glove. Inquiring the reason, I told her 'twas great odds between handling a dead goat and a living lady. Got it off. I told her I had one petition to ask of her—that was that she would take off the negative she laid on me the third of October; she readily answered she could not, and enlarged upon it; she told me of it so soon as she could; could not leave her house, children, neighbors, business. I told her she might do some good to help and support me. Mentioning Mrs. Gookin (Nath.), the Widow Weld was spoken of; said I had visited Mrs. Denison. I told her, "Yes!" Afterward I said if after a first and second vagary she would accept of me returning, her victorious kindness and good will would be very obliging. She thanked me for my book (Mr. Mayhew's sermon), but said not a word of the letter. When she insisted on the negative, I prayed there might be no more thunder and lightning, I should not sleep all night. I gave her Dr. Preston, *The Church's Marriage and the Church's Carriage,* which cose me 6ˢ at the sale. The door standing open, Mr. Airs came in, hung up his hat, and sat down. After awhile, Madam Winthrop moving, he went out. John Eyre looked in; I said, "How do ye?" or, "Your servant, Mr. Eyre," but heard no word from him. Sarah filled a glass of wine; she drank to me, I to her; she sent Juno home with me with a good lantern; I gave her 6ᵈ and bid her thank her mistress. In some of our discourse, I told her I had rather go to the stone house adjoining to her than to come to her against her mind. Told her the reason why I came every other night was lest I should drink too deep draughts of pleasure. She had talked of canary; her kisses were to me better than the best canary. Explained the expression concerning Columbus.

October 13. I tell my son and daughter Sewall that the weather was not so fair as I apprehended. Mr. Sewall preached very well in Mr. Wadsworth's turn. Mr. Williams of Weston and Mr. Odlin dine with us. Text was the excellency of the knowledge of Christ.

Friday, October 14. Made a dinner for my son and daughter Cooper. At table in the best room were Sister Stoddard, Sister Cooper, His Excellency, Mrs. Hannah Cooper, Brother Stoddard, Solomon Stoddard, Mr. Joseph

Sewall, Mr. Cooper, Mr. Sewall of Brookline, Mrs. Rand, Mrs. Gerrish, daughter of Brookline. Mr. Gerrish, Clark, and Rand sat at a side table.

October 15. I dine on fish and oil at Mr. Stoddard's. Capt. Hill wished me joy of my proceedings, *i.e.*, with M—— Winthrop; Sister Cooper applauded it, spake of visiting her; I said her complaisance of her visit would be obliging to me.

October 16. Lord's Day. I upbraided myself that could be so solicitous about earthly things, and so cold and indifferent as to the love of Christ, who is altogether lovely. Mr. Prince administered. Dined at my son's with Mr. Cutler and Mr. Shurtleff. Mr. Cutler preaches in the afternoon from Ezek. 16. 30: "How weak is thy heart." Son reads the order for the Thanksgiving.

October 17. Monday. Give Mr. Daniel Willard and Mr. Pelatiah Whittemore their oaths to their accounts, and Mr. John Briggs to his, as they are attorneys to Dr. Cotton Mather, administrator to the estate of Nathan Howell, deceased. In the evening I visited Madam Winthrop, who treated me courteously, but not in clean linen as sometimes. She said she did not know whether I would come again or no. I asked her how she could so impute inconstancy to me. (I had not visited her since Wednesday night, being unable to get over the indisposition received by the treatment received that night, and I *must* in it seemed to sound like a made piece of formality.) Gave her this day's *Gazette*. Heard David Jeffries say the Lord's Prayer, and some other portions of the Scriptures. He came to the door and asked me to go into chamber where his grandmother was tending little Katee, to whom she had given physic; but I chose to sit below. Dr. Noyes and his wife came in and sat a considerable time; had been visiting Son and Daughter Cooper. Juno came home with me.

October 18. Visited Madam Mico, who came to me in a splendid dress. I said, "It may be you have heard of my visiting Madam Winthrop," her sister. She answered, her sister had told her of it. I asked her good will in the affair. She answered, if her sister were for it, she should not hinder it. I gave her Mr. Homes's sermon. She gave me a glass of canary, entertained me with good discourse and a respectful remembrance of my first wife. I took leave.

October 19. Midweek. Visited Madam Winthrop; Sarah told me she was at Mr. Walley's, would not come home till late. I gave her Hannah 3 oranges with her duty, not knowing whether I should find her or no. Was ready to go home; but said if I knew she was there, I would go thither. Sarah seemed to speak with pretty good courage she would be there. I went and found her there, with Mr. Walley and his wife in the little room below. At 7 o'clock I mentioned going home; at 8 I put on my coat and quickly waited on her home. She found occasion to speak loud to the servant, as if she had a mind to be known. Was courteous to me, but took occasion to speak pretty earnestly about my keeping a coach. I said 'twould cost £100 per annum; she said 'twould cost but £40. Spake much against John Winthrop, his false-heartedness. Mr. Eyre came in and sat a while; I offered him Dr. Incr. Mather's *Sermons,* whereof Mr. Appleton's ordination sermon was one; said he had them already. I said I would give him another. Exit. Came away somewhat late.

October 20. Mr. Colman preaches from Luke 15. 10: "Joy among the angels"; made an excellent discourse.

At council, Col. Townsend spake to me of my hood: should get a wig. I said 'twas my chief ornament; I wore it for sake of the day. Brother Odlin, and Sam, Mary, and Jane Hirst dine with us. Promised to wait on the Governor about 7. Madam Winthrop not being at lecture, I went thither first; found her very serene with her daughter Noyes, Mrs. Dering, and the Widow Shipreeve, sitting at a little table, she in her armed chair. She drank to me, and I to Mrs. Noyes. After a while prayed the favor to speak with her. She took one of the candles and went into the best room, closed the shutters, sat down upon the couch. She told me Madam Usher had been there, and said the coach must be set on wheels, and not be rusting. She spake something of my needing a wig. Asked me what her sister said to me. I told her she said if her sister were for it, she would not hinder it. But I told her she did not say she would be glad to have me for her brother. Said, "I shall keep you in the cold"; and asked her if she would be within tomorrow night, for we had had but a running feat. She said she could not tell whether she should or no. I took leave. As were drinking at the governor's, he said in England the ladies minded little more than that they might have money, and coaches to ride in. I said, "And New England brooks its name." At which Mr. Dudley smiled. Governor said they were not quite so bad here.

October 21. Friday. My son the minister came to me P.M. by appointment and we pray one for another in the old chamber, more especially respecting my courtship. About 6 o'clock I go to Madam Winthrop's; Sarah told me her mistress was gone out, but did not tell me whither she went. She presently ordered me a fire; so I went in, having Dr. Sibb's *Bowels* with me to read. I read the two first sermons; still nobody came in. At last about 9 o'clock Mr. John Eyre came in; I took the opportunity to say to him as I had done to Mrs. Noyes before, that I hoped my visiting his mother would not be disagreeable to him; he answered me with much respect. When 'twas after 9 o'clock he of himself said he would go and call her, she was but at one of his brothers'; a while after I heard Madam Winthrop's voice, inquiring something about John. After a good while and clapping the garden door twice or thrice, she came in. I mentioned something of the lateness; she bantered me, and said I was later. She received me courteously. I asked when our proceedings should be made public; she said they were like to be no more public than they were already. Offered me no wine that I remember. I rose up at 11 o'clock to come away, saying I would put on my coat; she offered not to help me. I prayed her that Juno might light me home; she opened the shutter and said 'twas pretty light abroad, Juno was weary and gone to bed. So I came home by star light as well as I could. At my first coming in, I gave Sarah five shillings. I writ Mr. Eyre his name in his book with the date October 21, 1720. It cost me 8ˢ. *Jehovah jireh!* ["The Lord will provide"]. Madam told me she had visited M. Mico, Wendell, and William Clark of the South [Church].

October 22. Daughter Cooper visited me before my going out of town, stayed till about sunset. I brought her, going near as far as the Orange-tree. Coming back, near Leg's Corner, little David Jeffries saw me, and looking upon me very lovingly, asked me if I was going to see his grandmother. I said, "Not tonight." Gave him a penny and bid him present my service to his grandmother.

October 24. I went in the hackney coach through the Common, stopped at Madam Winthrop's (had told her I would take my departure from thence). Sarah came to the door with Katee in her arms; but I did not think to take notice of the child. Called her mistress. I told her, being encouraged by David Jeffries' loving eyes and sweet words, I was come to inquire whether she could find in her heart to leave that house and neighborhood, and go and dwell with me at the South End; I think she said softly, "Not yet." I told her it did not lie in my lands to keep a coach. If I should, I should be in danger to be brought to keep company with her neighbor Brooker (he was a little before sent to prison for debt). Told her I had an antipathy against those who would pretend to give themselves, but nothing of their estate. I would a proportion of my estate with myself. And I supposed she would do so. As to a periwig, my best and greatest friend, I could not possibly have a greater, began to find me with hair before I was born, and had continued to do so ever since; and I could not find in my heart to go to another. She commended the book I gave her, Dr. Preston, *The Church Marriage;* quoted him saying 'twas inconvenient keeping out of a fashion commonly used. I said the time and tide did circumscribe my visit. She gave me a dram of black-cherry brandy, and gave me a lump of the sugar that was in it. She wished me a good journey. I prayed God to keep her, and came away. Had a very pleasant journey to Salem.

October 25. Sent a letter of it to my son by Wakefield, who delivered it not till Wednesday; so he visited her not till Friday P.M. and then presented my service to her.

October 27. Kept the Thanksgiving at Salem. Mr. Fisk preached very well from Ephes. 5. 20: "Giving thanks always." Dine at Col. Brown's.

October 29. Hold court in the morn. Had a pleasant journey home a little before sunset.

October 30. Mrs. Phillips and her son sit in their pew.

October 31. She proves her husband's will. At night I visited Madam Winthrop about 6 P.M. They told me she was gone to Madam Mico's. I went thither and found she was gone; so returned to her house, read the epistles to the Galatians, Ephesians in Mr. Eyre's Latin Bible. After the clock struck 8, I began to read the 103 Psalm. Mr. Wendell came in from his warehouse. Asked me if I were alone. Spake very kindly to me, offered me to call Madam Winthrop. I told him she would be angry, had been at Mrs. Mico's; he helped me on with my coat, and I came home; left the *Gazette* in the Bible, which told Sarah of, bid her present my service to Mrs. Winthrop, and tell her I had been to wait on her if she had been at home.

November 1. I was so taken up that I could not go if I would.

November 2. Midweek. Went again, and found Mrs. Alden there, who quickly went out. Gave her about ½ pound of sugar almonds, cost 3^s per £. Carried them on Monday. She seemed pleased with them, asked what they cost. Spake of giving her a hundred pounds per annum if I died before her. Asked her what sum she would give me, if she should die first. Said I would give her time to consider of it. She said she heard as if I had given all to my children by deeds of gift. I told her 'twas a mistake, Point Judith was mine, etc. That in England, I owned, my father's desire was that it should go to my eldest son; 'twas £20 per annum; she thought 'twas forty. I think when I seemed to excuse pressing this, she seemed to think 'twas best to speak of it; a long winter was coming on. Gave me a glass or two of canary.

November 4th. Friday. Went again about 7 o'clock; found there Mr. John Walley and his wife; sat discoursing pleasantly. I showed them Isaac Moses's [an Indian] writing. Madam W. served comfits to us. After a while a table was spread, and supper was set. I urged Mr. Walley to crave a blessing; but he put it upon me. About 9 they went away. I asked Madam what fashioned necklace I should

present her with; she said, "None at all." I asked her
whereabout we left off last time, mentioned what I had
offered to give her, asked her what she would give me;
she said she could not change her condition, she had said
so from the beginning, could not be so far from her children,
the lecture. Quoted the Apostle Paul affirming that a single
life was better than a married. I answered that was for the
present distress. Said she had not pleasure in things of that
nature as formerly. I said, "You are the fitter to make me a
wife." If she held in that mind, I must go home and bewail my rashness in making more haste than good speed.
However, considering the supper, I desired her to be
within next Monday night, if we lived so long. Assented.
She charged me with saying that she must put away Juno
if she came to me; I utterly denied it, it never came in my
heart; yet she insisted upon it, saying it came in upon discourse about the Indian woman that obtained her freedom
this court. About 10 I said I would not disturb the good
orders of her house, and came away. She not seeming
pleased with my coming away. Spake to her about David
Jeffries; had not seen him.

Monday, November 7th. My son prayed in the old
chamber. Our time had been taken up by Son and Daughter Cooper's visit, so that I only read the 130th and 143rd
Psalm. 'Twas on the account of my courtship. I went to
Mad. Winthrop; found her rocking her little Katee in the
cradle. I excused my coming so late (near eight). She set
me an armed chair and cushion; and so the cradle was
between her armed chair and mine. Gave her the remnant
of my almonds; she did not eat of them as before, but
laid them away; I said I came to inquire whether she had
altered her mind since Friday, or remained of the same
mind still. She said, "Thereabouts." I told her I loved her,
and was so fond as to think that she loved me. She said
[she] had a great respect for me. I told her I had made
her an offer without asking any advice; she had so many
to advise with that 'twas a hindrance. The fire was come
to one short brand besides the block, which brand was
set up in end; at last it fell to pieces, and no recruit was
made. She gave me a glass of wine. I think I repeated again

that I would go home and bewail my rashness in making more haste than good speed. I would endeavor to contain myself, and not go on to solicit her to do that which she could not consent to. Took leave of her. As came down the steps she bid me have a care. Treated me courteously. Told her she had entered the 4th year of her widowhood. I had given her the *News-Letter* before. I did not bid her draw off her glove as sometime I had done. Her dress was not so clean as sometime it had been. *Jehovah jireh!*

Midweek, November 9th. Dine at Brother Stoddard's; were so kind as to inquire of me if they should invite Madam Winthrop; I answered, "No."

December 17 [1727]. I was surprised to hear Mr. Thacher of Milton, my old friend, prayed for as dangerously sick. Next day, December 18: I am informed by Mr. Gerrish that my dear friend died last night, which I doubt bodes ill to Milton and the Province, his dying at this time, though in the 77th year of his age. *Deus avertat omen!* ["God avert the omen!"]

December 22 [1727]. The day after the fast, was interred. . . . I was inclined before, and having a pair of gloves sent me, I determined to go to the funeral if the weather proved favorable, which it did; and I hired Blake's coach with four horses. My son, Mr. Cooper and Mr. Prince went with me. Refreshed there with meat and drink; got thither about half an hour past one. It was sad to see [death] triumphed over my dear friend! I rode in my coach to the burying place, not being able to get nearer by reason of the many horses. From thence went directly up the hill where the smith's shop, and so home very comfortably and easily, the ground being mollified. But when I came to my own gate, going in, I fell down, a board slipping under my left foot, my right leg raised off the skin and put me to a great deal of pain, especially when 'twas washed with rum. It was good for me that I was thus afflicted, that my spirit might be brought into a frame more suitable to the solemnity, which is apt to be too light. And by the loss of some of my skin and blood, I might be awakened to prepare for my own dissolution. . . . I have now been at the interment of 4 of my classmates. . . . Now

I can go to no more funerals of my classmates, nor none be
at mine; for the survivors, the Rev. Mr. Samuel Mather at
Windsor and the Rev. Mr. Taylor at Westfield, [are] one
hundred miles off, and are entirely enfeebled. I humbly
pray that Christ may be graciously present with us all
three, both in life and in death, and then we shall safely
and comfortably walk through the shady valley that leads
to glory.

4. JOHN WILLIAMS, 1664–1729

[In New England outposts massacre by the Indians was
a constant threat, but still worse was the prospect of captivity. Captured children were known to go entirely
heathen and refuse to come back. Captives who kept the
faith and lived through the torment were, of course, pilgrims in the most dramatic sense, and many of them told
their stories, always within the frame of the Puritan conception of personal narrative.

John Williams, born at Roxbury, graduated from Harvard in 1683, and was called to Deerfield in 1686. The
massacre occurred in 1704, Williams was redeemed in
1706, and all his children were regained except a daughter, Eunice, who married an Indian. The town was re-
settled in 1707, and Williams went back, saying, "I must
return and look after my sheep in the wilderness." The
book was published in 1707 and remained in print for over
a century.]

THE REDEEMED CAPTIVE

On the twenty-ninth of February [1704], not long before
break of day, the enemy came in like a flood upon us, our
watch being unfaithful: an evil, whose awful effects, in a
surprisal of our fort, should bespeak all watchmen to avoid
as they would not bring the charge of blood upon themselves. They came to my house in the beginning of the
onset, and by their violent endeavors to break open doors

and windows, with axes and hatchets, awakened me out of sleep. On which I leapt out of bed, and running toward the door, perceived the enemy making their entrance into the house. I called to awaken two soldiers in the chamber, and returned towards my bedside for my arms; the enemy immediately broke into the room—I judge to the number of twenty, with painted faces and hideous acclamations. I reached up my hands to the bed-tester for my pistol, uttering a short petition to God: "For everlasting mercies for me and mine, on the account of the merits of our glorified redeemer"; expecting a present passage through the valley of the shadow of death, saying in myself (as Isa. 38. 10, 11): "I said, in the cutting off my days, I shall go to the gates of the grave: I am deprived of the residue of my years. I said, I shall not see the Lord, even the Lord, in the land of the living: I shall behold man no more with the inhabitants of the world." Taking down my pistol, I cocked it, and put it to the breast of the first Indian who came up; but my pistol missing fire, I was seized by three Indians, who disarmed me and bound me naked, as I was in my shirt, and so I stood for near the space of an hour; binding me, they told me they would carry me to Quebec. My pistol missing fire was an occasion of my life's being preserved; since which I have also found it profitable to be crossed in my own will. The judgment of God did not long slumber against one of the three which took me, who was a captain, for by sun-rising he received a mortal shot from my next neighbor's house: who opposed so great a number of French and Indians as three hundred, and yet were no more than seven men in an ungarrisoned house.

I cannot relate the distressing care I had for my dear wife, who had lain in but a few weeks before, and for my poor children, family, and Christian neighbors. The enemy fell to rifling the house, and entered in great numbers into every room of the house. I begged of God to remember mercy in the midst of judgment, that He would so far restrain their wrath as to prevent their murdering of us, that we might have grace to glorify His name, whether in life or death, and, as I was able, committed our state to God. The enemies who entered the house were all of them In-

dians and Macquas, insulted over me a while, holding up
hatchets over my head, threatening to burn all I had. But
yet God beyond expectation made us in a great measure
to be pitied: for though some were so cruel and barbarous
as to take and carry to the door two of my children and
murder them, as also a Negro woman, yet they gave me
liberty to put on my clothes, keeping me bound with a
cord on one arm, till I put on my clothes to the other; and
then changing my cord, they let me dress myself, and then
pinioned me again. Gave liberty to my dear wife to dress
herself and our children.

About sun an hour high, we were all carried out of the
house for a march, and saw many of the houses of my
neighbors in flames, perceiving the whole fort, one house
excepted, to be taken. Who can tell, what sorrows pierced
our souls when we saw ourselves carried away from God's
sanctuary, to go into a strange land, exposed to so many
trials? The journey being at least three hundred miles we
were to travel, the snow up to the knees, and we never
inured to such hardships and fatigues, the place we were
to be carried to a Popish country.

Upon my parting from the town they fired my house and
barn. We were carried over the river, to the foot of the
mountain, about a mile from my house, where we found a
great number of our Christian neighbors, men, women and
children, to the number of an hundred, nineteen of which
were afterward murdered by the way, and two starved
to death, near Cowass in a time of great scarcity or famine
the savages underwent there. When we came to the foot of
our mountain, they took away our shoes, and gave us, in
the room of them, Indian-shoes, to prepare us for our
travel. Whilst we were there, the English beat out a company that remained in the town, and pursued them to the
river, killing and wounding many of them; but the body of
the army, being alarmed, they repulsed those few English
that pursued them.

I am not able to give you an account of the number of
the enemy slain, but I observed after this night no great
insulting mirth, as I expected; and saw many wounded
persons, and for several days together they buried of their

party, and one of chief note among the Macquas. The Governor of Canada told me his army had that success with the loss but of eleven men, three Frenchmen, one of which was the Lieutenant of the army, five Macquas, and three Indians. But after my arrival at Quebec, I spoke with an Englishman who was taken the last war and married there, and of their religion, who told me they lost above forty, and that many were wounded. I replied, the Governor of Canada said they lost but eleven men. He answered, 'tis true, that there were but eleven killed outright at the taking of the fort, but that many others were wounded, among whom was the ensign of the French; but, said he, they had a fight in the meadow, and that in both engagements they lost more than forty. Some of the soldiers, both French and Indians then present, told me so (said he) adding, that the French always endeavor to conceal the number of their slain.

After this, we went up the mountain and saw the smoke of the fires in the town, and beheld the awful desolations of our town. And before we marched any further, they killed a sucking child of the English. There were slain by the enemy of the inhabitants of our town to the number of thirty-eight, besides nine of the neighboring towns. We traveled not far the first day: God made the heathen so to pity our children that, though they had several wounded persons of their own to carry upon their shoulders for thirty miles before they came to the river, yet they carried our children, incapable of traveling, upon their shoulders and in their arms. When we came to our lodging place, the first night, they dug away the snow and made some wigwams, cut down some of the small branches of spruce trees to lie down on, and gave the prisoners somewhat to eat; but we had but little appetite.

I was pinioned and bound down that night, and so I was every night whilst I was with the army. Some of the enemy who brought drink with them from the town, fell to drinking, and in their drunken fit they killed my Negro man, the only dead person I either saw at the town or in the way. In the night an Englishman made his escape; in the morning I was called for and ordered by the general to tell the English, that if any more made their escape, they would burn the rest of the prisoners.

He that took me was unwilling to let me speak with any of the prisoners as we marched; but on the morning of the second day (he being appointed to guard the rear), I was put into the hands of my other master, who permitted me to speak to my wife when I overtook her, and to walk with her to help her in her journey. On the way we discoursed of the happiness of them who had a right to "an house not made with hands, eternal in the heavens; and God for a father and friend"; as also, that it was our reasonable duty quietly to submit to the will of God, and to say, "The will of the Lord be done." My wife told me her strength of body began to fail, so that I must expect to part with her, saying, she hoped God would preserve my life and the life of some, if not of all, of our children, with us; and commended to me, under God, the care of them. She never spoke any discontented word as to what had befallen us, but with suitable expressions, justified God in what had befallen us.

We soon made a halt, in which time my chief surviving master came up, upon which I was put upon marching with the foremost, and so made to take my last farewell of my dear wife, the desire of my eyes and companion in many mercies and afflictions. Upon our separation from each other, we asked for each other grace sufficient, for what God should call us to. After our being parted from one another, she spent the few remaining minutes of her stay in reading the holy scriptures; which she was wont personally every day to delight her soul in reading, praying, meditating of, and over, by herself, in her closet, over and above what she heard out of them in our family worship.

I was made to wade over a small river, and so were all the English, the water above kneedeep, the stream very swift; and after that, to travel up a small mountain; my strength was almost spent before I came to the top of it. No sooner had I overcome the difficulty of that ascent but I was permitted to sit down and be unburdened of my pack; I sat pitying those who were behind and entreated my master to let me go down and help up my wife; but he refused, and would not let me stir from him. I asked each of the prisoners (as they passed by me) after her, and heard that in passing through the abovesaid river, she fell down and was plunged over head and ears in the water, after which she traveled not far, for at the foot of this mountain, the cruel and bloodthirsty savage who took her, slew her with his hatchet at one stroke. The tidings of which were very awful; and yet such was the hard-heartedness of the adversary, that my tears were reckoned to me as a reproach. My loss, and the loss of my children was great: our hearts were so filled with sorrow that nothing but the comfortable hopes of her being taken away in mercy, to herself, from the evils we were to see, feel and suffer under (and joined to the assembly of the "spirits of just men made perfect," to rest in peace and "joy unspeakable, and full of glory," and the good measure of God thus to exercise us), could have kept us from sinking under at that time. That scripture (Job 1. 21): "Naked came I out of my mother's womb, and naked shall I return thither: the Lord gave, and the Lord hath taken away, blessed be the name of the Lord," was brought to my mind; and from it, that an "afflicting God was to be glorified"; with some other places of scripture, to persuade to a patient bearing my afflictions. . . .

[At Quebec:] The next morning the bell rang for mass: my master bid me go to church. I refused; he threatened me, and went away in a rage. At noon the Jesuits sent for me to dine with them; for I ate at their table all the time I was at the fort. And after dinner, they told me, the Indians would not allow of any of their captives staying in their wigwams whilst they were at church; and were resolved by force and violence to bring us all to church, if we would not go without. I told them it was highly unreasonable so to impose upon those who were of a contrary religion, and to force us to be present at such service as we abhorred, was nothing becoming Christianity. They replied, they were savages, and would not hearken to reason, but would have their wills; said also, if they were in New England themselves, they would go into the churches to see their ways of worship. I answered, the case was far different, for there was nothing (themselves being judges) as to matter or manner of worship, but what was according to the word of God in our churches; and therefore it could not be an offense to any man's conscience. But among those there were "idolatrous superstitions" in worship. They said: "Come and see, and offer us conviction, of what is superstitious in worship." To which I answered, that I was not to do evil that good might come on it, and that forcing in matters of religion was hateful. They answered, the Indians were resolved to have it so, and they could not pacify them without my coming; and they would engage they should offer no force or violence to cause any compliance with their ceremonies.

The next mass, my master bid me go to church; I objected; he arose and forcibly pulled me out by head and shoulders out of the wigwam to the church that was nigh the door. So I went in and sat down behind the door, and there saw a great confusion, instead of any Gospel order, for one of the Jesuits was at the altar, saying mass in a tongue unknown to the savages, and the other, between the altar and the door, saying and singing prayers among the Indians at the same time; and many others were at the same time saying over their *Pater Nosters* and *Ave Mary*, by tale from their chaplet or beads on a string. At our going out, we smiled at their devotion so managed, which was offensive to them; for they said we made a derision of their worship.

When I was here, a certain savage died; one of the Jesuits told me; "She was a very holy woman, who had not committed one sin in twelve years." After a day or two, the Jesuits asked me what I thought of their way, how I saw it? I told them, I thought Christ said of it (as Mark 7. 7, 8, 9): "Howbeit, in vain do they worship me, teaching for doctrines the commandments of men. For laying aside the commandment of God, ye hold the tradition of men, as the washing of pots and cups: and many other such like things ye do. And he said unto them, full well ye reject the commandment of God, that ye may keep your own tradition." They told me, they were not the commandments of men, but apostolical traditions, of equal authority with the holy scriptures, and that after my death, I would bewail my not praying to the virgin Mary, and that I should find the want of her intercession for me with her son, judging me to hell for asserting the scriptures to be a perfect rule of faith. And said, I abounded in my own sense, entertaining explications contrary to the sense of the Pope, regularly sitting with a general council, explaining scripture, and making articles of faith. I told them, it was my comfort that Christ was to be my judge and not they at the great day; and as for their censuring and judging of me, I was not moved with it.

One day a certain savage, taken prisoner in Philip's war, who had lived at Mr. Buckley's at Weathersfield, called Ruth, who could speak English very well, who had been often at my house but was now proselyted to the Romish faith, came into the wigwam and with her an English maid who was taken the last war, who was dressed up in Indian apparel, could not speak one word of English, who said she could neither tell her own name, or the name of the place from whence she was taken. These two talked in the Indian dialect with my master a long time; after which my master bade me cross myself. I told him I would not; he commanded me several times, and I as often refused. Ruth said: "Mr. Williams, you know the scripture, and therefore act against your own light, for you know the scripture saith, 'Servants obey your masters'; he is your master and you his servant." I told her she was ignorant, and knew not the meaning of the scripture, telling her, I was not to disobey the great God to obey any master, and that I was ready to suffer for God if called thereto. On which she talked to my master; I suppose she interpreted what I said. My master took hold of my hand to force me to cross myself; but I struggled with him, and would not suffer him to guide my hand. Upon this he pulled off a crucifix from his own neck and bade me kiss it; but I refused once and again; he told me, he would dash out my brains with his hatchet if I refused. I told him I should sooner choose death than to sin against God; then he ran and caught up his hatchet, and acted as though he would have dashed out my brains; seeing I was not moved, he threw down his hatchet, saying, he would first bite off all my nails if I still refused. I gave him my hand and told him I was ready to suffer; he set his teeth in my thumb nail and gave a grip with his teeth, and then said: "No good minister, no love God, as bad as the devil," and so left off. I have reason to bless God who strengthened me to withstand; by this he was so discouraged as never more to meddle with me about my religion.

CHAPTER FIVE

POETRY

1. ANNE BRADSTREET, 1612–1672

[Puritanism was not an anti-intellectual fundamentalism; it was a learned, scholarly movement that required on the part of the leaders, and as much as possible from the followers, not only knowledge but a respect for the cultural heritage. Being good classicists, they read Latin and Greek poetry, and tried their hands at composing verses of their own. The amount they wrote, even amid the labor of settling a wilderness, is astonishing.

Of course, the Puritan aesthetic restricted the Puritan poet. He could not surrender himself to sensual delights, and the code of the plain style would apply to his rhythms as well as to his prose. Consequently little of this production speaks readily to the modern reader, but every collection of American poetry must salute the lyrics of Anne Bradstreet.

The daughter of Thomas Dudley, she lived as a girl in the comfort of the mansion of the Earl of Lincolnshire, was married at sixteen to Simon Bradstreet, and came with the Great Migration in 1630 to New England, "where," she says, "I found a new world and new manners, at which my heart rose." However, she continues: "After I was convinced it was the way of God, I submitted to it and joined the church at Boston." Later the Bradstreets became pioneers of North Andover; she raised a large family and in her few moments of leisure wrote a series of long, recondite poems on such conventional subjects as the seasons and the four monarchies. These are competent, cultured, though to our taste a bit stiff; they show intensive reading in such modern poets as Spenser and Sidney. Her brother-in-law took them to England and published them in 1650 under the revealingly boastful title, *The Tenth Muse Lately sprung up in America. Or, Severall Poems, compiled with great variety of Wit and Learning, full of delight.*

If these show that a Puritan could combine deep piety with a genial culture, more importantly Anne Bradstreet's occasional lyrics, inspired by the native setting or the homely incidents of her daily life, show that a Puritan could further combine piety with sexual passion, love of children and good furniture, humor—that the female Puritan, in short, could be both a Puritan and a woman of great charm.

These lyrics were printed after her death at Boston in 1678 under the title, *Several Poems Compiled . . . By a Gentlewoman in New-England.*]

SEVERAL POEMS

The Author to Her Book

Thou ill-formed offspring of my feeble brain,
Who after birth didst by my side remain
Till snatched from thence by friends, less wise than true,
Who thee abroad exposed to public view,
Made thee in rags, halting to th' press to trudge,
Where errors were not lessened (all may judge).
At thy return my blushing was not small,
My rambling brat (in print) should mother call;
I cast thee by as one unfit for light,
Thy visage was so irksome in my sight;
Yet being mine own, at length affection would
Thy blemishes amend, if so I could:
I washed thy face, but more defects I saw,
And rubbing off a spot, still made a flaw.
I stretched thy joints to make thee even feet,
Yet still thou run'st more hobbling than is meet;
In better dress to trim thee was my mind,
But nought save home-spun cloth in th' house I find.

In this array, 'mongst vulgars mayst thou roam;
In critics' hands, beware thou dost not come.
And take thy way where yet thou art not known.
If for thy father asked, say thou hadst none;
And for thy mother—she, alas, is poor,
Which caused her thus to send thee out of door.

The Flesh and the Spirit

In secret place where once I stood
Close by the banks of lacrim flood,
I heard two sisters reason on
Things that are past and things to come.
One Flesh was called, who had her eye
On worldly wealth and vanity;
The other Spirit, who did rear
Her thoughts unto a higher sphere.
"Sister," quoth Flesh, "what liv'st thou on—
Nothing but meditation?
Doth contemplation feed thee, so
Regardlessly to let earth go?
Can speculation satisfy
Notion without reality?
Dost dream of things beyond the moon,
And dost thou hope to dwell there soon?
Hast treasures there laid up in store,
That all in th' world thou count'st but poor?
Art fancy sick, or turned a sot,
To catch at shadows which are not?
Come, come, I'll show unto thy sense
Industry hath its recompense.
What canst desire but thou mayst see
True substance in variety?
Dost honor like? Acquire the same,
As some to their immortal fame,
And trophies to thy name erect
Which wearing time shall ne'er deject.
For riches dost thou long full sore?
Behold enough of precious store;

Earth hath more silver, pearls, and gold
Than eyes can see or hands can hold.
Affect'st thou pleasure? Take thy fill;
Earth hath enough of what you will.
Then let not go what thou mayst find
For things unknown, only in mind."

Spirit: "Be still, thou unregenerate part;
Disturb no more my settled heart,
For I have vowed (and so will do)
Thee as a foe still to pursue,
And combat with thee will and must
Until I see thee laid in th' dust.
Sisters we are, yea, twins we be,
Yet deadly feud 'twixt thee and me;
For from one father are we not:
Thou by old Adam wast begot,
But my arise is from above,
Whence my dear Father I do love.
Thou speak'st me fair but hat'st me sore;
Thy flattering shows I'll trust no more.
How oft thy slave hast thou me made
When I believed what thou hast said,
And never had more cause of woe
Than when I did what thou bad'st do.
I'll stop mine ears at these thy charms
And count them for my deadly harms.
Thy sinful pleasures I do hate,
Thy riches are to me no bait,
Thine honors do nor will I love,
For my ambition lies above.
My greatest honor it shall be
When I am victor over thee
And triumph shall, with laurel head,
When thou my captive shalt be led.
How I do live thou need'st not scoff,
For I have meat thou know'st not of;
The hidden manna I do eat,
The word of life it is my meat.
My thoughts do yield me more content
Than can thy hours in pleasure spent.

Nor are they shadows which I catch,
Nor fancies vain at which I snatch;
But reach at things that are so high,
Beyond thy dull capacity.
Eternal substance I do see,
With which enrichèd I would be;
Mine eye doth pierce the heavens, and see
What is invisible to thee.
My garments are not silk nor gold
Nor such like trash which earth doth hold,
But royal robes I shall have on
More glorious than the glist'ring sun.
My crown not diamonds, pearls, and gold,
But such as angels' heads infold.
The city where I hope to dwell
There's none on earth can parallel;
The stately walls both high and strong
Are made of precious jasper stone;
The gates of pearl both rich and clear;
And angels are for porters there;
The streets thereof transparent gold,
Such as no eye did e'er behold;
A crystal river there doth run,
Which doth proceed from the Lamb's throne;
Of life there are the waters sure,
Which shall remain forever pure;
Nor sun nor moon they have no need,
For glory doth from God proceed;
No candle there, nor yet torchlight,
For there shall be no darksome night.
From sickness and infirmity
For evermore they shall be free,
Nor withering age shall e'er come there,
But beauty shall be bright and clear.
This city pure is not for thee,
For things unclean there shall not be.
If I of heaven may have my fill,
Take thou the world, and all that will."

Epitaph on a Patriot

Within this tomb a patriot lies
That was both pious, just, and wise,
To truth a shield, to right a wall,
To sectaries a whip and maul,
A magazine of history,
A prizer of good company,
In manners pleasant and severe;
The good him loved, the bad did fear.
And when his time with years was spent,
If some rejoiced, more did lament.

Before the Birth of One of Her Children

All things within this fading world hath end,
Adversity doth still our joys attend;
No ties so strong, no friends so dear and sweet,
But with death's parting blow is sure to meet.
The sentence past is most irrevocable,
A common thing, yet oh, inevitable.
How soon, my dear, death may my steps attend,
How soon 't may be thy lot to lose thy friend
We both are ignorant; yet love bids me
These farewell lines to recommend to thee,
That when that knot's untied that made us one,
I may seem thine, who in effect am none.
And if I see not half my days that's due,
What nature would, God grant to yours and you.
The many faults that well you know I have,
Let be interred in my oblivion's grave;
If any worth or virtue were in me,
Let that live freshly in thy memory;
And when thou feel'st no grief, as I no harms,
Yet love thy dead, who long lay in thine arms.
And when thy loss shall be repaid with gains,
Look to my little babes, my dear remains.
And if thou love thyself, or loved'st me,

These O protect from stepdame's injury.
And if chance to thine eyes shall bring this verse,
With some sad sighs honor my absent hearse;
And kiss this paper for thy love's dear sake,
Who with salt tears this last farewell did take.

To My Dear and Loving Husband

If ever two were one, then surely we.
If ever man were loved by wife, then thee.
If ever wife was happy in a man,
Compare with me, ye women, if you can.
I prize thy love more than whole mines of gold,
Or all the riches that the East doth hold.
My love is such that rivers cannot quench,
Nor ought but love from thee give recompense.
Thy love is such I can no way repay;
The heavens reward thee manifold, I pray.
Then, while we live, in love let's so persever,
That when we live no more we may live ever.

A Letter to Her Husband, Absent upon Public Employment

My head, my heart, mine eyes, my life—nay more,
My joy, my magazine of earthly store:
If two be one, as surely thou and I,
How stayest thou there, whilst I at Ipswich lie?
So many steps head from the heart to sever,
If but a neck, soon should we be together.
I like the earth this season mourn in black;
My sun is gone so far in's Zodiac,
Whom whilst I 'joyed, nor storms nor frosts I felt,
His warmth such frigid colds did cause to melt.
My chilled limbs now numbed lie forlorn:
Return, return, sweet sol, from Capricorn.
In this dead time, alas, what can I more
Than view those fruits which through thy heat I bore?

Which sweet contentment yields me for a space
True living pictures of their father's face.
O strange effect! Now thou art southward gone,
I weary grow, the tedious day so long:
But when thou northward to me shalt return,
I wish my sun may never set, but burn
Within the Cancer of my glowing breast,
The welcome house of him, my dearest guest.
Where ever, ever, stay, and go not thence
Till nature's sad decree shall call thee hence:
Flesh of thy flesh, bone of thy bone,
I here, thou there, yet both but one.

Verses upon the Burning of Our House, July 10th, 1666

In silent night, when rest I took,
For sorrow near I did not look.
I wakened was with thundering noise
And piteous shrieks of dreadful voice.
That fearful sound of "Fire!" and "Fire!"
Let no man know, is my desire.

I, starting up, the light did spy,
And to my God my heart did cry
To strengthen me in my distress,
And not to leave me succorless;
Then coming out, beheld apace
The flame consume my dwelling-place.

And when I could no longer look
I blest His name that gave and took,
That laid my goods now in the dust;
Yea, so it was, and so 'twas just—
It was His own; it was not mine.
Far be it that I should repine.

He might of all justly bereft,
But yet sufficient for us left.

When by the ruins oft I passed
My sorrowing eyes aside did cast,
And here and there the places spy
Where oft I sat, and long did lie.

Here stood that trunk, and there that chest;
There lay that store I counted best;
My pleasant things in ashes lie,
And them behold no more shall I.
Under thy roof no guest shall sit,
Nor at thy table eat a bit;

No pleasant tale shall e'er be told,
Nor things recounted done of old;
No candle e'er shall shine in thee,
Nor bridegroom's voice e'er heard shall be.
In silence ever shalt thou lie.
Adieu, adieu; all's vanity.

Then straight I 'gan my heart to chide:
And did thy wealth on earth abide?
Didst fix thy hope on mouldering dust,
The arm of flesh didst make thy trust?
Raise up thy thoughts above the sky,
That dunghill mists away may fly.

Thou hast an house on high erect;
Framed by that mighty Architect,
With glory richly furnished,
Stands permanent though this be fled.
It's purchasèd, and paid for, too,
By Him who hath enough to do—

A price so vast as is unknown,
Yet, by His gift, is made thine own.
There's wealth enough; I need no more.
Farewell, my pelf; farewell, my store;
The world no longer let me love.
My hope and treasure lie above.

As Weary Pilgrim, Now at Rest

As weary pilgrim, now at rest,
  Hugs with delight his silent nest;
His wasted limbs now lie full soft
  That miry steps have trodden oft;
Blesses himself to think upon
  His dangers past and travails done;
The burning sun no more shall heat,
  Nor stormy rains on him shall beat;
The briars and thorns no more shall scratch,
  Nor hungry wolves at him shall catch;
He erring paths no more shall tread
  Nor wild fruits eat instead of bread;
For waters cold he doth not long,
  For thirst no more shall parch his tongue;
No rugged stones his feet shall gall,
  Nor stumps nor rocks cause him to fall;
All cares and fears he bids farewell
  And means in safety now to dwell:
A pilgrim I on earth, perplexed
  With sins, with cares and sorrows vexed,
By age and pains brought to decay,
  And my clay house mould'ring away.
Oh! how I long to be at rest
  And soar on high among the blest!
This body shall in silence sleep;
  Mine eyes no more shall ever weep;
No fainting fits shall me assail,
  Nor grinding pains, my body frail;
With cares and fears ne'er cumbered be,
  Nor losses know, nor sorrows see.
What though my flesh shall there consume?
  It is the bed Christ did perfume;
And when a few years shall be gone,
  This mortal shall be clothed upon;
A corrupt carcass down it lies,
  A glorious body it shall rise;
In weakness and dishonor sown,

In power 'tis raised by Christ alone.
Then soul and body shall unite
    And of their maker have the sight,
Such lasting joys shall there behold
    As ear ne'er heard nor tongue e'er told.
Lord, make me ready for that day!
    Then come, dear bridegroom, come away!

2. ANNE BRADSTREET, 1612–1672

[One can hardly appreciate the charm of Anne Bradstreet's lyrics unless he fully comprehends that they were
written by the same woman who, having been too occupied
with house affairs to keep a diary, bequeathed to her children these *Meditations,* which she composed, she says,
"when my soul hath been refreshed with consolations which
the world knows not." Though they might more properly
appear with the prose of Chapter Three, there is an advantage in printing them alongside the poetry that also came
out of these supernal consolations.]

MEDITATIONS

For My Dear Son Simon Bradstreet

Parents perpetuate their lives in their posterity, and their
manners in their imitation. Children do naturally rather
follow the failings than the virtues of their predecessors,
but I am persuaded better things of you. You once desired
me to leave something for you in writing that you might
look upon when you should see me no more. I could think
of nothing more fit for you, nor of more ease to myself, than
these short meditations following. Such as they are I bequeath to you: small legacies are accepted by true friends,
much more by dutiful children. I have avoided encroach-
ing upon others' conceptions, because I would leave you
nothing but mine own; though in value they fall short of
all in this kind, yet I presume they will be better prized

by you for the author's sake. The Lord bless you with grace here, and crown you with glory hereafter, that I may meet you with rejoicing at that great day of appearing, which is the continual prayer of

Your affectionate mother,

March 20, 1664.   A.B.

1

There is no object that we see, no action that we do, no good that we enjoy, no evil that we feel or fear, but we may make some spiritual advantage of all; and he that makes such improvement is wise, as well as pious.

2

Many can speak well, but few can do well. We are better scholars in the theory than the practical part, but he is a true Christian that is a proficient in both.

3

Youth is the time of getting, middle age of improving, and old age of spending; a negligent youth is usually attended by an ignorant middle age, and both by an empty old age. He that hath nothing to feed on but vanity and lies must needs lie down in the bed of sorrow.

4

A ship that bears much sail, and little or no ballast, is easily overset; and that man whose head hath great abilities, and his heart little or no grace, is in danger of foundering.

5

It is reported of the peacock that, priding himself in his gay feathers, he ruffles them up; but, spying his black feet, he soon lets fall his plumes: so he that glories in his gifts and adornings should look upon his corruptions, and that will damp his high thoughts.

6

The finest bread hath the least bran; the purest honey, the least wax; and the sincerest Christian, the least self-love.

7

The hireling that labors all the day comforts himself that when night comes he shall both take his rest and receive his reward: the painful Christian that hath wrought hard in God's vineyard and hath born the heat and drought of the day, when he perceives his sun apace to decline, and the shadows of his evening to be stretched out, lifts up his head with joy, knowing his refreshing is at hand.

8

Downy beds make drowsy persons, but hard lodging keeps the eyes open. A prosperous state makes a secure Christian, but adversity makes him consider.

9

Sweet words are like honey: a little may refresh, but too much gluts the stomach.

10

Diverse children have their different natures: some are like flesh which nothing but salt will keep from putrefaction; some again like tender fruits that are best preserved with sugar. Those parents are wise that can fit their nurture according to their nature.

11

That town which thousands of enemies without hath not been able to take, hath been delivered up by one traitor within; and that man, which all the temptations of Satan without could not hurt, hath been foiled by one lust within.

12

Authority without wisdom is like a heavy axe without an edge, fitter to bruise than polish.

13

The reason why Christians are so loath to exchange this world for a better is because they have more sense than faith: they see what they enjoy, they do but hope for that which is to come.

14

If we had no winter, the spring would not be so pleasant: if we did not sometimes taste of adversity, prosperity would not be so welcome.

15

A low man can go upright under that door where a taller is glad to stoop: so a man of weak faith and mean abilities may undergo a cross more patiently than he that excels him both in gifts and graces.

16

That house which is not often swept makes the cleanly inhabitant soon loathe it; and that heart which is not continually purifying itself is not fit temple for the spirit of God to dwell in.

17

Few men are so humble as not to be proud of their abilities; and nothing will abase them more than this: "What hast thou, but what thou hast received? Come, give an account of thy stewardship?"

18

He that will undertake to climb up a steep mountain with a great burden on his back will find it a wearisome, if not an impossible task: so he that thinks to mount to heaven clogged with the cares and riches of this life, 'tis no wonder if he faint by the way.

31

Iron till it be thoroughly heated is incapable to be wrought: so God sees good to cast some men into the furnace of affliction, and then beats them on His anvil into what frame He pleases.

32

Ambitious men are like hops that never rest climbing so long as they have anything to stay upon: but take away their props, and they are of all the most dejected.

36

Sore laborers have hard hands, and old sinners have brawny consciences.

38

Some children are hardly weaned: although the teat be rubbed with wormwood or mustard, they will either wipe it off or else suck down sweet and bitter together. So it is with some Christians: let God embitter all the sweets of this life that so they might feed upon more substantial food; yet they are so childishly sottish that they are still hugging and sucking these empty breasts, that God is forced to hedge up their way with thorns, or lay affliction on their loins, that so they might shake hands with the world before it bid them farewell.

50

Sometimes the sun is only shadowed by a cloud that we cannot see his luster, although we may walk by his light. But when he is set, we are in darkness till he arise again. So God doth sometimes veil His face but for a moment, that we cannot behold the light of His countenance as at some other time; yet He affords so much light as may direct our way, that we may go forwards to the city of habitation. But when He seems to set and be quite gone out of sight, then must we needs walk in darkness and see no light; yet then must we trust in the Lord, and stay upon our God. And when the morning (which is the appointed time) is come, the Sun of Righteousness will arise with healing in His wings.

53

He that is to sail into a far country, although the ship, cabin, and provision be all convenient and comfortable for him, yet he hath no desire to make that his place of residence, but longs to put in at that port where his business lies. A Christian is sailing through this world unto his heavenly country, and here he hath many conveniences and comforts; but he must beware of desiring to make this the place of his abode, lest he meet with such tossings that may cause him to long for shore before he sees land. We must, therefore, be here as strangers and pilgrims, that we may plainly declare that we seek a city above, and wait all the days of our appointed time till our change shall come.

62

As man is called the little world, so his heart may be called the little commonwealth: his more fixed and resolved thoughts are like to inhabitants; his slight and flitting thoughts are like passengers that travel to and fro continually. Here is also the great court of justice erected, which is always kept by conscience, who is both accuser, excuser, witness and judge, whom no bribes can pervert, nor flattery cause to favor; but as he finds the evidence, so he absolves or condemns. Yea, so absolute is this court of judicature that there is no appeal from it—no, not to the court of heaven itself. For if our conscience condemn us, He also, who is greater than our conscience, will do it much more. But he that would have the boldness to go to the throne of grace to be accepted there must be sure to carry a certificate from the court of conscience, that he stands right there.

64

We see in orchards some trees so fruitful that the weight of their burden is the breaking of their limbs; some again are but meanly loaden, and some have nothing to show but leaves only, and some among them are dry stocks. So is it in the church, which is God's orchard: there are some eminent Christians that are so frequent in good duties that many times the weight thereof impairs both their bodies and estates; and there are some (and they sincere ones too) who have not attained to that fruitfulness, although they aim at perfection. And again, there are others that have nothing to commend them but only a gay profession; and these are but leavy Christians, which are in as much danger of being cut down as the dry stocks—for both cumber the ground.

65

We see in the firmament there is but one sun among a multitude of stars, and those stars also to differ much, one from the other, in regard of bigness and brightness: yet all receive their light from that one sun. So is it in the church both militant and triumphant: there is but one Christ, who is the sun of righteousness, in the midst of an innumerable company of saints and angels. Those saints have their degrees even in this life—some are stars of the first magnitude, and some of a less degree; and others (and they indeed the most in number) but small and obscure. Yet all receive their luster (be it more or less) from that glorious sun that enlightens all in all. And, if some of them shine so bright while they move on earth, how transcendently splendid shall they be when they are fixed in their heavenly spheres!

77

God hath by His providence so ordered that no one country hath all commodities within itself, but what it wants another shall supply, that so there may be a mutual commerce through the world. As it is with countries, so it is with men: there was never yet any one man that had all excellences. Let his parts, natural and acquired, spiritual and moral, be never so large, yet he stands in need of something which another man hath—perhaps meaner than himself: which shows us perfection is not below, as also that God will have us beholden one to another.

3. MICHAEL WIGGLESWORTH, 1631–1705

[It has long been a custom to make fun of *The Day of Doom* as incarnating the repulsive joylessness that modern generations insist on attributing to the Puritans. However, it must be remembered that Michael Wigglesworth was versifying a conception which all Christians had accepted for centuries with similar literalness, the day of the last judgment, as can be seen in sculptures as unsophisticated as his lines on the west front of medieval cathedrals. In fact, Wigglesworth's purpose was identical with that of those sculptors, to give to the people a representation of the dreadful event toward which all creation moves in an imagery they could immediately comprehend. So he used the lilting ballad meter they all knew. He himself was a man of much greater culture, and in this work was deliberately stepping down to the popular level.

Eighteen hundred copies were printed at Cambridge in 1662, and not one survives: they were read to pieces. The work was many times reprinted, and may be said to be the first American best-seller, to be replaced a century later with, interestingly enough, Benjamin Franklin's *The Way to Wealth*.

Wigglesworth was born in England, brought to New England as a child; he graduated from Harvard in 1651. From 1656 to 1705 he was pastor in Malden, also serving the town as physician.]

THE DAY OF DOOM

1

Still was the night, serene and bright,
  when all men sleeping lay;
Calm was the season, and carnal reason
  thought it would last for ay.
Soul, take thine ease, let sorrow cease,
  much good thou hast in store;
This was their song, their cups among,
  the evening before.

2

Wallowing in all kind of sin,
   vile wretches lay secure;
The best of men had scarcely then
   their lamps kept in good ure;
Virgins unwise, who through disguise
   amongst the best were numbered,
Had closed their eyes; yea, and the wise
   through sloth and frailty slumbered.

3

Like as of old, when men grow bold,
   God's threatenings to contemn,
Who stopped their ear and would not hear
   when mercy warnèd them,
But took their course without remorse
   till God began to pour
Destruction the world upon
   in a tempestuous shower.

4

They put away the evil day,
   and drowned their cares and fears,
Till drowned were they and swept away
   by vengeance unawares.
So at the last, whilst men slept fast
   in their security,
Surprised they are in such a snare
   as cometh suddenly.

5

For at midnight broke forth a light,
   which turned the night to day,
And speedily a hideous cry
   did all the world dismay.
Sinners awake, their hearts do ache,
   trembling their loins surpriseth,
Amazed with fear by what they hear,
   each one of them ariseth.

6

They rush from beds with giddy heads,
 and to their windows run,
Viewing this light which shone more bright
 than doth the noonday sun.
Straightway appears (they see't with tears)
 the Son of God most dread,
Who with his train comes on amain
 to judge both quick and dead.

7

Before his face the heavens give place,
 and skies are rent asunder,
With mighty voice and hideous noise,
 more terrible than thunder.
His brightness damps heaven's glorious lamps,
 and makes them hide their heads;
As if afraid and quite dismayed,
 they quit their wonted steads.

8

Ye sons of men that durst contemn
 the threat'nings of God's word,
How cheer you now? your hearts, I trow,
 are thrilled as with a sword.
Now atheist blind, whose brutish mind
 a God could never see,
Dost thou perceive, dost thou believe
 that Christ thy judge shall be?

9

Stout courages, whose hardiness
 could death and hell outface,
Are you as bold, now you behold
 your judge draw near apace?
They cry, "No, no, alas and woe,
 our courage all is gone;
Our hardiness, foolhardiness,
 hath us undone, undone."

10

No heart so bold but now grows cold
  and almost dead with fear,
No eye so dry but now can cry
  and pour out many a tear.
Earth's potentates and pow'rful states,
  captains and men of might,
Are quite abashed, their courage dashed
  at this most dreadful sight.

11

Mean men lament, great men do rent
  their robes and tear their hair;
They do not spare their flesh to tear
  through horrible despair.
All kindreds wail; their hearts do fail;
  horror the world doth fill
With weeping eyes and loud outcries,
  yet knows not how to kill.

12

Some hide themselves in caves and delves
  and places under ground,
Some rashly leap into the deep
  to 'scape by being drowned,
Some to the rocks (O senseless blocks!)
  and woody mountains run,
That there they might this fearful sight
  and dreaded presence shun.

13

In vain do they to mountains say,
  "Fall on us and us hide
From Judge's ire, more hot than fire,
  for who may it abide?"
No hiding place can from his face
  sinners at all conceal,
Whose flaming eye hid things does spy
  and darkest things reveal.

14

The Judge draws nigh, exalted high
    upon a lofty throne,
Amidst the throng of angels strong,
    like Israel's holy one.
The excellence of whose presence
    and awful majesty
Amazeth Nature and every creature
    doth more than terrify.

15

The mountains smoke, the hills are shook,
    the earth is rent and torn,
As if she should be clean dissolved
    or from her center borne.
The sea doth roar, forsake the shore,
    and shrinks away for fear.
The wild beasts flee into the sea,
    so soon as he draws near.

16

Whose glory bright, whose wondrous might,
    whose power imperial
So far surpass whatever was
    in realms terrestrial,
That tongues of men (nor angels' pen)
    cannot the same express,
And therefore I must pass it by,
    lest speaking should transgress.

17

Before his throne a trump is blown,
    proclaiming the day of doom,
Forthwith he cries, "Ye dead, arise,
    and unto judgment come."
No sooner said but 'tis obeyed;
    sepulchers opened are;
Dead bodies all rise at his call,
    and 's mighty power declare.

18

Both sea and land, at his command,
    their dead at once surrender;
The fire and air constrained are
    also their dead to tender.
The mighty word of this great lord
    links body and soul together,
Both of the just and the unjust,
    to part no more forever.

19

The same translates from mortal states
    to immortality
All that survive and be alive,
    i' th' twinkling of an eye;
That so they may abide for aye
    to endless weal or woe,
Both the renate and reprobate
    are made to die no more.

20

His wingèd hosts fly through all coasts
    together gathering
Both good and bad, both quick and dead,
    and all to judgment bring,
Out of their holes those creeping moles,
    that hid themselves for fear,
By force they take, and quickly make
    before the Judge appear.

21

Thus every one before the throne
    of Christ the Judge is brought,
Both righteöus and impious,
    that good or ill hath wrought.
A separation and diff'ring station
    by Christ appointed is
(To sinners sad) 'twixt good and bad,
    'twixt heirs of woe and bliss. . . .

54

There Christ demands at all their hands
    a strict and straight account
Of all things done under the sun,
    whose number far surmount
Man's wit and thought; they all are brought
    unto this solemn trial,
And each offense with evidence,
    so that there's no denial.

55

There's no excuse for their abuse,
    since their own consciences
More proof give in of each man's sin,
    than thousand witnesses.
Though formerly this faculty
    had grossly been abusèd
(Men could it stifle, or with it trifle,
    when as it them accusèd),

56

Now it comes in, and every sin
    unto men's charge doth lay;
It judgeth them and doth condemn,
    though all the world say nay.
It so stingeth and tortureth,
    it worketh such distress,
That each man's self against himself,
    is forcèd to confess.

57

It's vain moreover for men to cover
    the least iniquity;
The Judge hath seen, and privy been
    to all their villainy.
He unto light and open sight
    the work of darkness brings;
He doth unfold both new and old,
    both known and hidden things.

58

All filthy facts and secret acts,
  however closely done
And long concealed, are there revealed
  before the mid-day sun.
Deeds of the night, shunning the light,
  which darkest corners sought,
To fearful blame and endless shame
  are there most justly brought.

59

And as all facts and grosser acts,
  so every word and thought,
Erroneous notions and lustful motion,
  are unto judgment brought.
No sin so small and trivial
  but hither it must come,
Nor so long past, but now at last
  it must receive a doom. . . .

188

The Judge is strong; doers of wrong
  cannot his power withstand.
None can by flight run out of sight
  nor 'scape out of his hand.
Sad is their state, for advocate
  to plead their cause there's none—
None to prevent their punishment,
  or misery bemoan.

189

O dismal day! whither shall they
  for help and succor flee?
To God above, with hopes to move
  their greatest enemy?
His wrath is great, whose burning heat
  no floods of tears can slake:
His word stands fast, that they be cast
  into the burning lake. . . .

195

Unto the saints with sad complaints
    should they themselves apply?
They're not dejected nor aught affected
    with all their misery.
Friends stand aloof and make no proof
    what prayers or tears can do;
Your godly friends are now more friends
    to Christ than unto you.

196

What tender love men's hearts did move
    unto a sympathy,
And bearing part of other's smart
    in their anxiety,
Now such compassion is out of fashion,
    and wholly laid aside;
No friends so near but saints to hear
    their sentence can abide.

197

One natural brother beholds another
    in this astonished fit,
Yet sorrows not thereat a jot,
    nor pities him a whit.
The godly wife conceives no grief,
    nor can she shed a tear
For the sad state of her dear mate
    when she his doom doth hear.

198

He that was erst a husband pierced
    with sense of wife's distress,
Whose tender heart did bear a part
    of all her grievances,
Shall mourn no more as heretofore
    because of her ill plight,
Although he see her now to be
    a damned forsaken wight.

199

The tender mother will own no other
    of all her numerous brood
But such as stand at Christ's right hand
    acquitted through his blood.
The pious father had now much rather
    his graceless son should lie
In hell with devils, for all his evils
    burning eternally,

200

Than God most high should injury
    by sparing him sustain,
And doth rejoice to hear Christ's voice
    ajudging him to pain:
Who having all, both great and small,
    convinced and silenced,
Did then proceed their doom to read,
    and thus it uttered:

201

"Ye sinful wights and cursed sprights
    that work iniquity,
Depart together from me forever
    to endless misery.
Your portion take in yonder lake
    where fire and brimstone flameth;
Suffer the smart which your desert
    as its due wages claimeth." . . .

206

That word "Depart," maugre their heart,
    drives every wicked one,
With mighty power, the self-same hour
    far from the Judge's throne.
Away they're chased by the strong blast
    of his death-threatening mouth;
They flee full fast, as if in haste
    although they be full loath.

207

As chaff that's dry and dust doth fly
    before the northern wind,
Right so are they chased away,
    and can no refuge find.
They hasten to the pit of woe,
    guarded by angels stout,
Who to fullfil Christ's holy will
    attend this wicked rout,

208

Whom having brought, as they are taught,
    unto the brink of hell
(That dismal place far from Christ's face
    where death and darkness dwell,
Where God's fierce ire kindleth the fire,
    and vengeance feeds the flame
With piles of wood and brimstone flood,
    that none can quench the same),

209

With iron bands they bind their hands
    and cursed feet together,
And cast them all, both great and small,
    into that lake forever.
Where day and night, without respite,
    they wail and cry and howl
For torturing pain which they sustain
    in body and in soul.

210

For day and night, in their despite,
    their torments' smoke ascendeth.
Their pain and grief have no relief,
    their anguish never endeth.
There must they lie and never die,
    though dying every day;
There must they dying ever lie,
    and not consume away.

211

Die fain they would, if die they could;
    but death will not be had.
God's direful wrath their bodies hath
    forever immortal made;
They live to lie in misery
    and bear eternal woe:
And live they must while God is just,
    that He may plague them so. . . .

219

The saints behold with courage bold
    and thankful wonderment
To see all those that were their foes
    thus sent to punishment.
Then do they sing unto their King
    a song of endless praise;
They praise His name and do proclaim
    that just are all His ways.

220

Thus with great joy and melody
    to heav'n they all ascend,
Him there to praise with sweetest lays,
    and hymns that never end;
Where with long rest they shall be blest,
    and naught shall them annoy,
Where they shall see as seen they be,
    and whom they love enjoy.

221

Oh, glorious place! where face to face
    Jehovah may be seen,
By such as were sinners while here,
    and no dark veil between!
Where the sunshine and light divine
    of God's bright countenance
Doth rest upon them every one,
    with sweetest influence!

222

Oh, blessèd state of the renate!
  Oh, wond'rous happiness,
To which they're brought beyond what thought
  can reach or words express!
Grief's watercourse and sorrow's source
  are turned to joyful streams;
Their old distress and heaviness
  are vanishèd like dreams.

223

For God above in arms of love
  doth dearly them embrace,
And fills their sprights with such delights
  and pleasures in His grace
As shall not fail, nor yet grow stale,
  through frequency of use;
Nor do they fear God's favor there
  to forfeit by abuse.

224

For there the saints are perfect saints,
  and holy ones indeed;
From all the sin that dwelt within
  their mortal bodies freed;
Made kings and priests to God through Christ's
  dear love's transcendency,
There to remain and there to reign
  with him eternally.

4. MICHAEL WIGGLESWORTH, 1631–1705

[That Wigglesworth was capable of a loftier vein in poetry than *The Day of Doom* is shown by this poetic jeremiad, composed in the year of a terrible drought, 1662. God here speaks the language of prophetic denunciation which all preachers upon New England's "declension" strove for, but few so magisterially attained. When in his own person Wigglesworth ends with an address to his dear-

est land, he betrays how subtly within the pattern of denunciation was conceived and cherished a patriotism, a love
of the new land, which it took these Englishmen some
decades to recognize, and which finally broke into ecstatic
utterance in Sewall's hymn to Plum Island.]

GOD'S CONTROVERSY WITH
NEW ENGLAND

Our temp'ral blessings did abound,
  But spiritual good things
Much more abounded, to the praise
  Of that great King of kings.
God's throne was here set up, here was
  His tabernacle pight;
This was the place and these the folk
  In whom He took delight.

Our morning stars shone all day long,
  Their beams gave forth such light
As did the noonday sun abash
  And's glory dazzle quite.
Our day continued many years
  And had no night at all;
Yea, many thought the light would last
  And be perpetual.

Such, O New England, was thy first,
  Such was thy best estate;
But, lo! a strange and sudden change
  My courage did amate.
The brightest of our morning stars
  Did wholly disappear;
And those that tarrièd behind
  With sackcloth covered were.

Moreover, I beheld and saw
  Our welkin overcast,
And dismal clouds for sunshine late

O'erspread from east and west.
The air became tempestuous;
The wilderness 'gan quake;
And from above with awful voice
Th'Almighty thund'ring spake:

"Are these the men that erst at My command
Forsook their ancient seats and native soil,
To follow Me into a desert land,
Contemning all the travel and the toil,
Whose love was such to purest ordinances
As made them set at nought their fair inheritances?

Are these the men that prizèd liberty
To walk with God according to their light,
To be as good as He would have them be,
To serve and worship Him with all their might,
Before the pleasures which a fruitful field,
And country flowing-full of all good things, could yield?

Are these the folk whom from the British Isles,
Through the stern billows of the wat'ry main,
I safely led so many thousand miles,
As if their journey had been through a plain,
Whom having from all enemies protected,
And through so many deaths and dangers well directed,

I brought and planted on the western shore,
Where nought but brutes and savage wights did swarm
(Untaught, untrained, untamed by virtue's lore)
That sought their blood, yet could not do them harm;
My fury's flail them threshed, My fatal broom
Did sweep them hence, to make My people elbow-room.

Are these the men whose gates with peace I crowned,
To whom for bulwarks I salvation gave,
Whilst all things else with rattling tumults sound,
And mortal frays send thousands to the grave?
Whilst their own brethren bloody hands embrewed
In brothers' blood, and fields with carcasses bestrewed?

Is this the people blest with bounteous store,
   By land and sea full richly clad and fed,
Whom plenty's self stands waiting still before,
   And poureth out their cups well temperèd?
For whose dear sake an howling wilderness
   I lately turned into a fruitful paradise?

Are these the people in whose hemisphere
   Such bright-beamed, glist'ring, sun-like stars I placed,
As by their influence did all things cheer,
   As by their light blind ignorance defaced,
As errors into lurking holes did fray,
   As turned the late dark night into a lightsome day?

Are these the folk to whom I milkèd out,
   And sweetness streamed from consolation's breast;
Whose souls I fed and strengthenèd throughout
   With finest spiritual food most finely dressed?
On whom I rainèd living bread from heaven,
   Withouten error's bane, or superstition's leaven?

With whom I made a covenant of peace,
   And unto whom I did most firmly plight
My faithfulness, if whilst I live I cease
   To be their guide, their God, their full delight;
Since them with cords of love to Me I drew,
   Enwrapping in My grace such as should them ensue?

Are these the men, that now Mine eyes behold,
   Concerning whom I thought, and whilom spake,
First heaven shall pass away together scrolled,
   Ere they My laws and righteous ways forsake,
Or that they slack to run their heavenly race?
   Are these the same? or are some others come in place?

If these be they, how is it that I find
   Instead of holiness, carnality;
Instead of heavenly frames, an earthly mind;
   For burning zeal, luke-warm indifferency;
For flaming love, key-cold dead-heartedness;

For temperance (in meat, and drink, and clothes),
    excess?

Whence cometh it that pride, and luxury,
    Debate, deceit, contentiön, and strife,
False-dealing, covetousness, hypocrisy,
    (With such like crimes) amongst them are so rife,
That one of them doth over-reach another?
    And that an honest man can hardly trust his brother?

How is it that security and sloth
    Amongst the best are common to be found?
That grosser sins, instead of grace's growth,
    Amongst the many more and more abound?
I hate dissembling shows of holiness.
    Or practice as you talk, or never more profess.

Judge not, vain world, that all are hypocrites
    That do profess more holiness than thou;
All foster not dissembling, guileful sprites,
    Nor love their lusts, though very many do.
Some sin through want of care and constant watch;
    Some with the sick converse till they the sickness catch.

Some, that maintain a real root of grace,
    Are overgrown with many noisome weeds,
Whose heart, that those no longer may take place,
    The benefit of due correction needs.
And such as these, however gone astray,
    I shall by stripes reduce into a better way.

Moreover some there be that still retain
    Their ancient vigor and sincerity;
Whom both their own and others' sins constrain
    To sigh, and mourn, and weep, and wail, and cry;
And for their sakes I have forborne to pour
    My wrath upon revolters to this present hour.

To praying saints I always have respect,
    And tender love, and pitiful regard;

Nor will I now in any wise neglect
  Their love and faithful service to reward;
Although I deal with others for their folly,
  And turn their mirth to tears that have been too jolly.

For think not, O backsliders, in your heart,
  That I shall still your evil manners bear;
Your sins Me press as sheaves do load a cart,
  And therefore I will plague you for this gear.
Except you seriously, and soon, repent,
  I'll not delay your pain and heavy punishment.

And who be those themselves that yonder show?
  The seed of such as name My dreadful Name!
On whom while 'ere compassion's skirt I threw
  Whilst in their blood they were, to hide their shame!
Whom My preventing love did ne'er Me take!
  Whom for Mine own I marked, lest they should me
    forsake!

I looked that such as these to virtue's lore
  (Though none but they) would have inclined their ear;
That they at least Mine image should have bore,
  And sanctified My name with awful fear.
Let pagan's brats pursue their lusts, whose meed
  Is death. For Christian's children are an holy seed.

But hear, O heavens! Let earth amazèd stand!
  Ye mountains melt, and hills come flowing down!
Let horror seize upon both sea and land!
  Let nature's self be cast into a stone!
I children nourished, nurtured, and upheld;
  But they against a tender Father have rebelled.

What could have been by me performèd more?
  Or wherein fell I short of your desire?
Had you but asked, I would have oped My store,
  And given what lawful wishes could require.
For all this bounteous cost I looked to see

Heaven-reaching hearts and thoughts, meekness,
    humility.". . .

Ah dear New England! dearest land to me!
    Which unto God has hitherto been dear—
And may'st be still more dear than formerly
    If to His voice thou wilt incline thine ear.

Consider well and wisely what the rod,
    Wherewith thou art from year to year chastised,
Instructeth thee: repent and turn to God,
    Who will not have His nurture be despised.

Thou still hast in thee many praying saints,
    Of great account and precious with the Lord,
Who daily pour out unto Him their plaints,
    And strive to please Him both in deed and word.

Cheer on, sweet souls, my heart is with you all,
    And shall be with you, maugre Satan's might.
And whereso'er this body be a thrall,
    Still in New England shall be my delight.

5. E.B.

[A people who lived so much in the presence of death,
and more urgently with the thought of death constantly
in their mind, were bound to use the death of every friend,
relative, or prominent man as an occasion for strengthening
their faith and courage. Hence they wrote innumerable
elegies. In 1721 the young Benjamin Franklin made hay
with the "receipt" for making a New England elegy. By
that time the plain style in verse had become so prosaic
that it invited such ridicule. But while the Puritans were
cautious about yielding themselves to a style in which a
play of words or conceits of wit distracted thought from
the substance, nevertheless there is evidence that some of
them had a hankering for "metaphysical" poetry which
they could not stifle, even though suspecting it to be sinful.

In 1663 Samuel Stone, Hooker's colleague in the Hartford pulpit, died, much loved and lamented. One "E.B." wrote a threnody upon "our church's second dark eclipse" which was later printed in a history of the colonies. "E.B." was probably Edward Bulkeley, son of Peter of Concord, but this is not certain. Whoever wrote it took a leap into the metaphysical wilderness, and wrought upon the name "Stone" as elaborate a conceit as any court wit of the century ever devised.]

A THRENODIA

A stone more than the Ebenezer famed:
Stone, splendent diamond, right orient named;
A cordial stone, that often cheerèd hearts
With pleasant wit, with Gospel rich imparts;
Whetstone, that edgified the obtusest mind—
Loadstone, that drew the iron heart unkind—
A ponderous stone, that would the bottom sound
Of scripture depths, and bring out arcans found;
A stone for kingly David's use so fit
As would not fail Goliath's front to hit;
A stone, an antidote, that brake the course
Of gangrene error by convincing force;
A stone acute, fit to divide and square;
A squarèd stone became Christ's building rare.

6. EDWARD TAYLOR, 1645?–1729

[The discovery of the manuscripts of Edward Taylor by Thomas H. Johnson in 1937 completely upset the established perspective on Puritan literature: here was a hitherto unknown poet of great distinction (who by now has taken an assured place in criticism), who in secret, over a long period of years, wrote in the most exquisite, the most subtle, of metaphysical veins. The mystery of this solitary labor in the wilderness is yet unsolved.

Little is known of Taylor's life. He was born in or near

Coventry, presumably about 1645, and came to New England as late as 1668. Possibly he had thus a better opportunity in his youth than had the average New England intellectual to come under the influence of Donne, Quarles, and other metaphysicals. Possibly for this reason, also, he was less bound to the plain style. He graduated from Harvard in 1671, a classmate and lifelong friend of Judge Sewell (cf. p. 255). He was ordained in the frontier town of Westfield, near Northampton; he arrived there in December of 1671, and served continuously, though because of King Philip's War he was not ordained until 1679. He married Elizabeth Fitch; none of their seven children survived him. By his second wife he had six children. As was often the case with the Puritan clergy, he served the town both as minister and physician. His grandson, Ezra Stiles, heard him described as "A man of small stature but firm: of quick passions—yet serious and grave." Though located so near to Solomon Stoddard, he was one of the two or three in the Valley who stood out against Stoddard's inovations (cf. pp. 221–22), which shows how much independence he possessed. However, he appears to have confined his opposition to communings with himself. Obviously he cherished his accumulated manuscripts, but left instructions in his will that nothing ever be published. Ezra Stiles ultimately deposited the four hundred pages, unopened, in the Yale College Library.

As little is known of Taylor's preaching as of Wise's since he published nothing in his lifetime. Sewall reports that on a visit to Boston he delivered a sermon worthy of Paul's Cross. From the poetry we see that he was a thoroughly orthodox federalist theologian, but his thinking upon the covenant is in a mode, stylistically speaking, which cannot elsewhere be matched in the colonies.

The central work in the collection is a series of poems that make up, not a connected whole, but a series in various forms and meters which compose a sequential exposition of Puritan cosmology. His own long title for the aggregation is: *God's Determinations Touching His Elect: And The Elects' Combat in Their Conversion, And Coming Up To God In Christ: Together With The Comfortable Effects*

Thereof. This is the true, lofty, Puritan version of *The Day of Doom,* on the level of the highest (or deepest) spiritual eloquence. In fascinating contrast to Wigglesworth's popularization of the theology, Taylor's profound analysis comes to a triumphant climax not with the distant judgment but with the present, living church. For him, the great drama is not the theatrical blast of the trumpet, but the agonizing pilgrimage of man into the fellowship of the saints.

Mr. Johnson issued *The Poetical Works of Edward Taylor* in 1939. These selections are made by his permission and that of the Princeton University Press.]

GOD'S DETERMINATIONS
TOUCHING HIS ELECT

The Preface

Infinity, when all things it beheld
In nothing, and of nothing all did build—
Upon what base was fixed the lath wherein
He turned this globe and riggaled it so trim?
Who blew the bellows of His furnace vast?
Or held the mould wherein the world was cast?
Who laid its corner-stone? Or whose command?
Where stand the pillars upon which it stands?
Who laced and filleted the earth so fine
With rivers like green ribbons smaragdine?
Who made the seas its selvage, and its locks
Like a quilt ball within a silver box?
Who spread its canopy? Or curtains spun?
Who in this bowling alley bowled the sun?
Who made it always when it rises set:
To go at once both down and up to get?
Who the curtain rods made for this tapestry?
Who hung the twinkling lanthorns in the sky?
Who? Who did this? Or who is He? Why, know
It's only Might Almighty this did do.

His hand hath made this noble work which stands

His glorious handiwork not made by hands.
Who spake all things for nothing—and with ease
Can speak all things to nothing, if He please.
Whose little finger at His pleasure can
Out-mete ten thousand worlds with half a span;
Whose Might Almighty can by half a looks
Root up the rocks and the hills by the roots,
Can take this mighty world up in His hand,
And shake it like a squitchen or a wand.
Whose single frown will make the heavens shake
Like as an aspen leaf the wind makes quake.
Oh! What a might is this! whose single frown
Doth shake the world as it would shake it down!
Which all from nothing fet, from nothing, all:
Hath all on nothing set, lets nothing fall.
Gave all to nothing-man indeed, whereby
Through nothing, man-all might Him glorify.
In nothing is embossed the brightest gem,
More precious than all preciousness in them.
But nothing-man did throw down all by sin,
And darkened that lightsome gem in him
   That now his brightest diamond is grown,
   Darker by far than any coalpit stone.

Prologue

Lord, can a crumb of earth the earth outweigh,
   Outmatch all mountains, nay, the crystal sky?
Imbosom in't designs that shall display
   And trace into the boundless Deity?
   Yea! hand, a pen whose moisture doth gild o'er
   Eternal glory with a glorious glore?

If it its pen had of an angel's quill,
   And sharpened on a precious stone ground tight,
And dipt in liquid gold, and moved by skill,
   In crystal leaves should golden letters write,
   It would but blot and blur, yea, jag and jar
   Unless Thou mak'st the pen, and scrivener.

I am this crumb of dust which is designed
   To make my pen unto Thy praise alone,
And my dull fancy I would gladly grind
   Unto an edge on Zion's precious stone,
   And write in liquid gold upon Thy name
   My letters, till Thy glory forth doth flame.

Let not th'attempts break down my dust, I pray,
   Nor laugh Thou them to scorn, but pardon give.
Inspire this crumb of dust till it display
   Thy glory through't, and then Thy dust shall live.
   Its failings then Thou'lt overlook, I trust,
   They being slips slipped from Thy crumb of dust.

Thy crumb of dust breathes two words from its breast:
   That Thou wilt guide its pen to write aright
To prove Thou art and that Thou art the best,
   And show Thy properties to shine most bright.
   And then Thy works will shine as flowers on stems,
   Or as in jewelry shops do gems.

The Forwardness of the Elect in the Work of Conversion

Those upon whom Almighty doth intend
His all-eternal glory to expend,
Lull'd in the lap of sinful nature snug,
Like pearls in puddles covered o'er with mud,
Whom, if you search, perhaps some few you'll find
That to notorious sins were ne'er inclined:
Some shunning some, some most, some great, some small;
Some this, that, or the other, some none at all.
But all, or almost all, you'st easily find
To all, or almost all, defects inclined:
To revel with the rabble rout who say,
"Let's hiss this piety out of our day."
And those whose frame is made of finer twine
Stand further off from grace than wash from wine.
Those who suck grace from th' breast are nigh as rare
As black swans that in milk-white rivers are.
Grace therefore calls them all, and sweetly woos.

Some, won, come in; the rest as yet refuse
And run away. Mercy pursues apace:
Then some cast down their arms, cry, "Quarter, grace!"
Some chased out of breath, drop down with fear,
Perceiving the pursuer drawing near.
The rest, pursued, divide into two ranks,
And this way one, and that the other pranks.

Then in comes Justice with her forces by her,
And doth pursue as hot as sparkling fire.
The right wing then begins to fly away,
But in the straits strong barricadoes lay.
They're therefore forced to face about and have
Their spirits quelled, and therefore quarter crave.
These, captived thus, Justice pursues the game
With all her troops, to take the other train:
Which, being chased in a peninsula
And followed close, they find no other way
To make escape but t'rally round about:
Which, if it fail them that they got not out,
They're forced into the infernal gulf alive,
Or hackt in pieces are, or took captive.
But spying Mercy stand with Justice, they
Cast down their weapons, and for quarter pray.
Their lives are therefore spared, yet they are ta'en
As th'other band, and prisoners must remain.
And so they must now Justice's captives be,
On Mercy's quarrel: Mercy sets not free.
    Their former captain is their deadly foe,
    And now, poor souls, they know not what to do.

Our Insufficiency to Praise God Suitably for His Mercy

Should all the world so wide to atoms fall,
    Should th' air be shred to motes: should we
    See all the earth hackt here so small
        That none could smaller be?
Should heaven and earth be atomized, we guess
The number of these motes were numberless.

But should we then a world each atom deem,
  Where dwell as many pious men
As all these motes the world could teem,
    Were it shred into them?
Each atom would the world surmount, we guess,
Whose men in number would be numberless.

But had each pious man as many tongues
  At singing all together then
The praise that to the Lord belongs,
    As all these atoms, men?
Each man would sing a world of praise, we guess,
Whose tongues in number would be numberless.

And had each tongue as many songs of praise
  To sing to the Almighty ALL,
As all these men have tongues to raise
    To Him their holy call?
Each tongue would tune a world of praise, we guess,
Whose songs in number would be numberless.

Nay, had each song as many tunes most sweet,
  Or one intwisting in't, as many
As all these tongues have songs most meet
    Unparalleled by any?
Each song a world of music makes, we guess,
Whose tunes in number would be numberless.

Now should all these conspire in us, that we
  Could breathe such praise to Thee, Most High:
Should we Thy sounding organs be
    To ring such melody?
Our music would the world of worlds outring,
Yet be unfit within Thine ears to ting.

Thou didst us mould, and us new-mould when we
  Were worse than mould we tread upon.
  Nay, nettles made by sin we be:
    Yet hadst compassion.

Thou hast pluckt out our stings; and by degrees
Hast of us, lately wasps, made lady-bees.

Though e'er our tongues Thy praises due can fan
　　A weevil with the world may fly:
　　　Yea, fly away; and with a span
　　　We may out-mete the sky.
Though what we can is but a lisp, we pray
Accept thereof: we have no better pay.

The Joy of Church-Fellowship Rightly Attended

　　In heaven soaring up, I dropt an ear
　　　On earth. And oh! sweet melody!
　　And listening, found it was the saints who were
　　　Encoacht for heaven that sang for joy.
　　　　For in Christ's coach they sweetly sing,
　　　　As they to glory ride therein.

　　Oh! joyous hearts! Enfired with holy flame!
　　　Is speech thus tasseled with praise?
　　Will not your inward fire of joy contain
　　　That it in open flames doth blaze?
　　　　For in Christ's coach saints sweetly sing,
　　　　As they to glory ride therein.

　　And if a string do slip by chance, they soon
　　　Do screw it up again: whereby
　　They set it in a more melodious tune
　　　And a diviner harmony.
　　　　For in Christ's coach they sweetly sing,
　　　　As they to glory ride therein.

　　In all their acts, public and private, nay,
　　　And secret too, they praise impart.
　　But in their acts divine and worship, they
　　　With hymns do offer up their heart.
　　　　Thus in Christ's coach they sweetly sing,
　　　　As they to glory ride therein.

Some few not in, and some whose time and place
   Block up this coach's way, do go
As travelers afoot: and so do trace
   The road that gives them right thereto;
   While in this coach these sweetly sing,
   As they to glory ride therein.

7. EDWARD TAYLOR, 1645?–1729

[Though the Puritan stripped the Lord's Supper of all
the ceremonial that surrounds the Anglican Communion or
the Catholic Mass, it remained a solemn, a momentous occasion. It was a monthly attestation of the Covenant of
Grace. Covenanted churches were founded on the doctrine
that participants had presumably been received into the
Covenant of Grace, but the question was put squarely up
to each communicant, to answer in the privacy of his soul.
If he was not really one of the gracious, then by partaking
of the Lord's Supper he did himself no good, but only, as
the Puritan phrase had it, "ate and drank damnation unto
himself." So, taking the sacrament, let alone administering
it, was a terrifying prospect—if, that is, one approached it
in a humble and contrite spirit.

Edward Taylor regarded the ordinance seriously; for
many years, on the night before he administered it, he
meditated upon the awful dilemma. He put these meditations into poetic form; it may be that because, in these
searching exercises, he yielded to the temptation to create
forms of his own, he at last forbade his children to let the
results be published.

If so, he also yielded to temptation at other times, and
wrote a few incidental lyrics which have now become minor
treasures of the English language.]

POEMS AND SACRAMENTAL MEDITATIONS

Meditation One

What love is this of Thine, that cannot be
    In Thine infinity, O Lord, confined,
Unless it in Thy very Person see
    Infinity and finity conjoined?
    What! hath Thy godhead, as not satisfied,
    Married our manhood, making it its bride?

Oh, matchless love! filling heaven to the brim!
    O'errunning it, all running o'er beside
This world! Nay, overflowing hell, wherein
    For Thine elect there rose a mighty tide!
    That there our veins might through Thy Person bleed
    To quench those flames that else would on us feed.

Oh! that my love might overflow my heart
    To fire the same with love! For love I would,
But oh! my straitened breast! my lifeless spark!
    My fireless flame! What chilly love and cold!
    In measure small! in manner chilly! See!
    Lord, blow the coal, Thy love enflame in me.

The Reflexion

Canticles 2. 1: "I am the rose of Sharon."

Lord, art Thou at the table-head above
    Meat, med'cine, sweetness, sparkling beauties, to
Enamor souls with flaming flakes of love,
    And not my trencher nor my cup o'erflow?
    Ben't I a bidden guest? Oh! sweat, mine eye;
    O'erflow with tears! Oh! draw thy fountains dry.

Shall I not smell thy sweet, oh! Sharon's rose?
    Shall not mine eye salute thy beauty? Why?

Shall thy sweet leaves their beauteous sweets upclose
   As half-ashamed my sight should on them lie?
Woe's me! For this my sighs shall be in grain,
   Offer'd on sorrow's altar for the same.

Had not my soul's (Thy conduit) pipes stopt been
   With mud, what ravishment would'st Thou convey?
Let grace's golden spade dig till the spring
   Of tears arise and clear this filth away.
   Lord, let Thy spirit raise my sighings till
   These pipes my soul do with Thy sweetness fill.

Earth once was paradise of heaven below,
   Till ink-faced sin had it with poison stockt
And chast this paradise away into
   Heav'ns upmost loft, and its glory lockt.
   But Thou, sweet Lord, has with Thy golden key
   Unlockt the door, and made a golden day.

Once at Thy feast I saw Thee pearl-like stand
   'Tween heaven and earth, where heaven's bright glory all
In streams fell on thee, as a floodgate, and
   Like sunbeams through thee on the world to fall.
   Oh! sugar sweet then! My dearest sweet Lord, I see
   Saints' heaven-lost happiness restored by thee.

Shall heaven and earth's bright glory all up lie,
   Like sunbeams bundled in the sun in Thee?
Dost Thou sit rose at table-head, where I
   Do sit, and carv'st no morsel sweet for me?
   So much before, so little now! Sprindge, Lord,
   Thy rosey leaves, and me their glee afford.

Shall not Thy rose my garden fresh perfume?
   Shall not Thy beauty my dull heart assail?
Shall not Thy golden gleams run through this gloom?
   Shall my black velvet mask Thy fair face veil?
   Pass o'er my faults. Shine forth, bright sun, arise!
   Enthrone thy rosey self within mine eyes.

Meditation Eight

John 6. 51: "I am the living bread."

I, kenning through astronomy divine
    The world's bright battlement, wherein I spy
A golden path my pencil cannot line
    From that bright throne unto my threshold lie,
    And while my puzzled thoughts about it pore,
    I find the bread of life in't at my door.

When that this bird of paradise, put in
    This wicker cage (my corpse) to tweedle praise,
Had peckt the fruit forbid, and so did fling
    Away its food, and lost its golden days,
    It fell into celestial famine sore,
    And never could attain a morsel more.

Alas! alas! poor bird! What wilt thou do?
    This creature's field no food for souls e'er gave.
And if thou knock at angels' doors, they show
    An empty barrel; they no soul-bread have.
    Alas! poor bird, the world's white loaf is done
    And cannot yield thee here the smallest crumb.

In this sad state, God's tender bowels run
    Out streams of grace; and He, to end all strife,
The purest wheat in heaven, his dear-dear Son,
    Grinds and kneads up into this bread of life,
    Which bread of life from heaven down came and stands
    Disht on thy table up by angels' hands.

Did God mould up this bread in heaven, and bake,
    Which from his table came, and to thine goeth?
Doth he bespeak thee thus? "This soul-bread take;
    Come, eat thy fill of this, thy God's white loaf.
    It's food too fine for angels; yet come, take
    And eat thy fill. It's heaven's sugar cake."

What grace is this, knead in this loaf? This thing,
    Souls are but petty things it to admire.
Ye angels, help! This fill would to the brim
    Heav'n's whelmed-down crystal meal-bowl, yea and
        higher.
    This bread of life, dropt in my mouth, doth cry,
    "Eat, eat me, soul, and thou shalt never die."

Meditation Thirty-eight

I John 2. 1: "And if any man sin, we have an
advocate with the Father."

Oh! What a thing is man? Lord, who am I?
    That Thou shouldst give him law (Oh! golden line)
To regulate his thoughts, words, life thereby?
    And judge him wilt thereby too in Thy time.
    A court of justice Thou in heaven hold'st
    To try his case while he's here housed on mould.

How do Thy angels lay before Thine eye
    My deeds both white and black I daily do?
How doth Thy court Thou panel'st there them try?
    But flesh complains: "What right for this? Let's know.
    For right or wrong, I can't appear unto't.
    And shall a sentence pass on such a suit?"

Soft; blemish not this golden bench or place.
    Here is no bribe, nor colorings to hide,
Nor pettifogger to befog the case;
    But justice hath her glory here well tried;
    Her spotless law all spotted cases tends,
    Without respect or disrespect them ends.

God's judge Himself, and Christ attorney is,
    The Holy Ghost registerer is found;
Angels the sergeants are, all creatures kiss
    The book, and do as evidence abound.

All cases pass according to pure law,
And in the sentence is no fret nor flaw.

What say'st, my soul? Here all thy deeds are tried.
    Is Christ thy advocate to plead thy cause?
Art thou His client? Such shall never slide.
    He never lost His case: He pleads such laws
    As carry do the same, nor doth refuse
    The vilest sinner's case that doth Him choose.

This is His honor, not dishonor. Nay,
    No habeas corpus 'gainst His clients came.
For all their fines His purse doth make down pay.
    He non-suits Satan's suit or casts the same.
    He'll plead thy case, and not accept a fee.
    He'll plead *sub forma pauperis* for thee.

My case is bad. Lord, be my advocate.
    My sin is red; I'm under God's arrest.
Thou hast the hit of pleading; plead my state.
    Although it's bad, Thy plea will make it best.
    If Thou wilt plead my case before the King,
    I'll wagon-loads of love and glory bring.

Meditation Three

(Second series)
Romans 5. 14: "[Adam] who is the figure of him that was
to come."

Like to the marigold I blushing close
    My golden blossoms when Thy sun goes down,
Moist'ning my leaves with dewy sighs, half froze
    By the nocturnal cold that hoars my crown.
    Mine apples ashes are in apple shells,
    And dirty too—strange and bewitching spells!

When, Lord, mine eye doth spy Thy grace to beam,
    Thy mediatorial glory in the shine,

Out-spouted so from Adam's typic stream
    And emblemized in Noah's polished shrine,
    Thine theirs outshines so far it makes their glory
    In brightest colors seem a smoky story.

But when mine eye full of these beams doth cast
    Its rays upon my dusty essence thin,
Impregnate with a spark divine defaced,
    All candied o'er with leprosy of sin,
    Such influences on my spirits light
    Which them as bitter gall or cold ice smite.

My bristled sins hence do so horrid 'pear,
    None but Thyself (and Thou decked up must be
In Thy transcendent glory sparkling clear)
    A mediator unto God for me.
    So high they rise, faith scarce can toss a sight
    Over their head upon Thyself to light.

Is't possible such glory, Lord, e'er should
    Center its love on me, sin's dunghill else?
My case up take, make it its own? Who would
    Wash with his blood my blots out? Crown his shelf
    Or dress his golden cupboard with such ware?
    This makes my pale-faced hope almost despair.

Yet let my titmouse's quill suck in
    Thy grace's milk pails some small drop; or cart
A bit or splinter of some ray, the wing
    Of grace's sun springed out, into my heart,
    To build there wonder's chapel, where Thy praise
    Shall be the psalms sung forth in gracious lays.

Meditation Twenty-six

(Second series)

Unclean, unclean, my Lord, undone, all vile,
    Yea, all defiled,—what shall Thy servant do?

Unfit for Thee, not fit for holy soil,
  Nor for communion of saints below.
  A bag of botches, lump of loathsomeness;
  Defiled by touch, by issue: leprous flesh.

Thou wilt have all that enter to Thy fold
  Pure clean and bright, whiter than whitest snow,
Better refined than most refined gold:
  I am not so, but foul,—what shall I do?
  Shall Thy church doors be shut, and shut out me?
  Shall not church-fellowship my portion be?

How can it be? Thy churches do require
  Pure holiness. I am all filth, alas!
Shall I defile them, tumbled thus in mire?
  Or they me cleanse before I current pass?
  If thus they do, where is the nitre bright
  And soap they offer me to wash me white?

The brisk red heifer's ashes, when calcined,
  Mixt all in running water, is too weak
To wash away my filth. The doves assign'd
  Burnt, and sin-offerings ne'er do the feat,
  But as they emblemize the fountain spring,
  Thy blood, my Lord, set ope' to wash off sin.

Oh! richest grace! Are Thy veins then tapt
  To ope' this holy fountain (boundless sea)
For sinners here to lavor off (all sapt
  With sin) their sins and sinfulness away?
  In this bright crystal, crimson fountain flows
  What washeth whiter than the swan or rose.

Oh! wash me, Lord, in this choice fountain, white,
  That I may enter, and not sully here
Thy Church, whose floor is paved with graces bright,
  And hold church-fellowship with saints most clear.
  My voice, all sweet, with their melodious lays
  Shall make sweet music blossomed with Thy praise.

Housewifery

Make me, O Lord, Thy spinning-wheel complete.
   Thy holy Word my distaff make for me;
Make mine affections Thy swift flyers neat;
   And make my soul Thy holy spool to be;
    My conversation make to be Thy reel,
    And reel the yarn thereon spun of Thy wheel.

Make me Thy loom then; knit therein this twine;
   And make Thy Holy Spirit, Lord, wind quills;
Then weave the web Thyself. The yarn is fine.
   Thine ordinances make my fulling mills.
    Then dye the same in heavenly colors choice,
    All pinked with varnished flowers of paradise.

Then clothe therewith mine understanding, will,
   Affections, judgment, conscience, memory,
My words and actions, that their shine may fill
   My ways with glory and Thee glorify.
    Then mine apparel shall display before Ye
    That I am clothed in holy robes for glory.

The Ebb and Flow

When first Thou on me, Lord, wrought'st Thy sweet print,
   My heart was made Thy tinder-box.
   My 'ffections were Thy tinder in't,
    Where fell Thy sparks by drops.
These holy sparks of heavenly fire that came
Did ever catch and often out would flame.

But now my heart is made Thy censer trim,
   Full of Thy golden altar's fire,
   To offer up sweet incense in
    Unto Thyself entire:
I find my tinder scarce Thy sparks can feel
That drop out from Thy holy flint and steel.

Hence doubts outbud, for fear Thy fire in me
  'S a mocking *ignis fatuus,*
    Or lest Thine altar's fire out be.
      It's hid in ashes thus.
Yet when the bellows of Thy spirit blow,
Away mine ashes: then Thy fire doth glow.

Upon a Spider Catching a Fly

Thou sorrow, venom elf—
  Is this thy play,
To spin a web out of thyself
  To catch a fly?
    For why?

I saw a pettish wasp
  Fall foul therein:
Whom yet thy whorl-pins did not hasp,
  Lest he should fling
    His sting.

But as afraid, remote
  Didst stand hereat,
And with thy little fingers stroke
  And gently tap
    His back.

Thus gently him didst treat
  Lest he should pet,
And in a froppish, aspish heat
  Should greatly fret
    Thy net.

Whereas the silly fly,
  Caught by its leg,
Thou by the throat took'st hastily,
  And 'hind the head
    Bite dead.

This goes to pot, that not:
    Nature doth call.
Strive not above what strength hath got,
    Lest in the brawl
        Thou fall.

This fray seems thus to us:
    Hell's spider gets
His entrails spun to whipcords thus,
    And wove to nets,
        And sets

To tangle Adam's race
    In's stratagems
To their destructions, spoiled, made base
    By venom things—
        Damned sins.

But mighty, gracious Lord,
    Communicate
Thy grace to break the cord—afford
    Us glory's gate
        And state.

We'll nightingale sing like,
    When perched on high
In glory's cage, Thy glory bright:
    Yea, thankfully,
        For joy.

CHAPTER SIX

LITERARY AND EDUCATIONAL IDEALS

1. RICHARD MATHER, 1596–1669

[In their purified church service Puritan congregations
sang a psalm. Soon after Massachusetts Bay was settled,
a committee of ministers, the chief of whom was Richard
Mather, began work on a translation, and it was undoubtedly he who wrote the preface when *The Whole Booke of
Psalmes Faithfully Translated into English Metre* was sent
to press, the first book to be printed at Cambridge, in 1640.
Seventeen hundred copies were issued, of which few survive today; those that do fetch fantastic prices. In the
course of the next century, some twenty-five editions were
called for.

The preface is a frank expression of the difficulties the
Puritan conscience faced when introducing into the religious life anything so sensual as rhyme and meter. In the
statement of rhetorical principles it also succinctly defines
the plain style.]

THE BAY PSALM BOOK

The singing of psalms, though it breathe forth nothing
but holy harmony and melody, yet such is the subtlety of
the Enemy—and the enmity of our nature against the Lord
and His ways—that our hearts can find matter of discord
in this harmony, and crotchets of division in this holy
melody.

For, there have been three questions especially stirring

concerning singing: First, what psalms are to be sung in the churches—whether David's and other scripture psalms or the psalms invented by the gifts of godly men in every age of the church? Secondly, if scripture psalms, whether in their own words or in such meter as English poetry is wont to run in? Thirdly, by whom are they to be sung—whether by the whole church together with their voices, or by one man singing alone and the rest joining in silence and in the close saying amen?

Touching the first, certainly the singing of David's psalms was an acceptable worship of God, not only in his own but in succeeding times. . . .

As for the scruple that some take at the translation of the Book of Psalms into meter, because David's psalms were sung in his own words without meter, we answer: First, there are many verses together in several psalms of David which run in rhythms, . . . which shows at least the lawfulness of singing psalms in English rhythms.

Secondly, the psalms are penned in such verses as are suitable to the poetry of the Hebrew language and not in the common style of such other books of the Old Testament as are not poetical. Now, no Protestant doubteth but that all the books of the scripture should by God's ordinance be extant in the mother tongue of each nation, that they may be understood of all: hence the psalms are to be translated into our English tongue. And if in our English tongue we are to sing them, then, as all our English songs according to the course of our English poetry do run in meter, so ought David's psalms to be translated into meter, that so we may sing the Lord's songs, as in our English tongue, so in such verses as are familiar to an English ear—which are commonly metrical. And as it can be no just offense to any good conscience to sing David's Hebrew songs in English words, so neither to sing his poetical verses in English poetical meter. Men might as well stumble at singing the Hebrew psalms in our English tunes, and not in the Hebrew tunes, as at singing them in English meter, which are our verses, and not in such verses as are generally used by David according to the poetry of the Hebrew language. But the truth is, as the Lord hath hid from us the Hebrew tunes, lest we should think ourselves bound to imitate them, so also the course and frame, for the most part, of their Hebrew poetry—that we might not think ourselves bound to imitate that; but that every nation without scruple might follow, as the grave sort of tunes of their own country songs, so the graver sort of verses of their own country poetry.

Neither let any think that for the meter's sake we have taken liberty or poetical license to depart from the true and proper sense of David's words in the Hebrew verses. No, but it hath been one part of our religious care and faithful endeavor to keep close to the original text. . . .

If therefore the verses are not always so smooth and elegant as some may desire or expect, let them consider that God's altar needs not our polishing (Exod. 20). For we have respected rather a plain translation than to smooth our verses with the sweetness of any paraphrase: and so have attended conscience rather than elegance, fidelity rather than poetry, in translating the Hebrew words into English language and David's poetry into English meter; that so we may sing in Sion the Lord's songs of praise according to His own will—until He take us from hence, and wipe away all our tears, and bid us enter into our Master's joy to sing eternal halleluiahs.

2. *NEW ENGLAND'S FIRST FRUITS*

[Puritanism, we have seen, had no intention of rejecting the intellectual heritage of antiquity and of the Renaissance. It insisted upon the absolute necessity for a learned ministry, and strove to educate the common man so that he could read the Bible and comprehend a learned discourse. No other colonizers in the English-speaking world have provided for higher education so soon upon their arrival as those in Massachusetts Bay. The General Court made an appropriation of £400 in October of 1636 for a college, and the first class of nine members graduated in 1642. The next year an account of Harvard College and of the class was printed in London, *New England's First*

Fruits. This was a pardonable boast, proving to orthodox Puritans at home that the colonizers had not intellectually degenerated, even though in a wilderness. Also, since some of the sectaries then emerging were proclaiming a religion of the heart that needed no help from "humane learning," the tract announced New England's adherence to the conservative ideal.]

NEW ENGLAND'S FIRST FRUITS

After God had carried us safe to New England, and we had builded our houses, provided necessaries for our livelihood, reared convenient places for God's worship, and settled the civil government, one of the next things we longed for and looked after was to advance learning and perpetuate it to posterity, dreading to leave an illiterate ministry to the churches when our present ministers shall lie in the dust. And as were thinking and consulting how to effect this great work, it pleased God to stir up the heart of one Mr. Harvard (a godly gentleman and a lover of learning, there living amongst us) to give the one half of his estate (it being in all about £1700) towards the erecting of a college, and all his library. After him, another gave £300, others after them cast in more, and the public hand of the state added the rest. The college was, by common consent, appointed to be at Cambridge (a place very pleasant and accommodate) and is called (according to the name of the first founder) Harvard College.

The edifice is very fair and comely within and without, having in it a spacious hall (where they daily meet at common lectures, exercises), and a large library with some books to it, the gifts of divers of our friends, their chambers and studies also fitted for and possessed by the students, and all other rooms of office necessary and convenient, with all needful offices thereto belonging. And by the side of the College, a fair grammar school, for the training up of young scholars and fitting of them for academical learning, that still as they are judged ripe they may be received into the College. Of this school, Master Corlet is the master, who hath very well approved himself for his abilities, dexterity and painfulness, in teaching and education of the youth under him.

Over the College is Master Dunster placed as president, a learned, conscionable and industrious man, who hath so trained up his pupils in the tongues and arts, and so seasoned them with the principles of divinity and Christianity, that we have to our great comfort (and in truth, beyond our hopes) beheld their progress in learning and godliness also. The former of these hath appeared in their public declamations in Latin and Greek, and disputations logical and philosophical, which they have been wont (besides their ordinary exercises in the College hall), in the audience of the magistrates, ministers and other scholars, for the probation of their growth in learning, upon set days, constantly once every month, to make and uphold. The latter hath been manifested in sundry of them by the savory breathings of their spirits in godly conversation, insomuch that we are confident, if these early blossoms may be cherished and warmed with the influence of the friends of learning and lovers of this pious work, they will, by the help of God, come to happy maturity in a short time.

Over the College are twelve overseers chosen by the General Court: six of them are of the magistrates, the other six of the ministers, who are to promote the best good of it, and (having a power of influence into all persons in it) are to see that every one be diligent and proficient in his proper place.

Rules and precepts that are observed in the College:

1. When any scholar is able to understand Tullius [Cicero] or such like classical Latin author *extempore,* and make and speak true Latin in verse and prose, *suo ut aiunt marte* ["to stand, as they say, on his own feet"], and decline perfectly the paradigms of nouns and verbs in the Greek tongue, let him then, and not before, be capable of admission into the College.

2. Let every student be plainly instructed and earnestly pressed to consider well: the main end of his life and

studies is "to know God and Jesus Christ, which is eternal life" (John 17. 3), and therefore to lay Christ in the bottom, as the only foundation of all sound knowledge and learning.

And seeing the Lord only giveth wisdom, let everyone seriously set himself by prayer in secret to seek it of Him (Prov. 2. 3).

3. Everyone shall so exercise himself in reading the scriptures twice a day that he shall be ready to give such an account of his proficiency therein, both in theoretical observations of the language and logic, and in practical and spiritual truths, as his tutor shall require, according to his ability: seeing "the entrance of the word giveth light; it giveth understanding unto the simple" (Psal. 119. 130).

4. That they, eschewing all profanation of God's name, attributes, word, ordinances and times of worship, do study with good conscience carefully to retain God and the love of His truth in their minds. Else, let them know that (notwithstanding their learning) God may give them up "to strong delusions" (II Thess. 2. 11, 12), and in the end "to a reprobate mind" (Rom. 1. 28).

5. That they studiously redeem the time, observe the general hours appointed for all the students, and the special hours for their own classes; and then diligently attend the lectures, without any disturbance by word or gesture. And if in anything they doubt, they shall inquire as of their fellows, so (in case of "non-satisfaction") modestly of their tutors.

6. None shall, under any pretense whatsoever, frequent the company and society of such men as lead an unfit and dissolute life.

Nor shall any, without his tutor's leave or (in his absence) the call of parents or guardians, go abroad to other towns.

7. Every scholar shall be present in his tutor's chamber at the seventh hour in the morning, immediately after the sound of the bell, at his opening the scripture and prayer; so also at the fifth hour at night, and then give account of his own private reading (as aforesaid in particular the third), and constantly attend lectures in the hall at the hours appointed. But if any (without necessary impedi-

ment) shall absent himself from prayer or lectures, he shall be liable to admonition, if he offend above once a week.

8. If any scholar shall be found to transgress any of the laws of God or the school, after twice admonition, he shall be liable, if not *adultus*, to correction; if *adultus*, his name shall be given up to the overseers of the College, that he may be admonished at the public monthly act.

The time and order of their studies (unless experience shall show cause to alter):

The second and third day of the week, read lectures, as followeth:

To the first year, at eight of the clock in the morning, logic the first three quarters, physics the last quarter.

To the second year, at the ninth hour, ethics and politics, at convenient distances of time.

To the third year, at the tenth, arithmetic and geometry the three first quarters, astronomy the last.

Afternoon:

The first year disputes at the second hour.

The second year at the third hour.

The third year at the fourth, every one in his art.

The fourth day, read Greek:

To the first year, the etymology and syntax, at the eighth hour.

To the second, at the ninth hour, *prosodia* and *dialects*.

Afternoon:

The first year, at second hour, practice the precepts of grammar in such authors as have variety of words.

The second year, at third hour, practice in poesy. . . .

The third year perfect their theory before noon, and exercise style, composition, imitation, epitome, both in prose and verse, afternoon.

The fifth day, read Hebrew and the Eastern tongues:

Grammar to the first year, hour the eighth.

To the second, Chaldee at the ninth hour.
To the third, Syriac at the tenth hour.

Afternoon:

The first year, practice in the Bible at the second hour.
The second, in Ezra and Daniel at the third hour.
The third, at the fourth hour in Trostius's New Testament.

The sixth day, read rhetoric to all at the eighth hour:
Declamations at the ninth. So ordered that every scholar may declaim once a month. The rest of the day, *vacat rhetoricis studiis* ["is given over to the study of rhetoric"].

The seventh day, read divinity catechetical at the eighth hour; commonplaces at the ninth hour.

Afternoon:

The first hour read history in the winter, the nature of plants in the summer.

The sum of every lecture shall be examined before the new lecture be read.

Every scholar that on proof is found able to read the originals of the Old and New Testament into the Latin tongue, and to resolve them logically, withal being of godly life and conversation, and at any public act hath the approbation of the overseers and master of the College, is fit to be dignified with his first degree.

Every scholar that giveth up in writing a system or synopsis, or summa, of logic, natural and moral philosophy, arithmetic, geometry and astronomy, and is ready to defend his theses or propositions, withal skilled in the originals as abovesaid, and of godly life and conversation, and so approved by the overseers and master of the College at any public act, is fit to be dignified with his second degree.

3. MICHAEL WIGGLESWORTH, 1631–1705

[As part of their training in rhetoric, undergraduates were required to deliver orations. Michael Wigglesworth spoke this one in his senior year, 1650. Though it nowhere mentions pulpit oratory as the primary end of eloquence, his listeners would assume that preaching was the chief branch of oratory. It expounds the Protestant conception of the spoken word as the "means" of conversion, and shows with what care language had to be studied and handled in order that it might serve that purpose.]

THE PRAISE OF ELOQUENCE

How sweetly doth eloquence even enforce truth upon the understanding and subtly convey knowledge into the mind, be it never so dull of conceiving and sluggish in yielding its assent! So that let a good orator put forth the utmost of his skill, and you shall hear him so lay open and unfold, so evidence and demonstrate from point to point what he hath in hand, that he will make a very block understand his discourse. Let him be to give a description of something absent or unknown, how strangely doth he realize and make it present to his hearers' apprehensions, framing in their minds as exact an idea of that which they never saw as they can possibly have of anything that they have been longest and best acquainted with! Or doth he take upon him to personate some others in word or deeds, why he presents his hearers not with a lifeless picture but with the living persons of those concerning whom he speaks. They see, they hear, they handle them, they walk, they talk with them, and what not. Or is he to speak about such things as are already known? Why should he here discourse after the vulgar manner, and deliver his mind as a cobbler would do? His hearers might then have some ground to say they knew as much as their orator could teach them. But by the power of eloquence, old truth receives a new habit; though its essence be the same, yet its visage is so altered that it may currently pass and be accepted as a novelty. The same verity is again and again perhaps set before the same guests, but dressed and dished up after a new manner, and every manner seasoned so well, that the intellectual parts may both without nauseating receive, and so oft as it doth receive, it still draw some fresh nourishing virtue from it. So that eloquence gives new luster and beauty, new strength, new vigor, new life unto truth, presenting it with such variety as refresheth, actuating it with such hidden powerful energy, that a few languid sparks are blown up to a shining flame.

And which is yet more: eloquence doth not only revive the things known, but secretly convey life into the hearer's understanding, rousing it out of its former slumber, quickening it beyond its natural vigor, elevating it above its ordinary conception. There are not only objects set before it, but eyes (after a sort) given it to see these objects in such wise as it never saw. Yea, it is strengthened as to apprehend that which is taught it, so of itself, with enlargement to comprehend many things which are not made known unto it. Hence it comes to pass that, after the hearing of a well-composed speech, lively expressed, the understanding of the auditor is so framed into the mould of eloquence, that he could almost go away and compose the like himself, either upon the same or another subject. And what's the reason of this? Why, his mind is transported with a kind of rapture, and inspired with a certain oratoric fury, as if the orator together with his words had breathed his soul and spirit into those that hear him.

These, and the like effects, hath eloquence upon the understanding. But furthermore, 'tis a fit bait to catch the will and affections. For hereby they are not only laid in wait for, but surprised; nor only surprised, but subdued; nor only subdued, but triumphed over. Yet eloquence beguiles with such honesty, subdues with such mildness, triumphs with such sweetness, that here to be surprised is nothing dangerous; here to be subject is the best freedom, this kind of servitude is more desirable than liberty. For whereas our untractable nature refuseth to be drawn, and a stiff will scorns to be compelled, yet by the power of well-composed speech, nature is drawn against the stream with delight, and the will after a sort compelled with its own consent. Although for a time it struggle and make resistance, yet at length it suffers itself to be vanquished and takes a secret contentment in being overcome.

In like manner, for the affections: look, as a mighty river augmented with excessive rains or winter snows, swelling above its wonted channel, bears down banks and bridges, overflows fields and hedges, sweeps away all before it that might obstruct its passage; so eloquence overturns, overturns all things that stand in its way, and carries them down with the irresistible stream of its all controlling power. Wonderful it were to speak of the several discoveries of the power in several affections: wonderful but to think, in general, how like a blustering tempest it one while drives before it the raging billows of this troubled ocean, how otherwhiles (as though it had them in fetters) it curbs and calms the fury at a word. And all this without offering violence to the parties so affected; nay, with a secret pleasure and delight it stirs men up to the greatest displeasure and distaste. Doth it affect with grief? Why, to be so grieved is no grievance. Doth it kindle coals, nay flames of fiery indignation? Why, those flames burn not, but rather cherish. Doth it draw tears from the eyes? Why, even tears flow with pleasure. For as is well said by one upon this point: *in omni animi motu etiam in dolore est quaedam jucunditas* ["In every activity of the spirit, yea even in sorrow, there is a certain pleasure"]. So potently, so sweetly doth eloquence command; and of a skillful orator in point of the affections, that may be spoken really, which the poet affirmeth fabulously of Aeolus, god of the winds. . . .

But I need instance no more. Some of you I hope will by this time assent unto what has been hitherto proved, that eloquence is of such useful concernment and powerful operation. But methinks I hear some still objecting: "'tis very true eloquence is a desirable thing, but what are we the better for knowing its worth unless we could hope ourselves to attain it? It is indeed a right excellent endowment, but 'tis not every capacity, nay scarce one of a hundredth that can reach it. How many men of good parts do we find that yet excel not here? Cicero indeed, a man in whom vast understanding and natural fluent facility of speech conspire together, no marvel if he make judges weep, and princes tremble. But to what purpose is it for a man of weak parts and mean abilities to labor after that which he is never like to compass? Had we not as good toss our caps against the wind as weary out ourselves in the pursuit of that which so few can reach to?"

Answer: To these I would answer: first, the reason why so few attain it is because there [are] few that indeed desire it. Hence they run not as if they meant to win, they pursue not as if they hoped to overtake. But secondly, let me answer them with Turner's words upon this very argument: *Negligentiam nostram arguit, qui cum non possimus, quod debemus, optimus, nolumus quod possimus, benè:* "We cannot do what we would, therefore will not do what we may." This savors of a slothful system. Because we cannot keep pace with the horsemen, shall we refuse to accompany the footmen? Because we cannot run, shall we sit down and refuse to go? We cannot reach so far as ourselves desire and as some others it may be attain; shall we not therefore reach as far as our endeavors may carry us? Because we cannot be orators *optimi*, do we content ourselves to be orators *pessimi*?

And as for those that have most excelled in this kind, whence had they their excellency? They did not come declaiming into the world; they were not born with orations in their mouths; eloquence did not sit upon their lips whilst they lay in their cradles; neither did they suck it from their mothers' breasts. But if you examine the matter, you shall find that by incredible pains and daily exercise, they even turned the course of nature into another channel, and cut out a way for the gentle stream of eloquence, where natural impediments seemed altogether to deny it passage, thereby effecting as much as another could brag: *Viam aut inveniam aut faciam* ["I shall either find a way or make one"].

Eminent in this respect is the example of the two best orators that fame has brought to our ears. Of Cicero, who when he had naturally a shrill, screaming, ill-tuned voice,

rising to such a note that it endangered his very life, yet
by art and industry he acquired such a commendable habit
as none with ease could speak more sweetly than he. And
Demosthenes, though he were naturally of a stammering
tongue, crazy-bodied and broken-winded and withal had
accustomed himself to a jetting uncomely deportment of
his body, or some part of it at least—when, to conclude,
he had scarce any part of an orator save only an ardent
desire to be an orator—yet by his indefatigable pains he
so overcame these natural defects as that he came to be
reputed prince of the Grecian eloquence. Though this was
not gotten without some futher difficulty and seeming vain
attempts: insomuch as he was several times quite discouraged and once threw all aside, despairing ever to become an orator, because the people laughed at his orations;
yet, notwithstanding, being heartened to it again by some
of his well-willers, he never left striving till he had won
the prize.

Go to, therefore, my fellow students (for to you I address my speech; my superiors I attempt not to speak to,
desiring rather to learn of them more of this nature, but) to
you give me leave to say: "Let no man hereafter tell me I
despair of excelling in the oratorical faculty, therefore 'tis
bootless to endeavor." Who more unlike to make an orator
than Demosthenes, except it were one who had no tongue
in his head? Yet Demosthenes became *orator optimus*. Tell
me not: "I have made trial once and again, but find my
labor fruitless." Thou art not the first that hast made an
onset and been repelled; neither canst thou presage what
renewed endeavors may produce. Would you then obtain
this skill? Take Demosthenes his course: gird up your loins,
put to your shoulders, and to it again, and again, and again;
let nothing discourage you. Know that to be a dunce, to be
a stammerer, unable to bring forth three or four sentences
hanging well together, this is an easy matter; but to become an able speaker: *Hic labor, hoc opus est* ["This is
the task, this is the work"]. Would you have your orations
please, such as need not be laughed at? Why, follow him
in that also. Let them be such as smell of the lamp, as was
said of his. Not slovenly I mean, but elaborate: *Diurnam*

industriam et nocturnis lucubrationibus elaboratae ["By
day hard work, by night unending toil, such as savor of
some pains"]. A good oration is not made at the first
thought, nor scarce at the first writing over. Nor is true
eloquence wont to hurry it out thick and threefold, as if
each word were running for a wager; nor yet to mutter or
whisper it out of a book, after a dreaming manner, with
such a voice as the orator can scantly hear himself speak:
but to utter it with lively affection, to pronounce it distinctly with audible voice.

4. COTTON MATHER, 1663–1728

[Cotton Mather, would-be conserver of standards of the
founders, nowhere more indicates how he himself was departing from them than by his experiments with a prose
style that was anything but "plain." He smarted under
criticisms of his bejeweled and convoluted sentences in the
Magnalia, and quickly became aware that the new century
was setting up the standard of a fresh simplicity. In 1726
he published at Boston a handbook for divinity students,
Manuductio ad Ministerium, which shows that in his old
age he was acutely aware of changing times. When he got
to the matter of style, he could not resist paying his respects to the "blades" who had jeered at him, but in the
course of defending himself he had inadvertently to confess the passing of the Puritan era by arguing for a
stylistic freedom that would permit every man to compose
in his own manner. Thus the reign of the "plain style," as
the founders had conceived it, was at an end, and a new
age in American writing could begin.]

OF STYLE

There has been a deal of ado about a style, so much
that I must offer you my sentiments upon it. There is a way
of writing wherein the author endeavors that the reader
may have something to the purpose in every paragraph.
There is not only a vigor sensible in every sentence, but the
paragraph is embellished with profitable references, even to

something beyond what is directly spoken. Formal and painful quotations are not studied, yet all that could be learnt from them is insinuated. The writer pretends not unto reading, yet he could not have writ as he does if he had not read very much in his time; and his composures are not only a cloth of gold, but also stuck with as many jewels as the gown of a Russian ambassador. This way of writing has been decried by many, and is at this day more than ever so, for the same reason that, in the old story, the grapes were decried that they were not ripe. A lazy, ignorant, conceited set of authors would persuade the whole tribe to lay aside that way of writing for the same reason that one would have persuaded his brethren to part with the incumbrance of their bushy tails. But however fashion and humor may prevail, they must not think that the club at their coffeehouse is all the world; but there will always be those who will in this case be governed by indisputable reason, and who will think that the real excellency of a book will never lie in saying of little—that the less one has for his money in a book, 'tis really the more valuable for it, and the less one is instructed in a book and the more superfluous margin and superficial harangue and the less of substantial matter one has in it, the more 'tis to be accounted of. And if a more massy way of writing be never so much disgusted at this day, a better gust will come on, as will some other thing, *quae jam cecidere* ["which now have fallen out of use"]. In the meantime, nothing appears to me more impertinent and ridiculous than the modern way (I cannot say rule, for they have none) of criticizing. The blades that set up for critics (I know not who constituted or commissioned them), they appear to me for the most part as contemptible as they are a supercilious generation. For indeed no two of them have the same style, and they are as intolerably cross-grained and severe in their censures upon one another as they are upon the rest of mankind. But while each of them, conceitedly enough, sets up for the standard of perfection, we are entirely at a loss which fire to follow. Nor can you easily find any one thing wherein they agree for their style, except perhaps a perpetual care to give us jejune and empty pages without such touches of erudition (to speak in the style of an ingenious traveler) as may make the discourses less tedious and more enriching to the mind of him that peruses them. There is much talk of a florid style obtaining among the pens that are most in vogue; but how often would it puzzle one, even with the best glasses, to find the flowers! And if they were to be chastised for it, it would be with much the same kind of justice as Jerome was for being a Ciceronian. After all, every man will have his own style which will distinguish him as much as his gait; and if you can attain to that which I have newly described, but always writing so as to give an easy conveyance unto your ideas, I would not have you by any scourging be driven out of your gait; but if you must confess a fault in it, make a confession like that of the lad unto his father while he was beating him for his versifying.

However, since every man will have his own style, I would pray that we may learn to treat one another with mutual civilities and condescensions and handsomely indulge one another in this as gentlemen do in other matters.

I wonder what ails people that they cannot let Cicero write in the style of Cicero and Seneca write in the (much other) style of Seneca, and own that both may please in their several ways. But I will freely tell you, what has made me consider the humorists that set up for critics upon style as the most unregardable set of mortals in the world is this: Far more illustrious critics than any of those to whom I am now bidding defiance, and no less men than your Erasmuses and your Grotiuses, have taxed the Greek style of the New Testament with I know not what solecisms and barbarisms (and how many learned folks have obsequiously run away with the notion) whereas 'tis an ignorant and an insolent whimsy which they have been guilty of. It may be (and particularly by an ingenious Blackwall, it has been) demonstrated that the gentlemen are mistaken in every one of their pretended instances; all the unquestionable classics may be brought in to convince them of their mistakes. Those glorious oracles are as pure Greek as ever was written in the world and so correct, so noble, so sublime is their style that never anything under the cope of Heaven but the Old Testament has equaled it.

A BRIEF BIBLIOGRAPHY

Because literary expression in Puritan New England was so bound up with theology and with political and ecclesiastical concerns, it can hardly be isolated from the social context. These suggestions for further study take account only of a few recent books and essays. For full listings, see Perry Miller and Thomas H. Johnson, *The Puritans*, for the years before 1939, and the annual bibliographies in *The New England Quarterly* for the years thereafter.

General Discussions

Baldwin, Alice, *The New England Clergy and the American Revolution* (1928).

Bridenbaugh, Carl, *Cities in the Wilderness: the First Century of Urban Life in America, 1625–1744* (1938).

Curti, Merle, *The Growth of American Thought* (1943).

Dexter, Henry M., *Congregationalism of the Last Three Hundred Years, as Seen in Its Literature* (1880).

Foster, Frank H., *A Genetic History of the New England Theology* (1907).

Griffiths, Olive M., *Religion and Learning* (1935).

Hall, Thomas C., *The Religious Background of American Culture* (1930).

Heimert, Alan, "Puritanism, the Wilderness, and the Frontier," *New England Quarterly*, XXVI (1953), 361–382.

Jantz, Harold S., *The First Century of New England Verse* (1944).

Levy, Babette M., *Preaching in the First Half Century of New England* (1945).

Michaelson, Robert S., "Changes in the Puritan Concept of Calling or Vocation," *New England Quarterly*, XXVI (1953), 315–336.

Miller, Perry, *Orthodoxy in Massachusetts* (1933).

———, "The Marrow of Puritan Divinity," *Publications of the Colonial Society of Massachusetts*, XXXII (1938), 247–300.

———, *The New England Mind: The Seventeenth Century* (1939, 1954).

——, *The New England Mind: From Colony to Province* (1953).

——, "The End of the World," *William and Mary Quarterly*, VIII (1951), 171–191.

——, "Errand into the Wilderness," *William and Mary Quarterly*, X (1953), 3–32.

Mitchell, W. Fraser, *English Pulpit Oratory from Andrewes to Tillotson* (1932).

Morgan, Edmund S., *The Puritan Family* (1944).

Morison, Samuel Eliot, *Builders of the Bay Colony* (1930).

——, *The Founding of Harvard College* (1935).

——, *Harvard College in the Seventeenth Century* (1936).

——, *The Puritan Pronaos* (1936).

Murdock, Kenneth B., "The Puritan Tradition in American Literature," in *The Reinterpretation of American Literature*, ed. Norman Foerster (1928).

——, *Literature and Theology in Colonial New England* (1949).

——, "Clio in the Wilderness: History and Biography in Puritan New England," *Church History*, XXIV (1955), 221–238.

Notestein, Wallace, *The English People on the Eve of Colonization, 1603–1630* (1954).

Park, Charles E., "Puritans and Quakers," *New England Quarterly*, XXVII (1954), 53–74.

Parrington, Vernon L., *Main Currents in American Thought*, Vol. I: *The Colonial Mind* (1927, 1955).

Piercy, Josephine K., *Studies in Literary Types in Seventeenth-Century America* (1939).

Rossiter, Clinton L., *Seedtime of the Republic* (1953).

Savelle, Max, *The Foundations of American Civilization* (1942).

Schneider, Herbert W., *The Puritan Mind* (1930).

Shipton, Clifford K., "Literary Leaven in Provincial New England," *New England Quarterly* IX (1936), 203–217.

Sweet, William W., *Religion in Colonial America* (1942).

Tyler, Moses C., *A History of American Literature during the Colonial Period, 1607–1765* (1878, 1897, 1949).

Walker, Williston, *Ten New England Leaders* (1901).

Winslow, Ola Elizabeth, *Meetinghouse Hill, 1630–1783* (1952).

Wright, Louis B., *The Atlantic Frontier* (1947).

Specific Discussions

WILLIAM BRADFORD

Bradford, Eugene F., "Conscious Art in Bradford's *History of Plymouth Plantation*," *New England Quarterly*, I (1928), 133–157.

ANNE BRADSTREET

Campbell, Helen S., *Anne Bradstreet and Her Times* (1891).

White, Elizabeth W., "The Tenth Muse—A Tercentenary Appraisal of Anne Bradstreet," *William and Mary Quarterly*, VIII (1951), 355–377.

THOMAS HOOKER

Walker, George L., *Thomas Hooker* (1891).

COTTON MATHER

Boas, Ralph P., and Louise Boas, *Cotton Mather: Keeper of the Puritan Conscience* (1928).

Holmes, Thomas J., *Cotton Mather: A Bibliography of His Works* (1940).

Marvin, Abijah P., *The Life and Times of Cotton Mather* (1892).

Wendell, Barrett, *Cotton Mather, the Puritan Priest* (1891, 1926).

INCREASE MATHER

Holmes, Thomas J., *Increase Mather: A Bibliography of His Works* (1931).

Murdock, Kenneth B., *Increase Mather, the Foremost American Puritan* (1925).

SAMUEL SEWALL

Chamberlain, Nathan H., *Samuel Sewall and the World He Lived In* (1897).

EDWARD TAYLOR

Blau, Herbert, "Heaven's Sugar Cake: Theology and Imagery in the Poetry of Edward Taylor," *New England Quarterly*, XXVI (1953), 337–360.

Brown, Wallace C., "Edward Taylor: an American Metaphysical," *American Literature*, XVI (1944), 186–197.

Johnson, Thomas H., "The Discovery of Edward Taylor's Poetry," *Colophon,* New Graphic Ser., I (1939), 101–106.

Lind, Sidney, "Edward Taylor: A Revaluation," *New England Quarterly,* XXI (1948), 518–530.

Pearce, Roy H., "Edward Taylor: the Poet as Puritan," *New England Quarterly,* XXIII (1950), 31–46.

Warren, Austin, "Edward Taylor's Poetry: Colonial Baroque," *Kenyon Review,* III (1941), 355–371.

Weathers, Willie T., "Edward Taylor, Hellenistic Puritan," *American Literature,* XVIII (1946), 18–26.

Wright, Nathalia, "The Morality Tradition in the Poetry of Edward Taylor," *American Literature,* XVIII (1946), 1–17.

MICHAEL WIGGLESWORTH

Matthiessen, F. O., "Michael Wigglesworth: A Puritan Artist," *New England Quarterly,* I (1928), 491–504.

JOHN WINTHROP

Winthrop, Robert C., *Life and Letters of John Winthrop* (1864–1867).

JOHN WISE

Cook, George A., *John Wise, Early American Democrat* (1952).

INDEX